VARGA

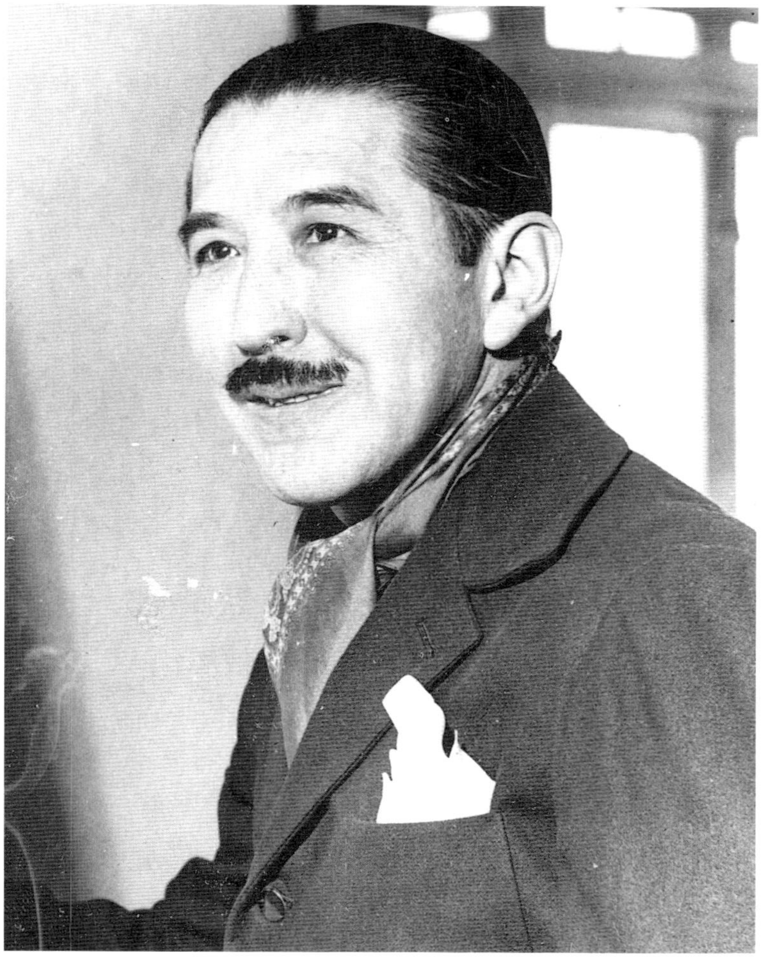

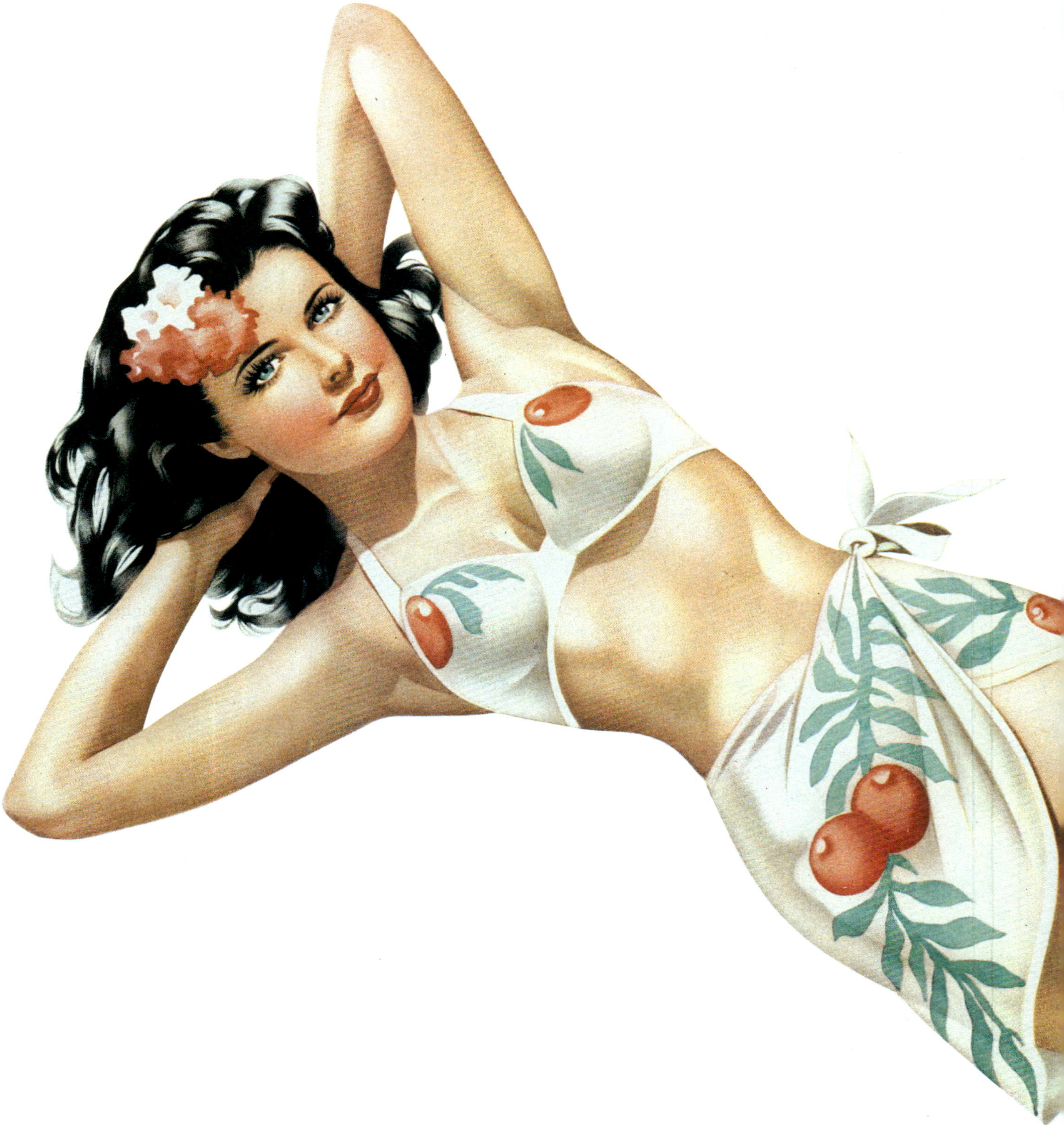

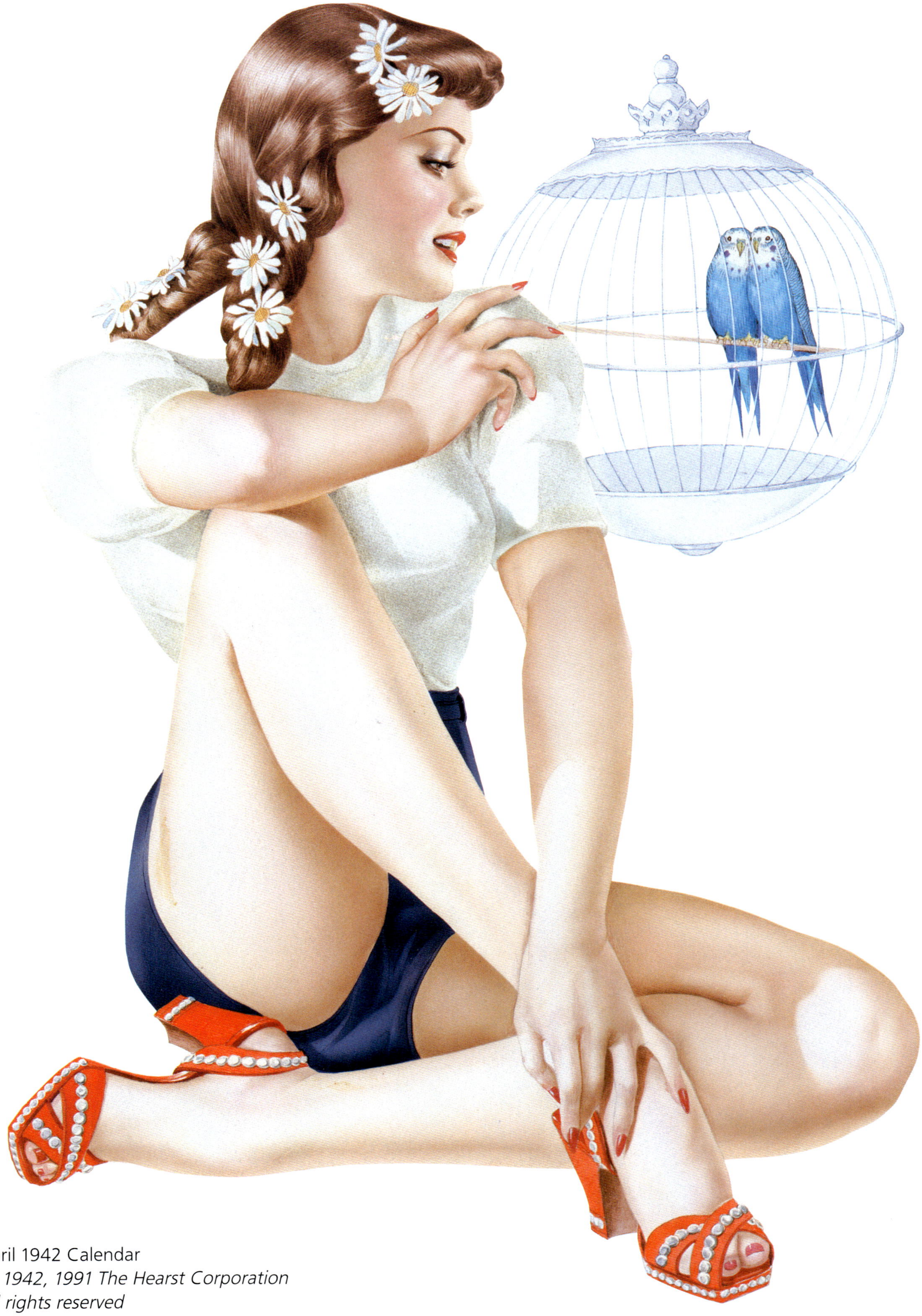

April 1942 Calendar

VARGA

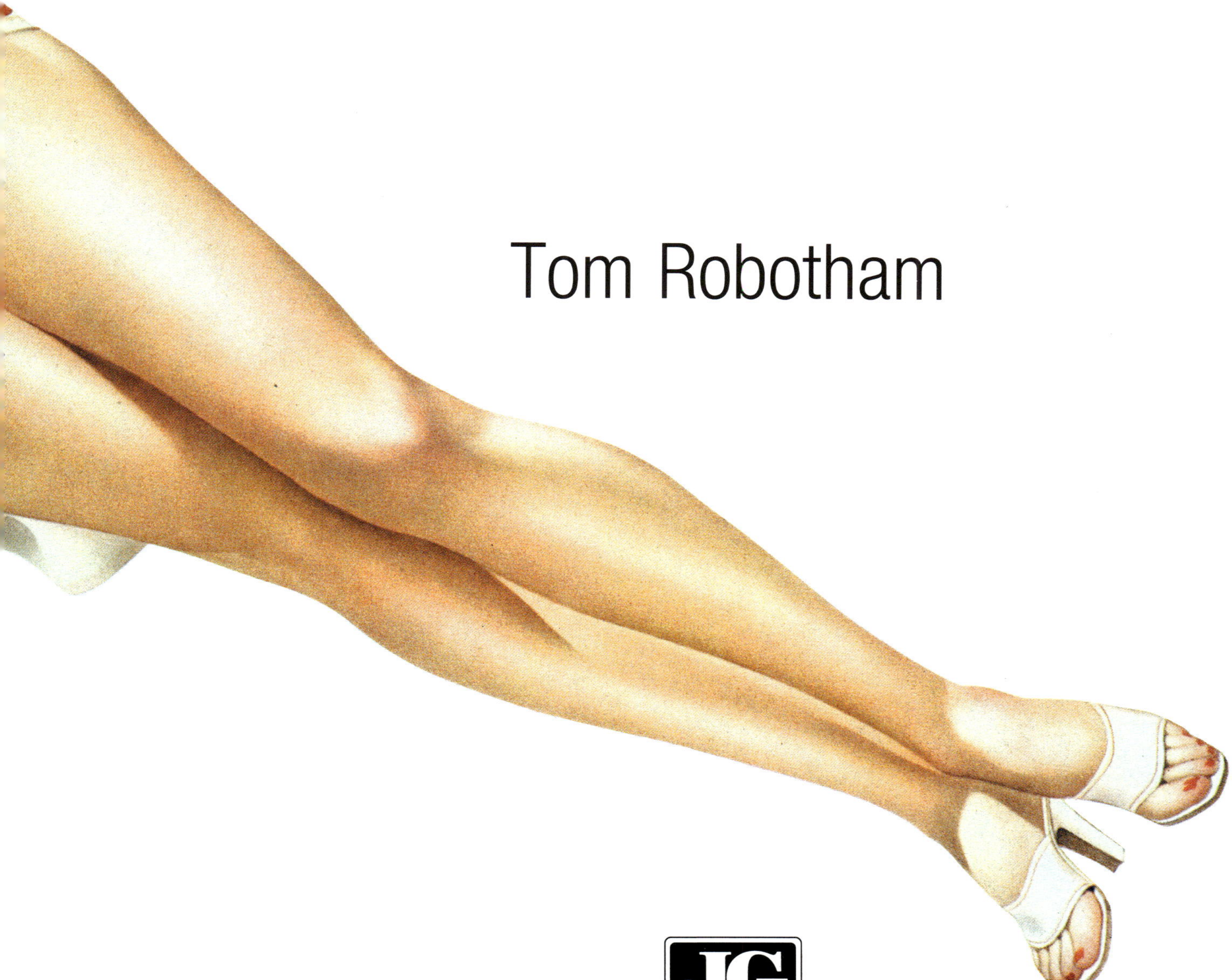

Tom Robotham

JG PRESS

Reprinted 2003 by
World Publications Group, Inc.
455 Somerset Avenue
North Dighton, MA 02764

ISBN 1-57215-324-5

Printed in Spain

Page 1: Alberto Vargas.

Pages 2-3: July 1945. *© 1945, 1991 The Hearst Corporation. All rights reserved.*

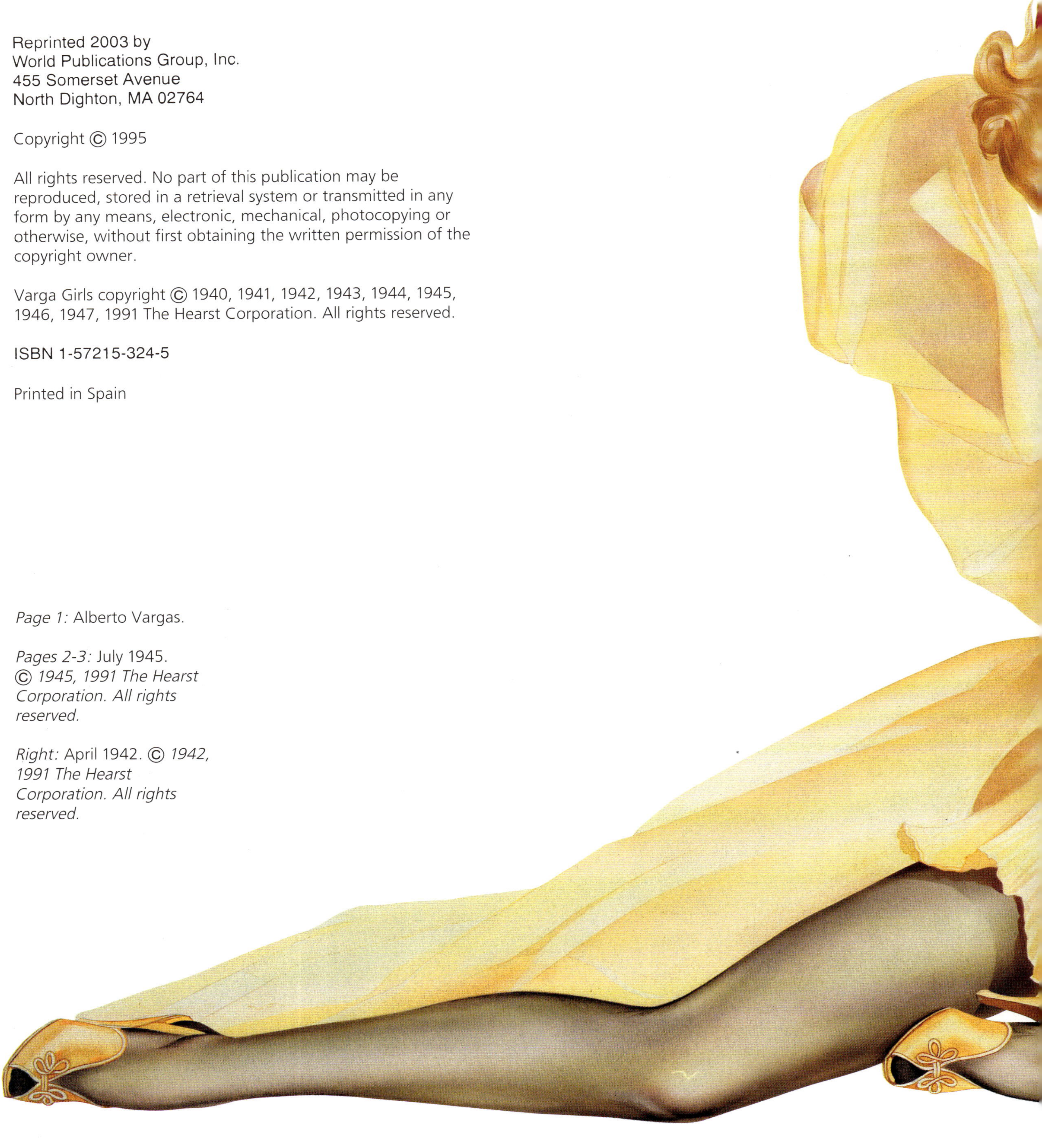

Right: April 1942. *© 1942, 1991 The Hearst Corporation. All rights reserved.*

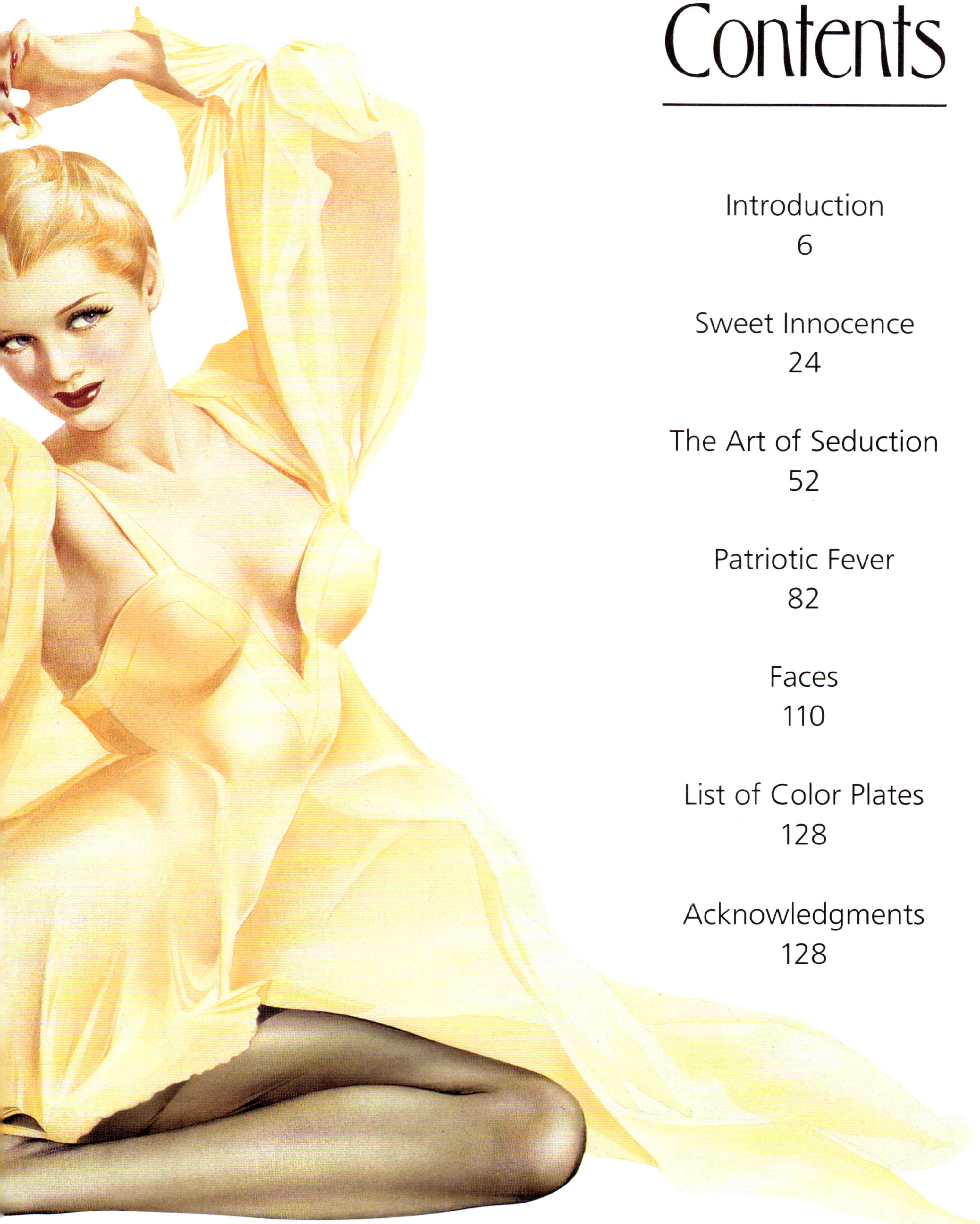

Contents

Introduction
6

Sweet Innocence
24

The Art of Seduction
52

Patriotic Fever
82

Faces
110

List of Color Plates
128

Acknowledgments
128

Introduction

The paintings of Alberto Vargas have been part of America's popular culture for four generations. In the 1920s, the work of the young Peruvian immigrant was used to promote the legendary *Ziegfeld Follies.* Half a century later, men of the baby-boom generation came to know and love the seductive Vargas Girl in the pages of *Playboy* magazine. But Vargas's greatest period by far was neither the roaring 1920s, nor the hedonistic 1970s. It was the five-year period that coincided with World War II: a time when young men – and women – looked forward to seeing Vargas's work each month in the pages of *Esquire*.

The Varga Girls, as Vargas's paintings in *Esquire* were called, were more than mere pinups: they were cultural icons, as familiar as the jokes of Bob Hope or the music of

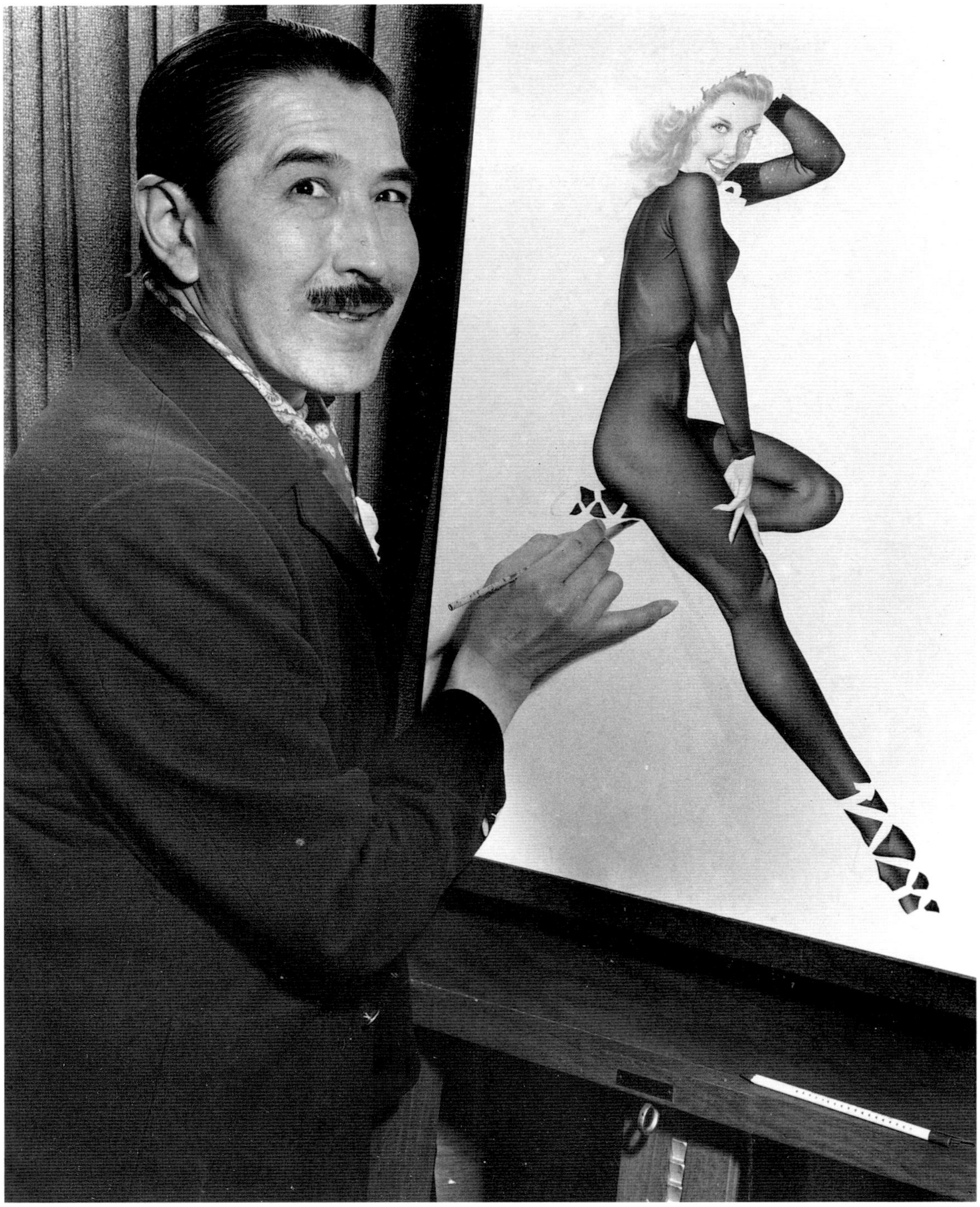

Left: Alberto Vargas in 1946.

Opposite right: The crew of the *Memphis Belle* is joined by military officials in Washington after the war. The morale-boosting practice of painting copies of Varga Girls on combat planes was common during World War II.

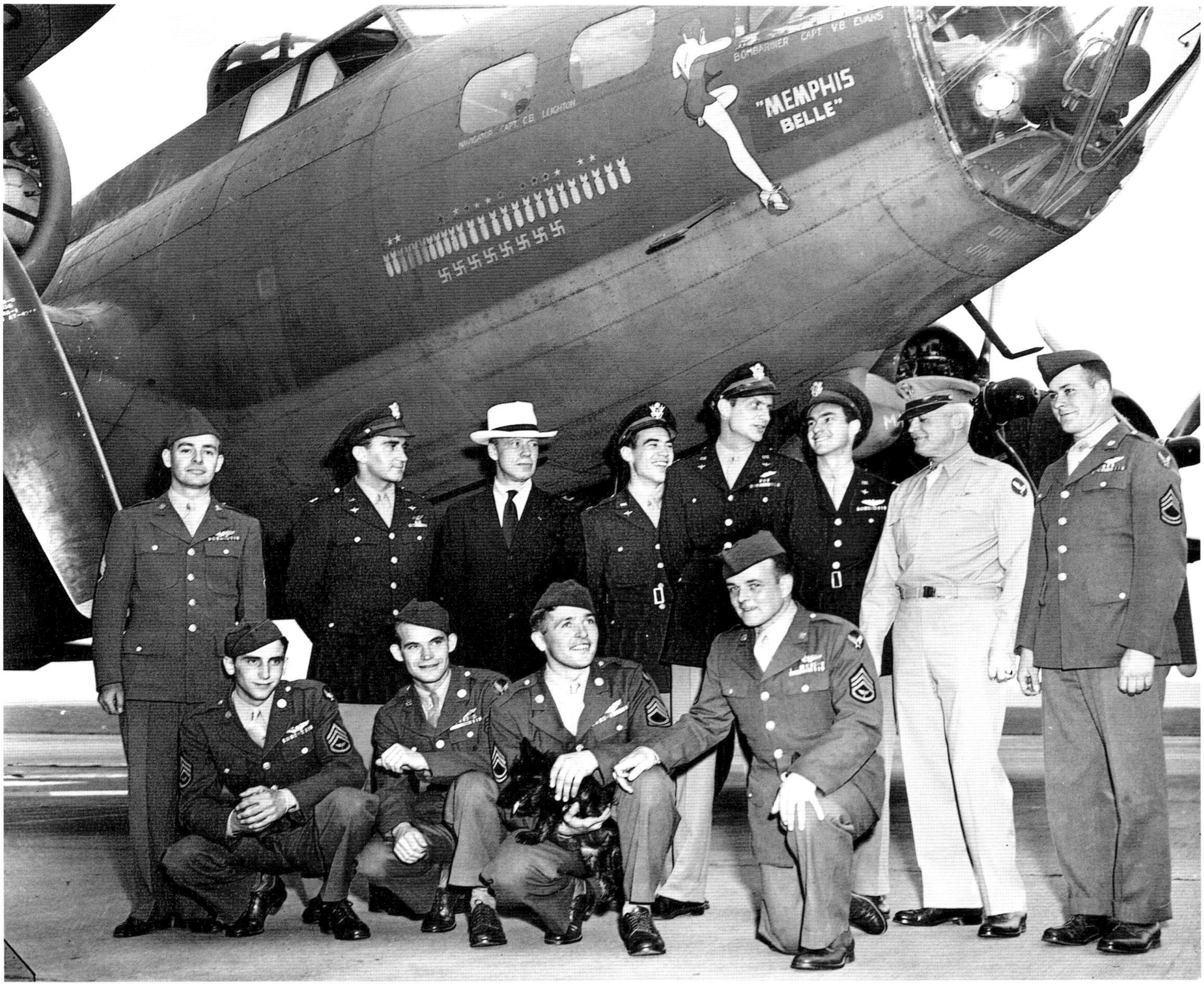

Glenn Miller. As such, they became closely associated with America's war effort. And, for a few short years, Vargas himself was an American hero.

Privately, Vargas was not entirely happy during those years. Having naïvely signed contracts without fully understanding them, he was forced to work for several years under a grueling schedule. The tension between the artist and the magazine culminated in a bitter court battle, and, by the late 1940s, the relationship was over. Vargas would later tell a friend that he'd succeeded "too fast for *Esquire*, and the publisher [David] Smart couldn't take it." But despite the resentment that Vargas felt for the rest of his life toward his one-time patron, he admitted that his years with *Esquire* were "the most satisfying" of his life. This book is an appreciation of Vargas's work during that period.

Joaquin Alberto Vargas y Chavez was born on 9 February 1896 in Arequipa, Peru, a mountain city about 500 miles southeast of Lima. Although the city itself was rather remote and untouched by cosmopolitan influences, Vargas was exposed at an early age to the artistic life. His father, Max, was a successful photographer, with studios in Arequipa and La Paz, Bolivia, and the young Alberto spent countless hours watching him work. By the time he reached early adolescence, Vargas was assisting his father. In particular, he had begun working with the airbrush, a tool he would eventually master and use to great effect on his paintings. Although the airbrush is now widely used by commercial artists to create silky-smooth surfaces and subtle contours, at that time it was a cumbersome tool. Indeed, it had been invented only a few years before Vargas was born. But Alberto learned to use it well, and while he initially employed it only to retouch photographs, he must have quickly realized its implications for painting.

Given Max's professional accomplishments, it would have been understandable if the younger Vargas had entered into a simple apprenticeship in his father's studio. When Vargas turned 14, however, his parents decided that he and his brother, Max Jr., should both study in Europe. Alberto was eventually enrolled in the prestigious Julien Studios in Geneva; his brother was to attend a different school in the same city to study banking and finance.

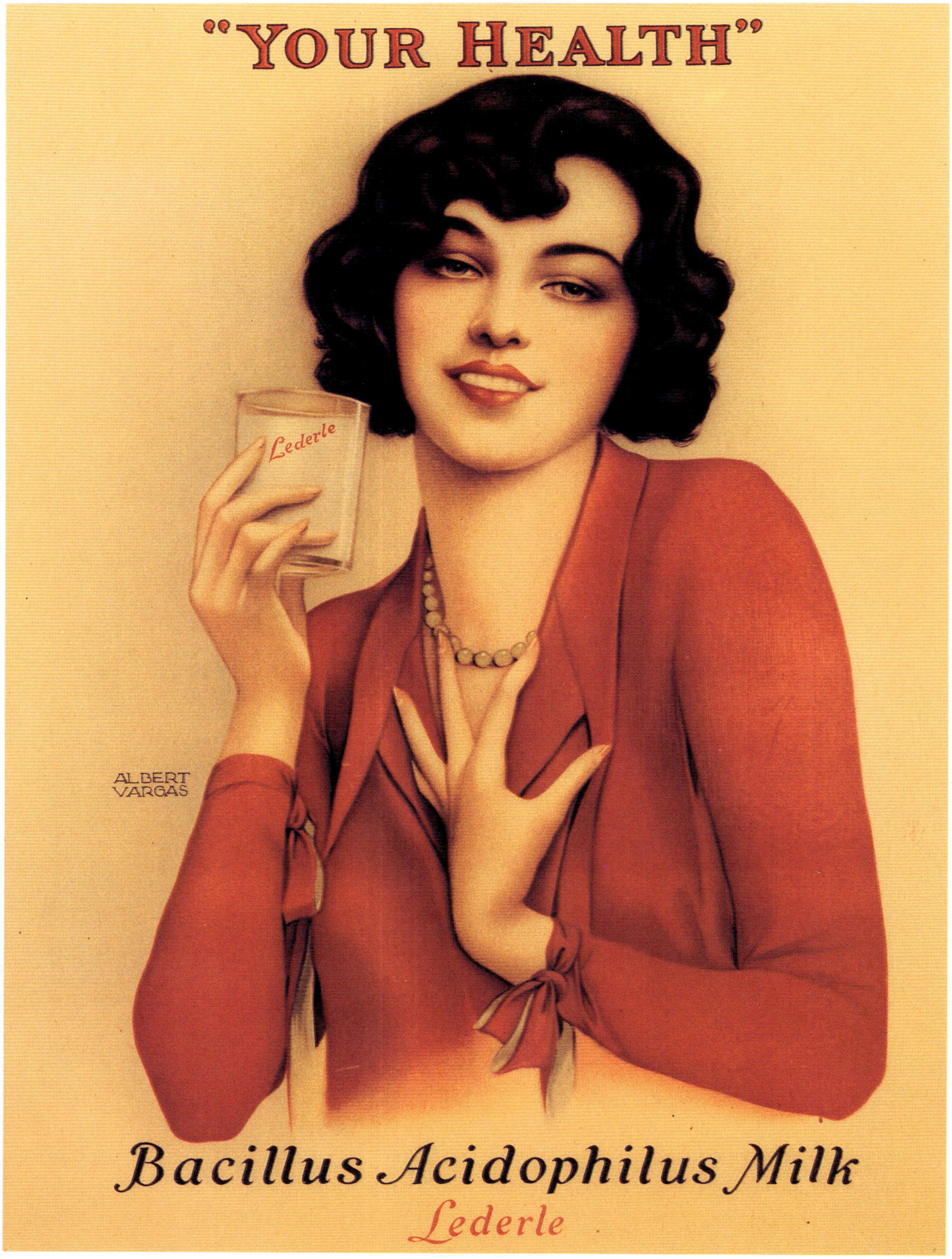

Left: An advertisement painted by Vargas in the early 1920s.

Right: Florenz Ziegfeld looks at photographs of aspiring show girls. Ziegfeld gave Vargas his first big break.

Opposite, bottom: A *Ziegfeld Follies* poster created by Vargas in 1922.

Accompanied by their father, the boys departed for Europe in 1911. Their initial stop was Paris, and it was here that Vargas was first exposed to the wider world of art. According to Vargas's friend and biographer, Reid Austin, Vargas quickly grew to admire the paintings of Ingres. But he was also taken with the work of popular illustrators, especially Raphael Kirchner, whose images of sensual young women adorned the pages of popular magazines. Vargas would later learn that Kirchner also supplied paintings to the *Ziegfeld Follies*. What he could not have imagined was that he would follow in his idol's footsteps.

For the next few years Vargas pursued his studies at a school outside Zurich, and in 1915 he finally began his apprenticeship at the Julien Studios. After a year in Geneva, Vargas's father informed Alberto that he was to continue his apprenticeship with a studio in London. While en route to England, however, he found that the war had severely restricted travel. Vargas concluded that he had no choice but to return to Peru and, in the fall of 1916, he boarded a ship bound for New York. Arrangements had been made for Max Jr. to meet him there, and at that point both boys would return home.

Vargas changed his plans shortly after arriving in the Big Apple. Like countless other young people, the Peruvian was excited by the pulse of the city. As Reid Austin has noted, Vargas was particularly attracted to the women of New

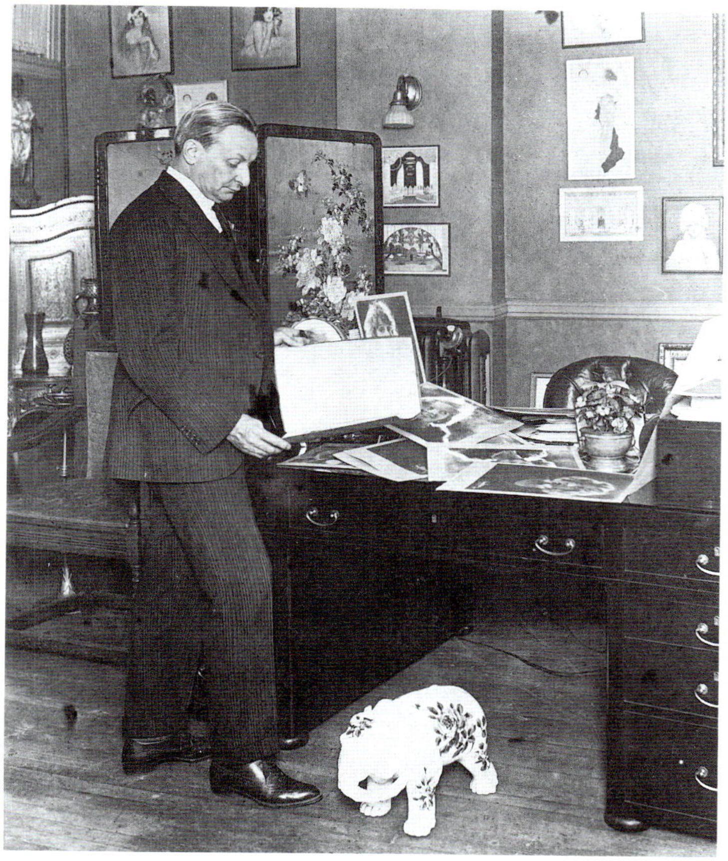

York. "From every building came torrents of girls," Vargas wrote. "I had never seen anything like it." Vargas noted that these American beauties, with their "self-assuredness and determination," were markedly different from the girls he had known in Europe. And he would eventually bestow these qualities upon his Varga Girls.

Vargas decided he could not leave New York, even if it meant cutting himself off from his father's financial assistance. His father, upon learning of Alberto's plans, wished him well but did indeed deny him any further financial support. Fortunately, Vargas was now skilled enough to begin his career as a commercial artist. After working for about a year as a photographer's retoucher, and later as an illustrator for a pattern company, Vargas sold his first freelance work. He was paid five dollars for each drawing. When he secured a few more clients, he quit his job with the pattern company and began supporting himself as a freelancer.

Vargas was impressed with the wide variety of illustrations of beautiful women that appeared in the popular magazines of the day. The most famous of these were the Gibson Girls, a series of woodcuts in *Life* and *Collier's*. Clad in knee-length dresses and black tights, these women appear at first glance to be very different from the Varga Girls. However, they had much in common: like many of the Varga Girls, the Gibson Girls had a sweet, open quality that represented, for the respective artists, an ideal of American womanhood. At the same time, Vargas continued to be inspired by the more worldly paintings of Raphael Kirchner and Maurice Milliere.

In the spring of 1919, Vargas got his first big break: a commission for a series of lobby paintings for the New Amsterdam Theater, home of the *Ziegfeld Follies*. Other such shows were also being produced at the time – notably the *Greenwich Village Follies*, which employed Vargas's future wife, Anna Mae Clift – but the productions of Florenz Ziegfeld defined the genre. In addition to featuring stunningly beautiful show girls, the *Follies* exploited the talents of a wide range of artists and performers, from Irving Berlin to W. C. Fields. The commission was an extraordinary opportunity for Vargas, and it marked the beginning of a very productive decade. Indeed, his association with Ziegfeld, and the status that came with it, led to many other freelance jobs, ranging from magazine work to private commissions for portraits.

As busy as he was during this period, Vargas somehow managed to find the time to paint purely for pleasure and artistic growth. Increasingly, his model was Anna Mae Clift. Vargas had met "Miss Clift" (as he called her for many years) about a year after his arrival in New York. It wasn't long before he fell in love with her, and the attraction appears to have been mutual. Nonetheless, the couple would not marry until 1930. By all accounts, they remained passionately in ove for the rest of their lives. In an undated poem to Anna Mae, Vargas writes of running his "quiv'ring hand 'round goddess contour o' your damascus flesh," and he refers to her "dim tender voice distilling lust into the brain." In spite of these feelings, however, he was always the gentleman in her presence, and in the presence of other women.

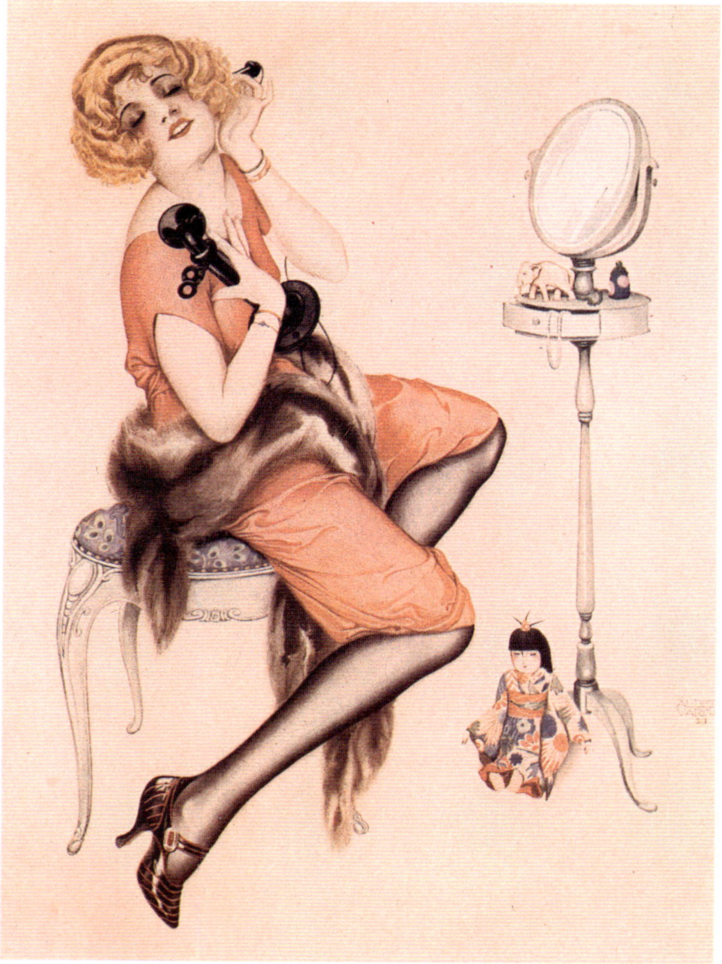

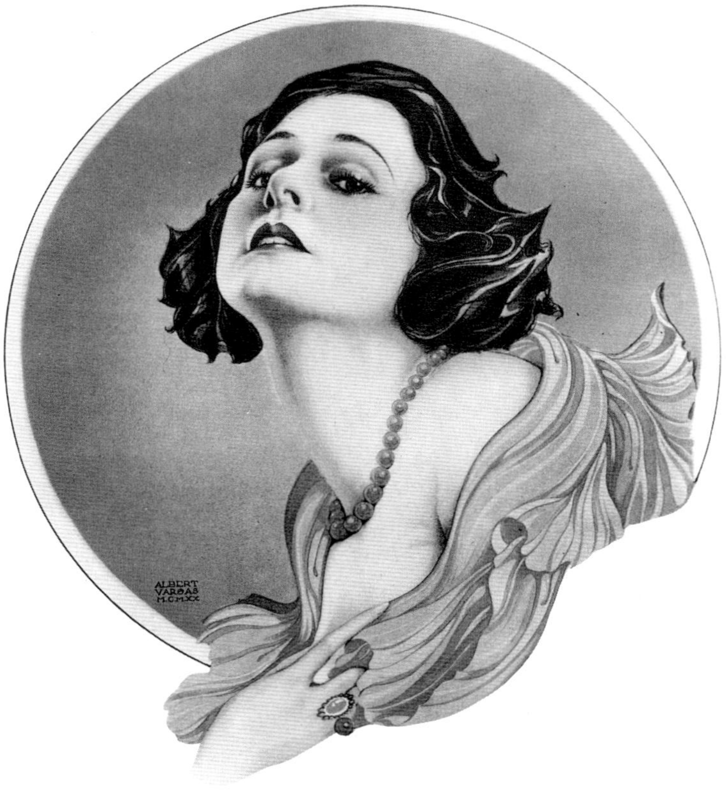

The beginning of Vargas's life with Anna Mae coincided with a sharp downturn in his professional fortunes. Changing tastes and national economic devastation put an end to the *Ziegfeld Follies*, and other types of work dried up as well. A handful of magazine and advertising jobs, along with the proceeds from Anna Mae's modeling, kept the couple afloat financially, but the next few years were very difficult, to say the least.

In 1934, Vargas's fortunes began to improve. That year, he obtained, among other jobs, a commission from the Fox Film Corporation to paint 13 star portraits. Vargas completed the job in the agreed-upon period of eight weeks, but continued to work in the studio's art department for the next few months. Among the portraits he painted during this period was one of the young Shirley Temple.

By 1935 Vargas had moved over to Warner Brothers, and by the end of the decade he had worked for every major studio. In September 1939, however, Vargas joined a unionization walkout, and the action cost him his reputation in Hollywood. Like most other people who spoke out for workers' rights at that time, he was branded a communist. Vargas's only option was to return to New York in an attempt to renew his contacts in the advertising

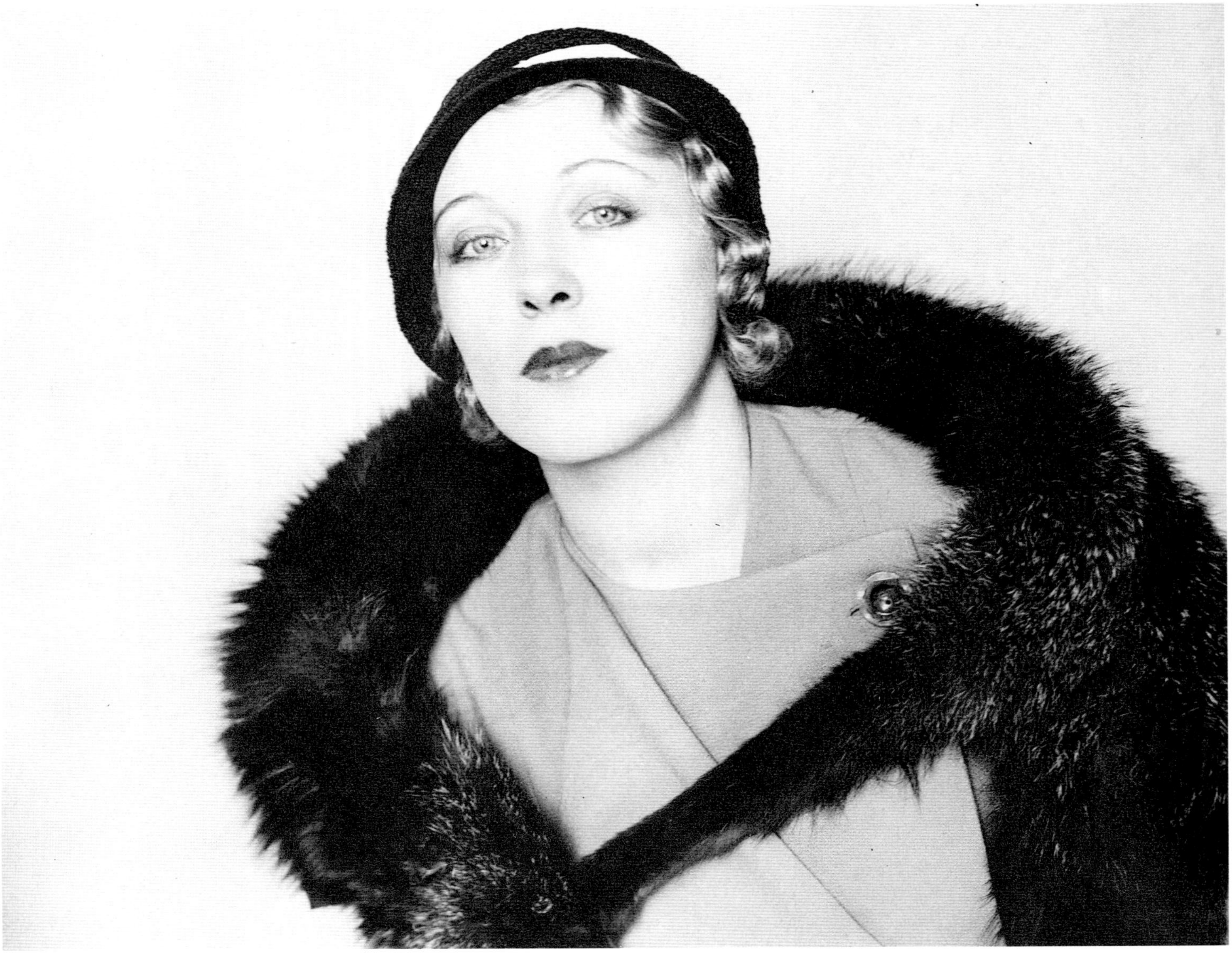

Left: A portrait of Norma Talmadge, painted by Vargas in 1919.

Opposite, bottom: Anna Mae Clift in 1930, the year she married Vargas.

Right: Anna Mae poses for a *Greenwich Village Follies* promotion in 1922.

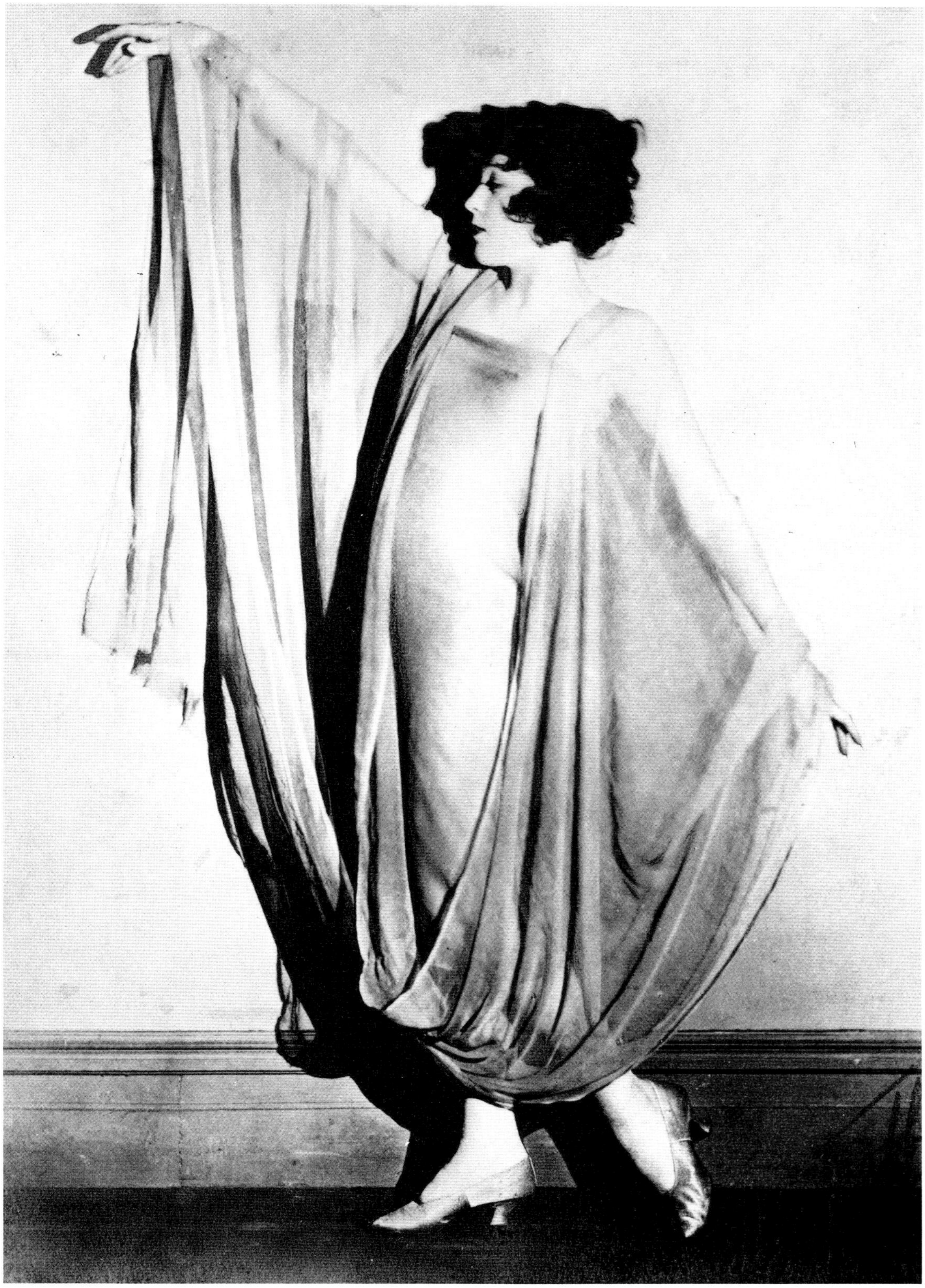

industry. During his first months there, the future continued to look bleak, but in June 1940 he got the biggest break of his career – a job offer from *Esquire*.

Esquire had been launched in 1933, perhaps the worst year of the Great Depression. But despite its exorbitant 50-cent cover price (*The Saturday Evening Post* cost a nickel), it was an immediate success. Its mixture of top-quality literature and journalism, "service" pieces on fashion and cars, and sexy, full-color cartoons, provided the perfect escape for Depression-weary men. As the 1930s wore on, the racy cartoons and drawings became an increasingly important part of the magazine's editorial mix, probably because the publisher was desperately trying to attract new readers. *Esquire*'s circulation peaked in 1937 at 728,000, but the following year it plunged to 453,000. In 1939, *Esquire* published its first pinup gatefolds featuring the work of an artist named George Petty.

Petty's cartoons had been part of the magazine since the first issue, and founding editor Arnold Gingrich considered them to be among "the truly distinguished elements of the magazine." But unlike Vargas, Petty was a tough businessman. *Esquire*'s publisher, David Smart, realized how valuable Petty was, and went out of his way to accommodate the artist. At the same time, however, he resented having to do so. As a result, Smart was more than open to the idea of replacing Petty with another artist by the time Vargas came along.

In the late spring of 1940, a friend of Vargas's, who had learned of the trouble between Petty and *Esquire*, arranged an appointment between Vargas and Sidney Carroll, head of the magazine's New York office. Carroll forwarded a sample of Vargas's work to David Smart, who was so

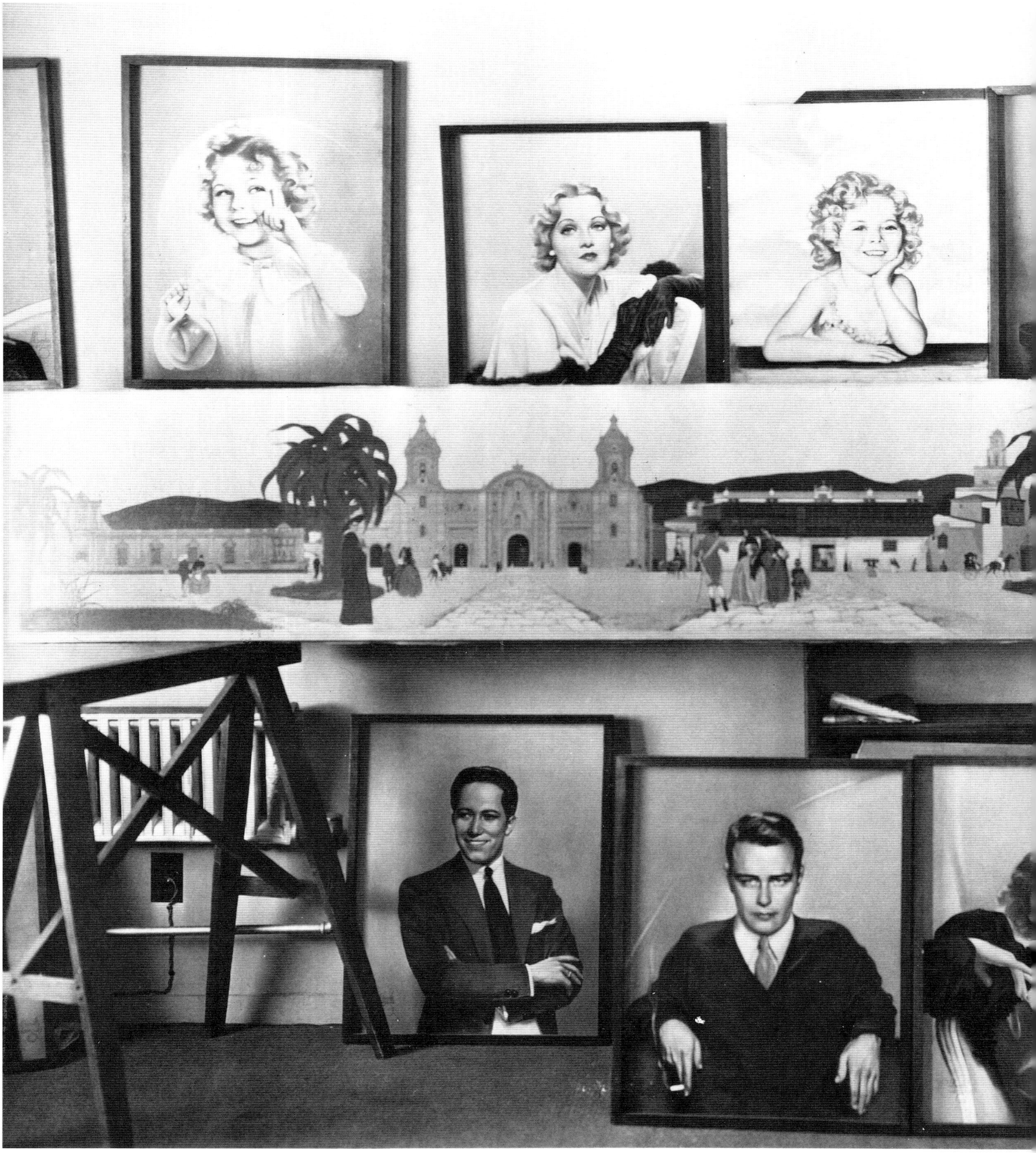

Below: Vargas poses with portraits he created for Fox Studios in the 1930s.

Right and below right: Storyboard drawings for the Warner Brothers movie *Juarez*, released in 1938.

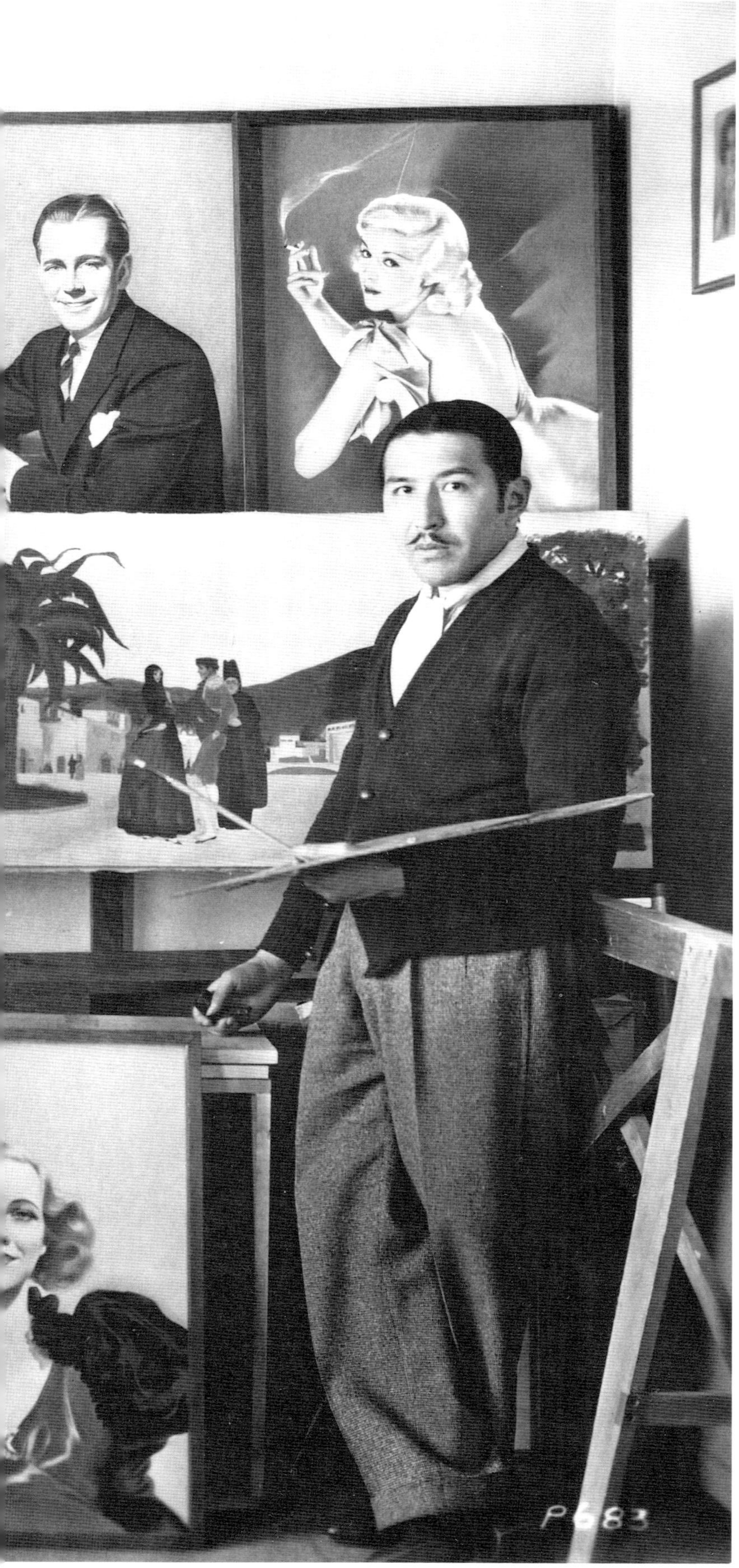

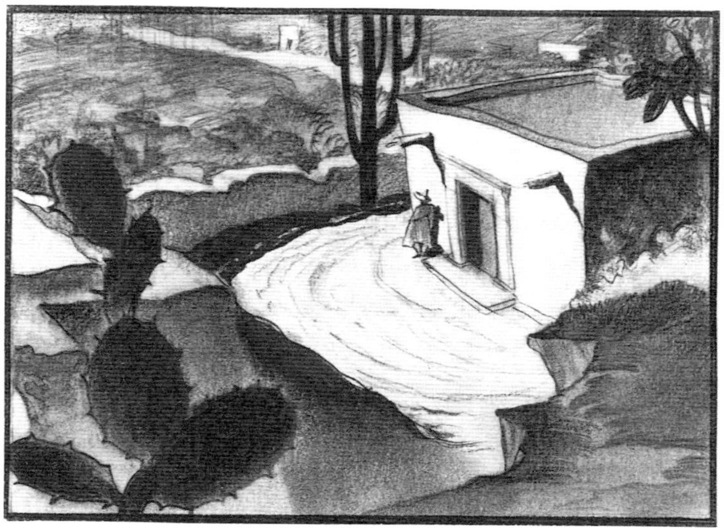

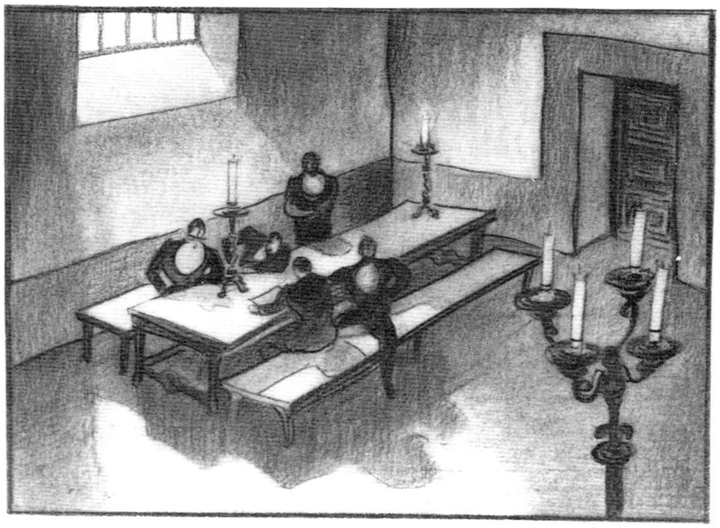

impressed that he traveled to New York to meet Vargas personally. By 20 June Vargas had signed his first contract with the magazine. The three-year contract stipulated that Vargas would receive a salary of $300 per month in exchange for "such art work as he is able to produce . . ." The vagueness of the contract left Vargas vulnerable to unfair demands but, as Reid Austin had noted, Vargas had no head for business. He was so happy to be working for such a prestigious magazine that it never occurred to him to try to negotiate any of the terms of the agreement or to argue when Smart told him to drop the "s" from his name. Varga, Smart said, sounded far better than Vargas.

The first Varga Girl, based on a sketch that was already in existence, was published in the October 1940 issue. In the previous issue, a full-page advertisement had alerted readers to the upcoming feature: "Every once in a while a new girl is born, fully grown and partially clothed, like Venus fresh risen from the sea," read the imaginative advertising copy.

"To the sinuous and faintly perfumed ranks of such women . . . *Esquire* introduces the Varga Girl . . . Her name joins those which over the centuries have made men stir uneasily in their beds, look critically at their wives, and wander to distant parts – pretending

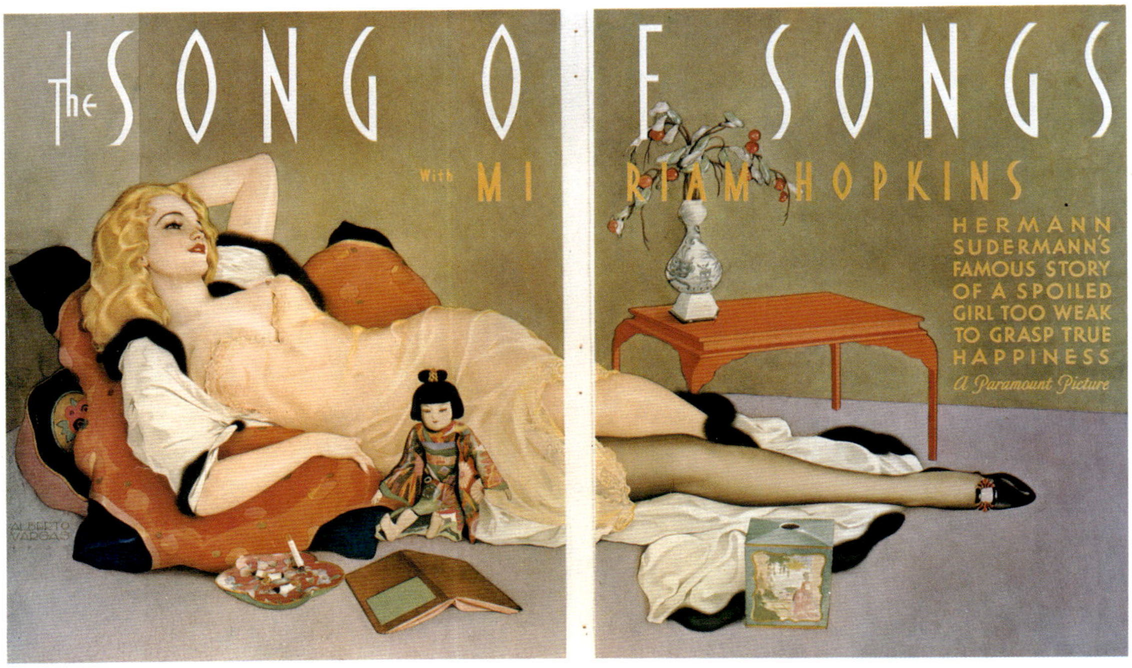

Left: Vargas's poster for the Paramount film, *The Song of Songs.*

Below: Vargas and *Esquire* publisher David Smart, second from right, with companions, look over a selection of Varga Girls.

to seek a Golden Fleece, a Holy Grail, a Fountain of Youth, or a Northwest Passage."

The Varga Girl may not have inspired men to wander the globe, but she did send them to their local newsstands. The circulation jumped, and the magazine was flooded with letters celebrating the new feature. Then, just two months after publishing the first gatefold, the magazine released the first Varga Girl calendar. "The calendar has become a national institution," Vargas wrote in his journal in January 1941. A national *sensation* might have been a more apt description at the time, but within a year or two the calendar would indeed become an institution.

During the first years of his association with *Esquire*, Vargas also began to produce work for the magazine's advertisers, including Jantzen Swimwear, Sealy Mattress Co., and several of the major movie studios. In 1942 Vargas created advertisements to promote M.G.M.'s *Du Barry Was a Lady*, starring Red Skelton and Lucille Ball. This assignment was especially gratifying for Vargas, since he had not

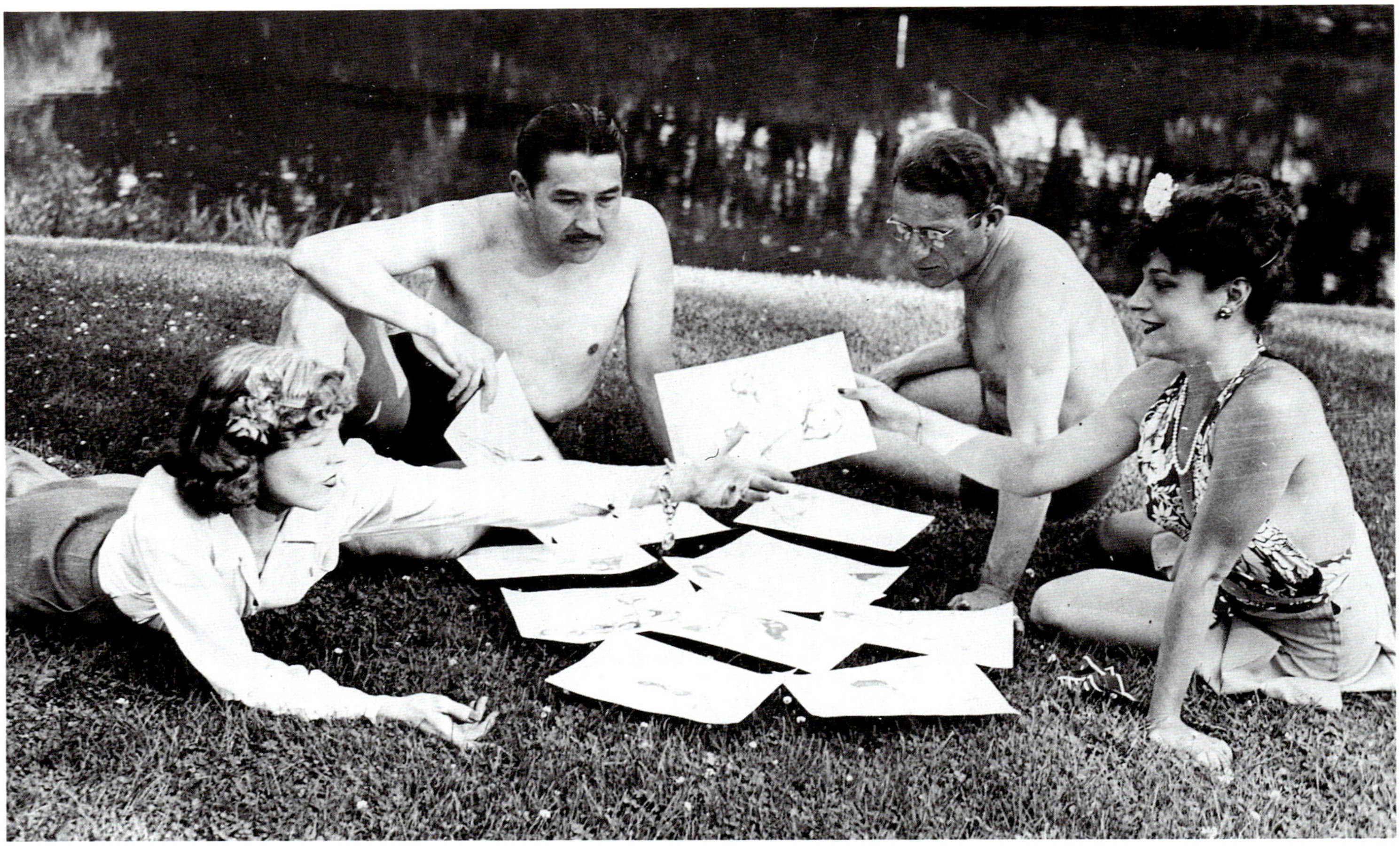

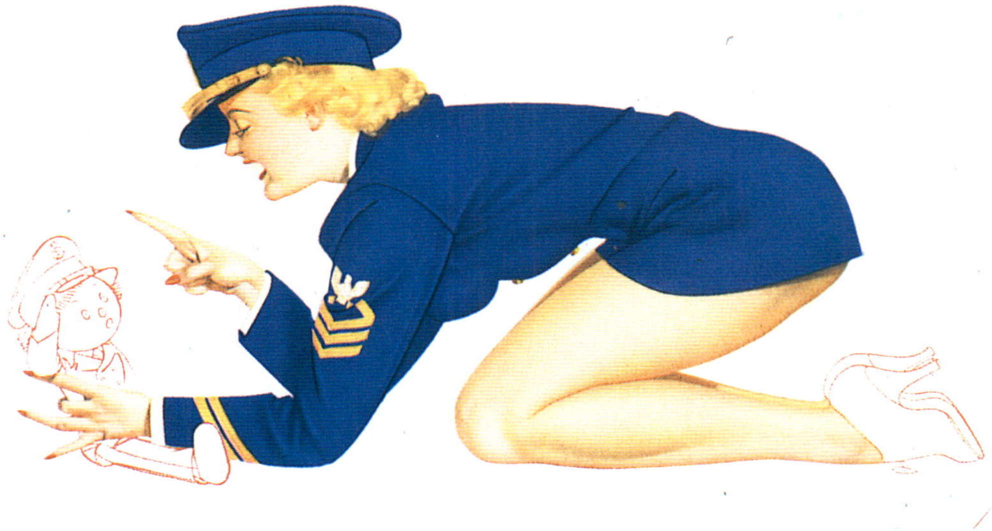

Left: A painting by George Petty, Vargas's predecessor at *Esquire*. *© 1991, The Hearst Corporation. All rights reserved.*

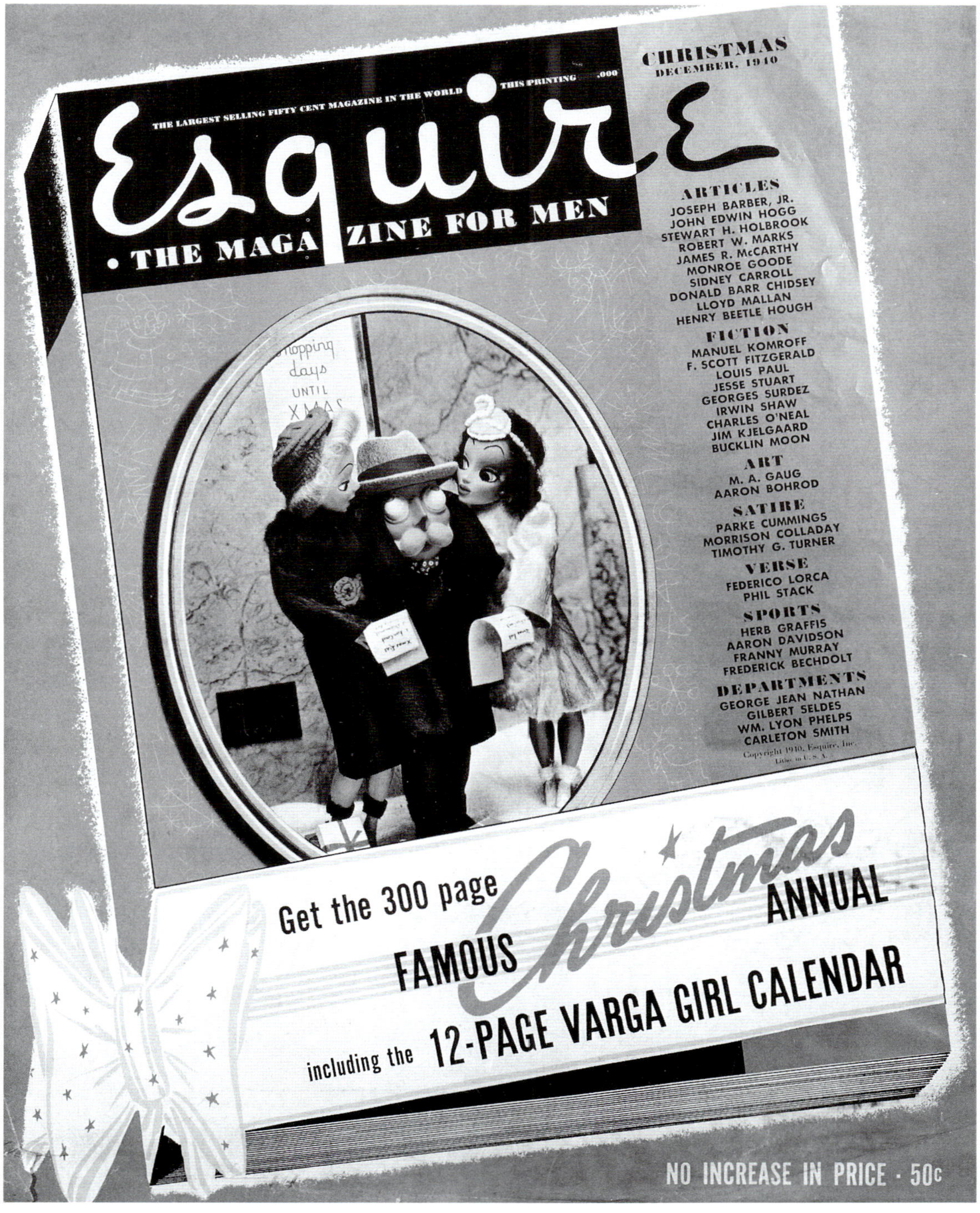

Right: The December 1940 issue of *Esquire* heavily promoted the first Varga Girl. *© 1991 The Hearst Corporation. All rights reserved.*

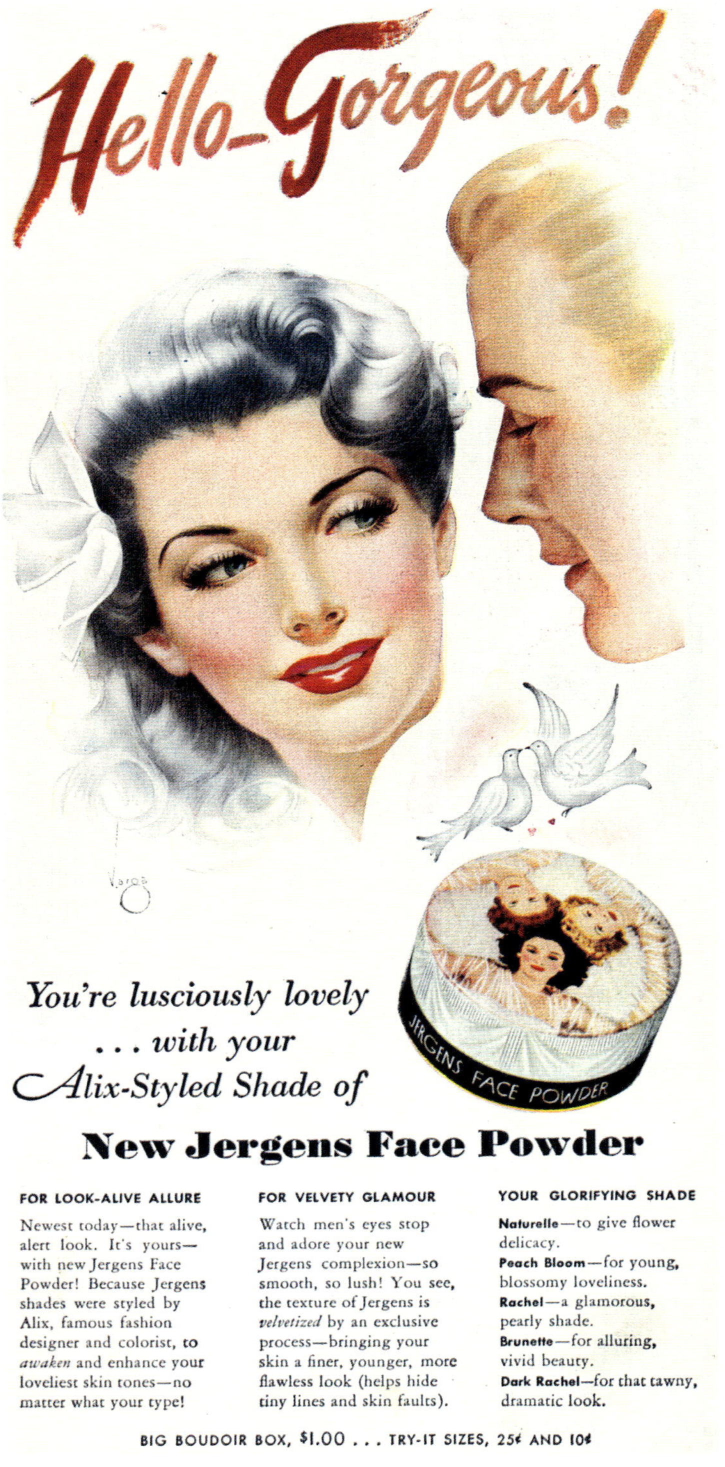

forgotten how shabbily he had been treated by the studios after participating in the union protests.

In spite of the importance of Vargas's advertising work, the *Esquire* gatefolds and calendars remained the most important part of his output. As already noted, the model for much of Vargas's pre-*Esquire* work had been Anna Mae. According to Reid Austin, however, Smart objected to this arrangement, and urged that she be replaced by a 15-year-old named Jeanne Dean. The move was significant: many of the paintings from these early years at *Esquire* reflect Dean's vivaciousness and innocent sensuality. The balance of these qualities made the Varga Girl extraordinarily popular, especially among the soldiers. And the war gave *Esquire* additional justification for publishing these pictures.

The Varga Girl had never been promoted as "art," but as long as the feature remained popular with soldiers, *Esquire* could claim that it was more than mere entertainment. After all, how could anyone object to something that so clearly "boosted the morale of our troops?" By 1942, *Esquire* was publishing special editions – without advertising – for distribution to U.S. troops stationed overseas. However, not everyone bought the morale-boosting argument. In August 1943, Postmaster General Frank C. Walker revoked *Esquire*'s second-class mailing privileges on the grounds that the magazine was not "published for the dissemination of information of a public character, or devoted to literature, the sciences, arts, or some special industry." The Varga Girl was not the only reason for this action, but she was certainly one of the key reasons. Walker's Catholic sensibilities were offended by the overt eroticism of the pinups, and he intended to undermine their popularity. As Peter Spielmann noted in a master's thesis on the magazine's history, *Esquire* could have continued to mail fourth-class, but at an additional cost of $500,000.

Esquire was not the only publication targeted by Walker, but it was the first one to fight the order. A board made up of assistant postmasters found unanimously in favor of *Esquire*, but Walker overruled the board and the case went to federal court. Fortunately for *Esquire*, the magazine

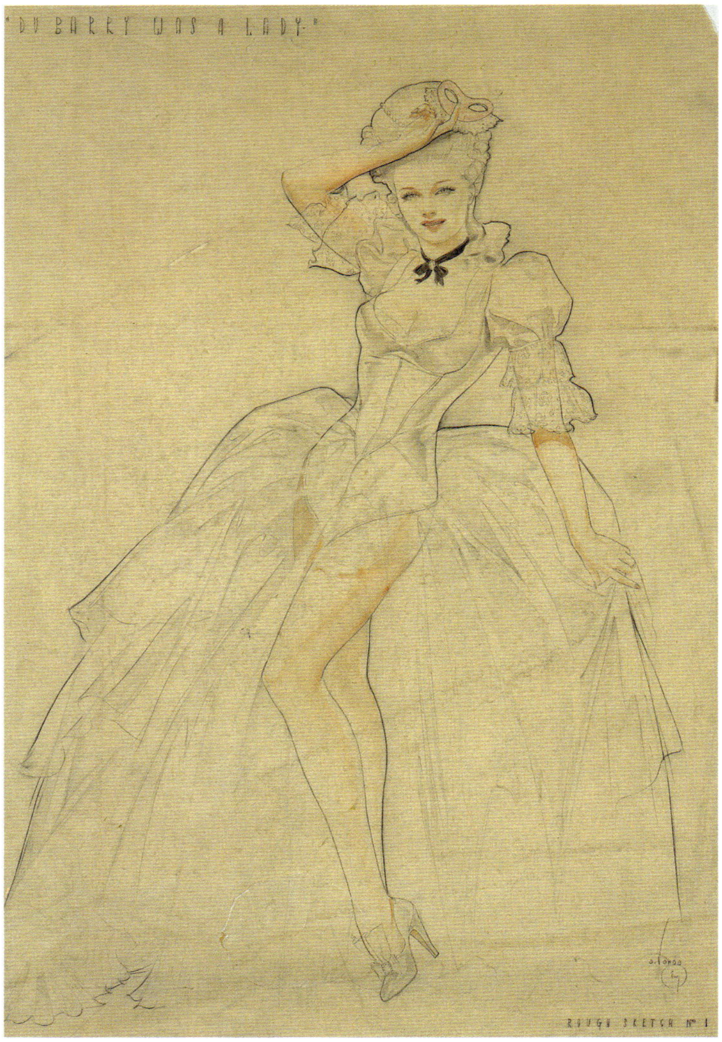

Opposite, top: One of many advertisements Vargas created while he was under contract to *Esquire*.

Opposite, bottom: Madame Du Barry, as sketched by Vargas. *© 1991 The Hearst Corporation. All rights reserved.*

Right: Vargas's favorite model, Jeanne Dean, rests, while the artist looks over a selection of his recent work.

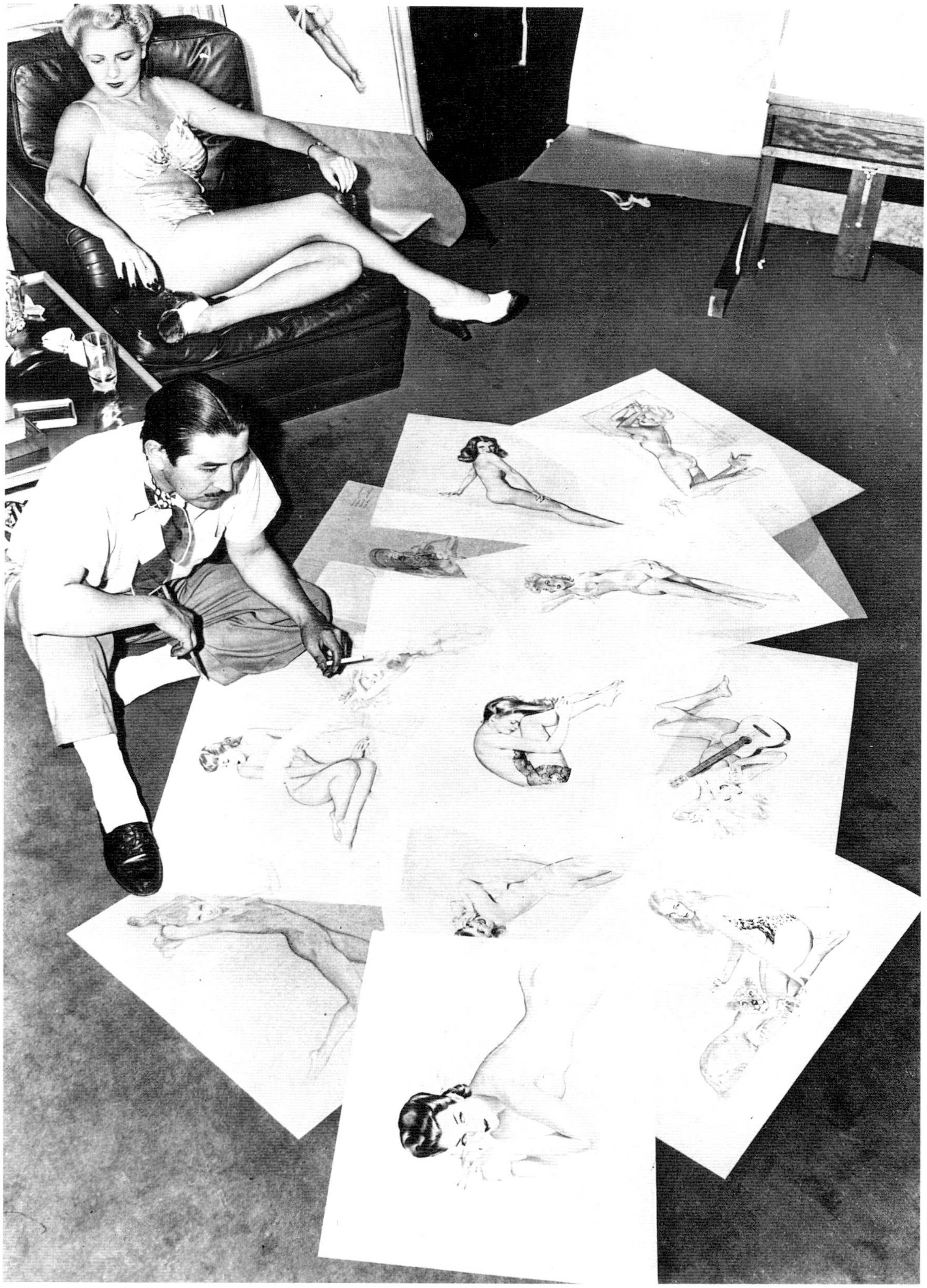

immediately won the right to distribute via second-class mail until the case was resolved. Finally, in 1946, the case went to the Supreme Court. Justice William O. Douglas, a lifelong staunch defender of the First Amendment, wrote the majority opinion in favor of the magazine.

Troublesome as the court case was for *Esquire*, in the end it helped boost the popularity of the magazine in general, and the Varga Girl in particular. A letter to the editor from an Air Corps lieutenant, published in *Esquire* while the court battle was raging, reflects the prevailing popular attitude toward the case. "The boys are more amused than worried over your case," the lieutenant wrote. "However, the possibility of *Esquire* along with other magazines losing their second-class mailing privileges is some what alarming . . . It is a real treat after a hard day . . . to sit in your tent and completely relax with *Esquire*." The soldier concluded that the charge of obscenity was plainly "absurd."

Esquire was popular among the soldiers for a variety of reasons (most really *did* read the articles). But the Varga Girl pinups and calendars, which could now be found in every barbershop across the land and in army barracks around the world, were certainly the highlight of the magazine for

Right: William C. O'Brien, attorney for the U.S. Post Office, shows a Varga Girl to Methodist Bishop Edwin Hughes during the trial to determine whether *Esquire*'s mailing privileges should be revoked.

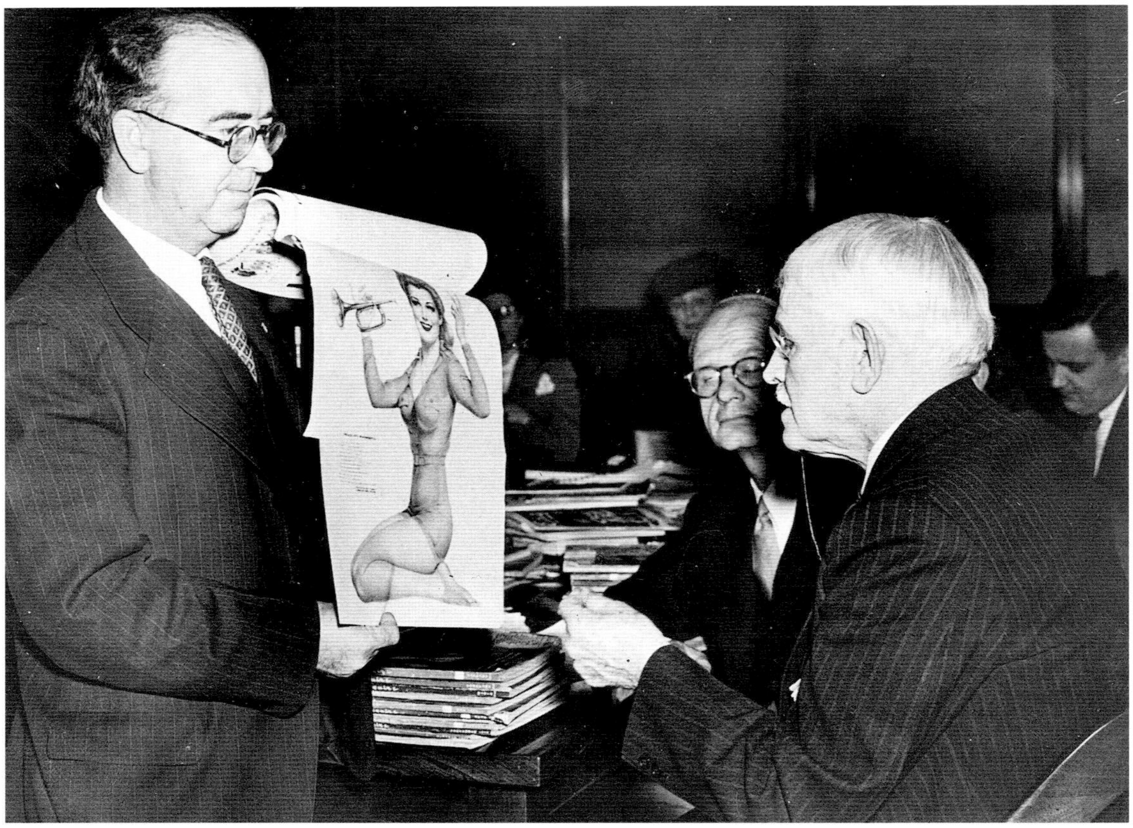

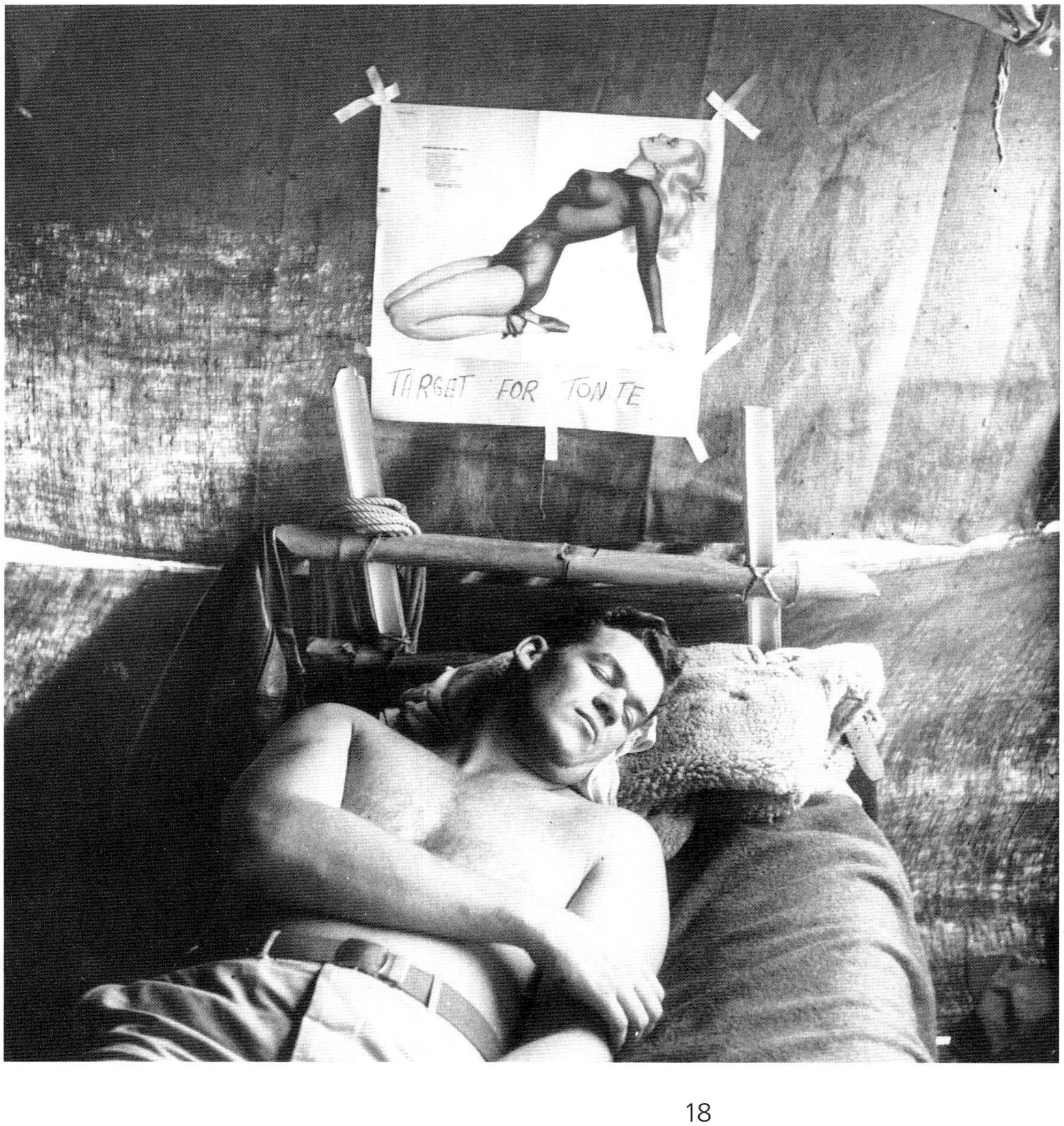

Left: An Army Air Corps pilot and his Varga Girl.

Right: One of Vargas's original drawings for the 1942 calendar.

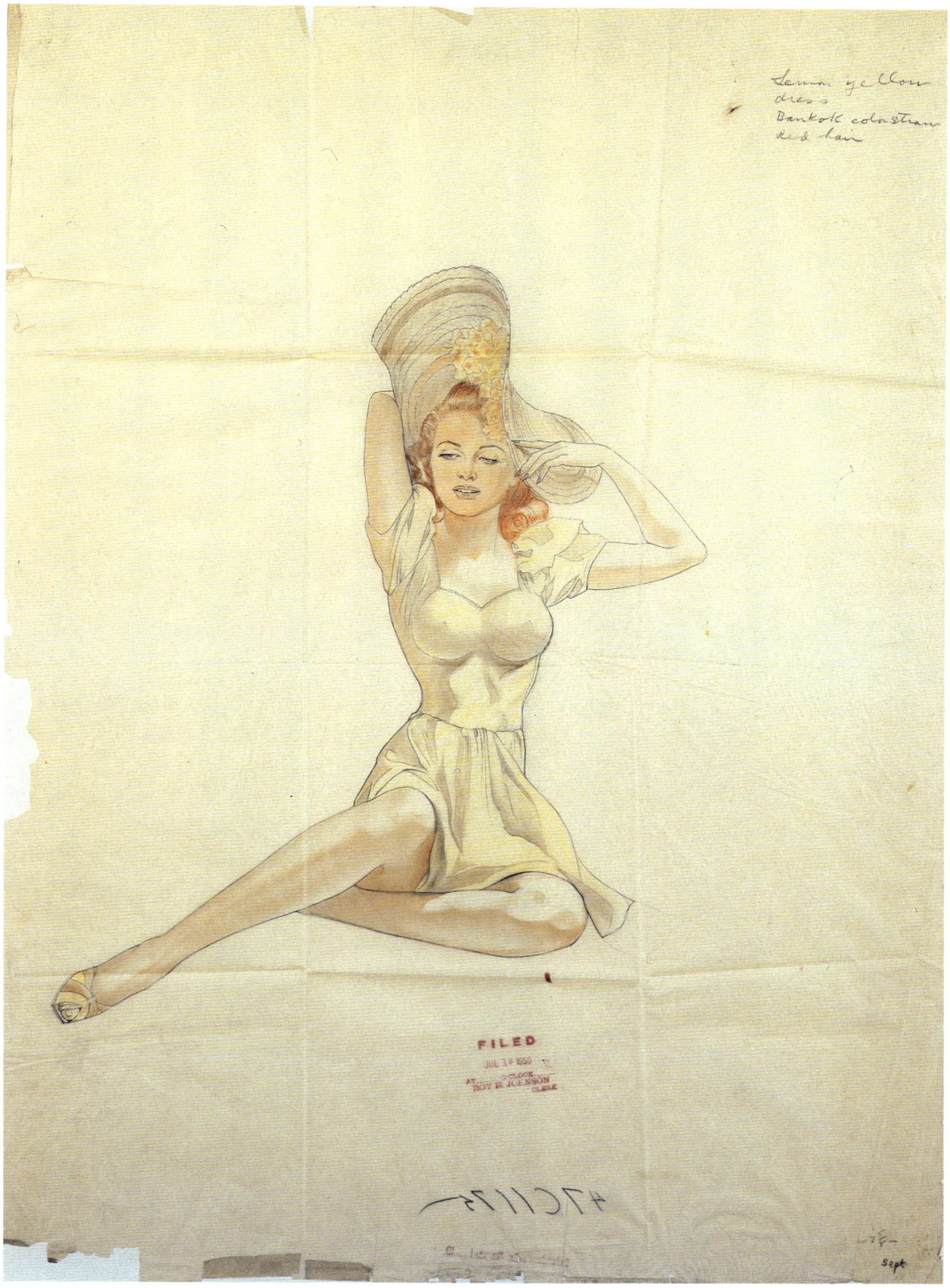

many readers. Their popularity was further demonstrated by *Esquire*'s success in selling Varga playing cards and other products bearing the artist's work.

Vargas received a substantial pay increase in his 1944 contract as a result of this success, but the agreement also called for a *minimum* of one painting a week. Vargas apparently did not read the contract before signing it. When Smart called the clause to his attention the following year, Vargas complained that the schedule was unrealistic. He continued working 16 to 18 hours a day in an attempt to keep up, but by the winter of 1946 tensions between the two men had reached breaking point.

According to Austin, the final meeting between Smart and Vargas began calmly, but when the subject of Vargas's work schedule and compensation came up, it degenerated into a ''smoldering, ugly shambles [and ended] with Smart's threat to see that Alberto never made another drawing for anyone in the United States.'' Immediately after the meeting, Smart ordered that the ''Varga Girl'' name be removed from the gatefolds that had not yet been published. The 1947 calendar also appeared under the label ''*Esquire* Girl.''

Shortly after the blowup, Vargas sued *Esquire*. A district court found in his favor, but the following August *Esquire* appealed against the decision and won. Additional suits and countersuits followed but, in the end, after four years of litigation, *Esquire* emerged victorious. The trial left Vargas deep in debt and legally unable to use his trademark name "Varga."

Throughout the 1950s Vargas barely managed to make a living, although he did experience one professional triumph: a trip to his native land at the invitation of the Peruvian government. The purpose of the trip was an exhibition of his work in Lima, and it couldn't have come at a better time. Vargas was received as a home-town hero.

The late 1950s also marked the beginning of a long-term relationship with Hugh Hefner and *Playboy* magazine. When Vargas approached Hefner in 1956 at the urging of Anna Mae, the young publishing entrepreneur was immediately impressed with the work he saw. Hefner told Vargas that he did not think he could use him on a regular basis, but he did agree to run a pictorial spread in 1957.

Regular work with *Playboy* did not begin until 1960, a year after Reid Austin arrived as associate art director for the magazine. Austin recalls how, "with embarrassing regularity," he would try to persuade Hefner to run Vargas's work. Eventually, Austin was successful: Vargas's work appeared in *Playboy* for the next two decades.

The artist's general contentment during this period was marred by one horrible event: the death of Anna Mae in November 1974. The loss was so devastating, according to Austin, that it greatly affected Vargas's ability to paint. *Playboy* nonetheless remained loyal to him, simply retouching his work when necessary.

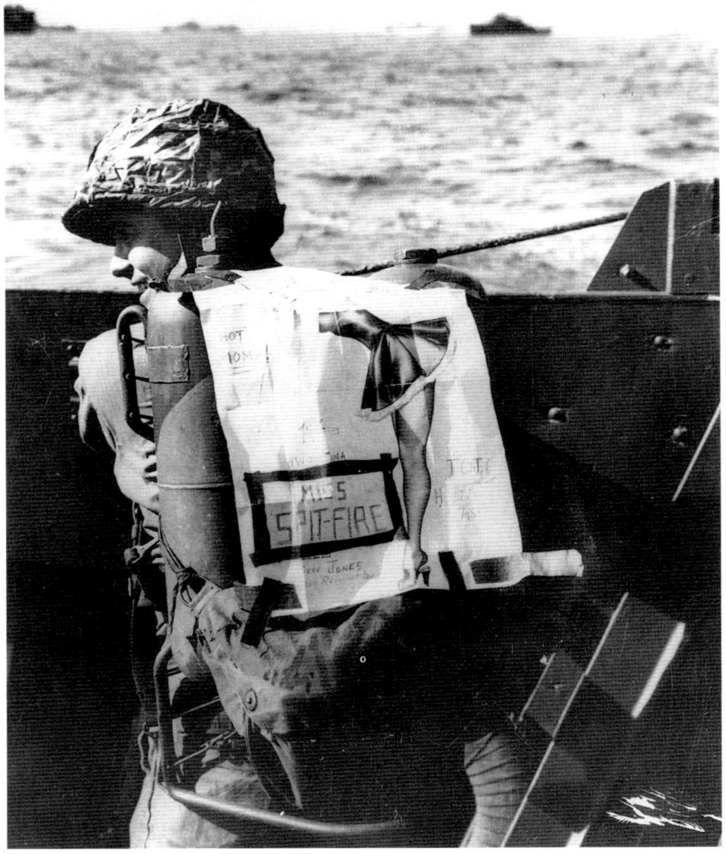

Vargas himself died in December 1982 at the age of 86, but his work lives on. Today, in fact, Vargas may have more admirers than at any time since the height of World War II. The San Francisco Art Exchange, more than any other

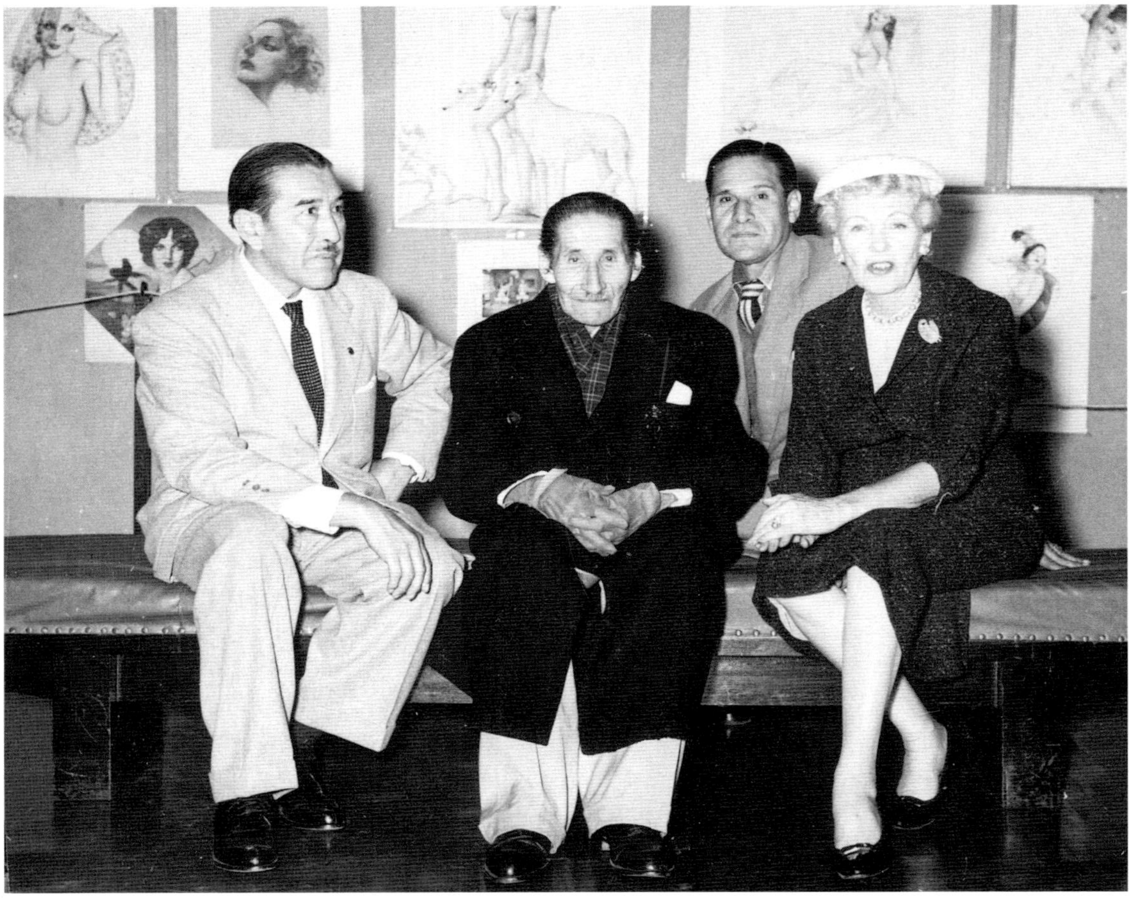

Above: Wherever American soldiers went during the war, they carried the Varga Girls with them. This G.I. was approaching Iwo Jima at the time the picture was taken.

Left: Alberto and Anna Mae are joined by his 88-year-old father, center, and his brother, during an exhibition of Vargas's work in Lima, Peru, in the 1950s.

Opposite: Vargas sketches a portrait of movie star Linda Darnell.

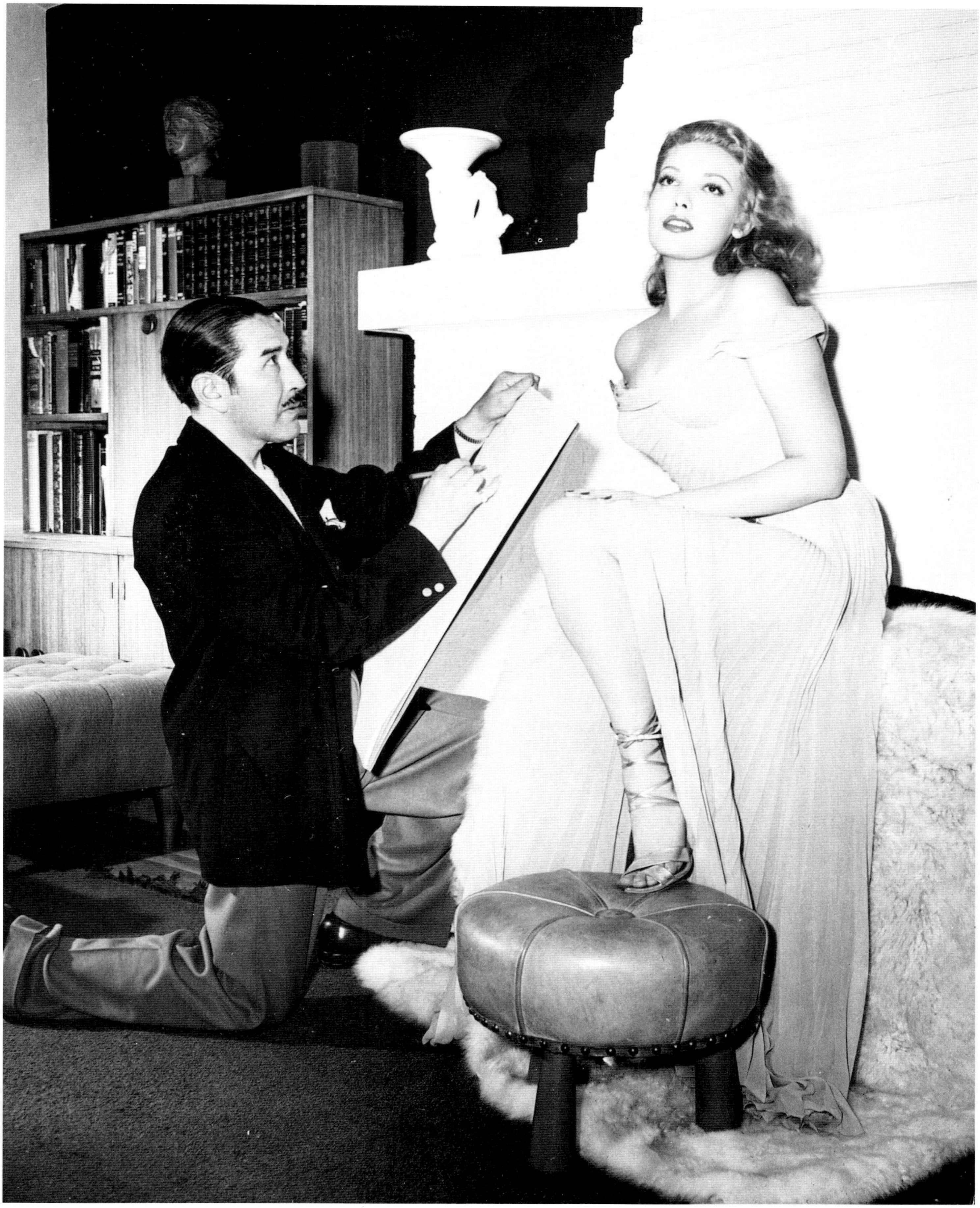

institution, deserves credit for helping to sustain interest in Vargas's work. In addition to exhibiting and selling Vargas originals from various periods of the artist's life, the gallery has successfully marketed limited-edition prints of the *Esquire* paintings. (The originals are housed in the Helen F. Spencer Museum at the University of Kansas.)

The continuing demand for these works is a testament to Vargas's artistic talents. Vargas, it has been said, was a

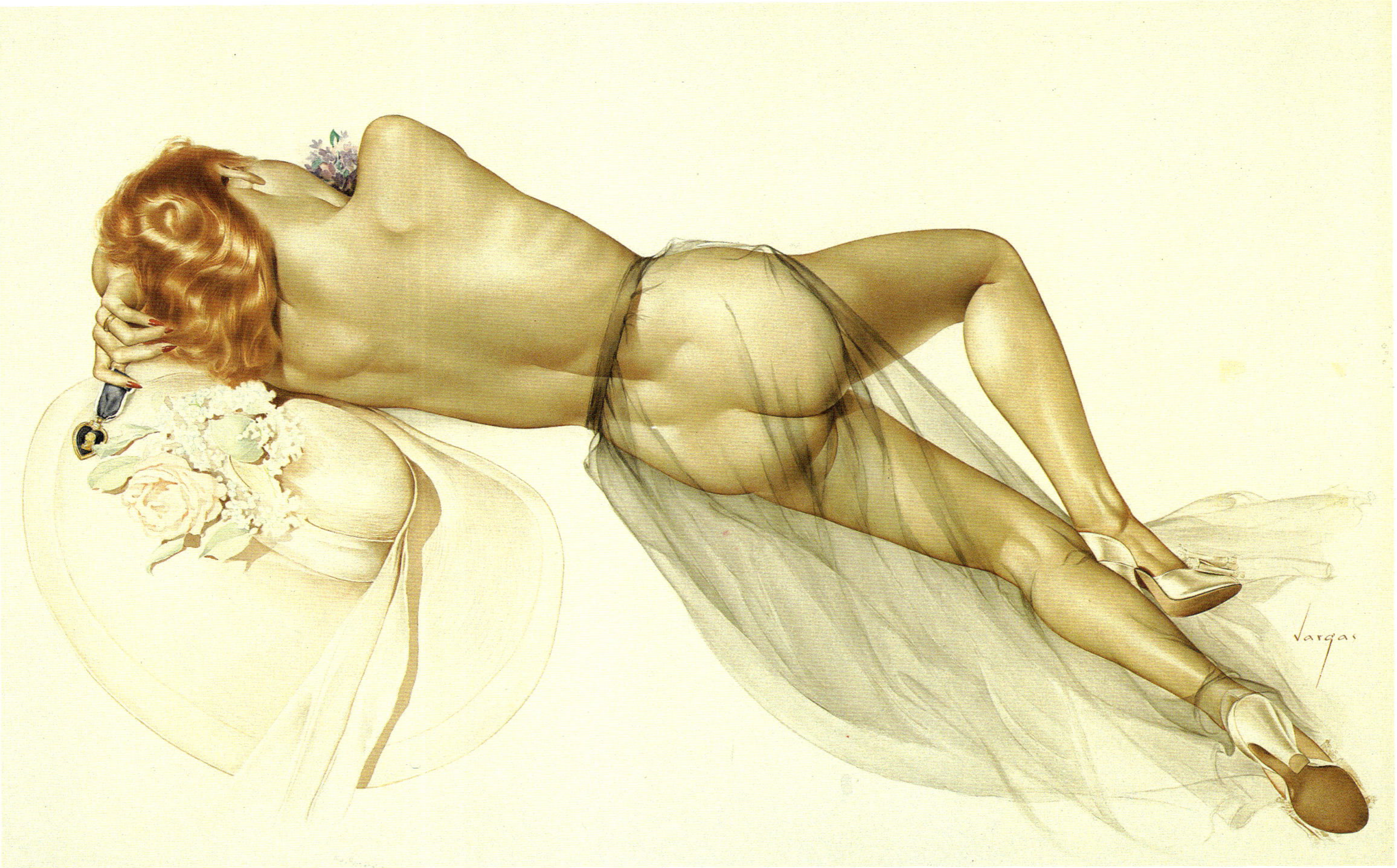

mere illustrator, not a true artist. But critics who make that assertion ignore the more subtle aspects of his paintings. Many people, for example, are so preoccupied with the Varga Girls' voluptuous bodies that they ignore Vargas's talent for painting faces. He had demonstrated this talent as early as the 1920s, when he painted a series of society portraits, and he went on to paint numerous celebrity portraits as well. But some of his best faces are those that he gave to his ''girls'' in *Esquire*. Indeed, it may come as a surprise to those people who are only superficially familiar with the Varga Girl paintings, that a number of them are *portraits*. Some, like the October 1941 gatefold featuring three women sporting military pins, are practically devoid of any overt sexuality. Others, like the January image from the 1942 calendar, are subtly seductive, despite the fact that they feature nothing but a face and a hand. Still others, like the February 1941 gatefold, are as infused with sensual passion as the most voluptuous full-body paintings. (This would be true even if Vargas had chosen to end the painting just below the neck.)

Many of the Varga Girls' faces are engaging primarily because of the intensity of their eyes. Indeed, the most alluring face is on one of his full-body paintings: the December 1944 gatefold. So penetrating are the woman's eyes, that the beauty of her figure is almost of secondary importance. On the other hand, Vargas often painted his ''girls'' with their eyes closed, and somehow still managed to bring them to life. In the case of the October 1944 calendar image, for example, the sensual delight apparent on

Above: Vargas's 1975 painting commemorating World War II.

Below: A society portrait painted by Vargas in 1928.

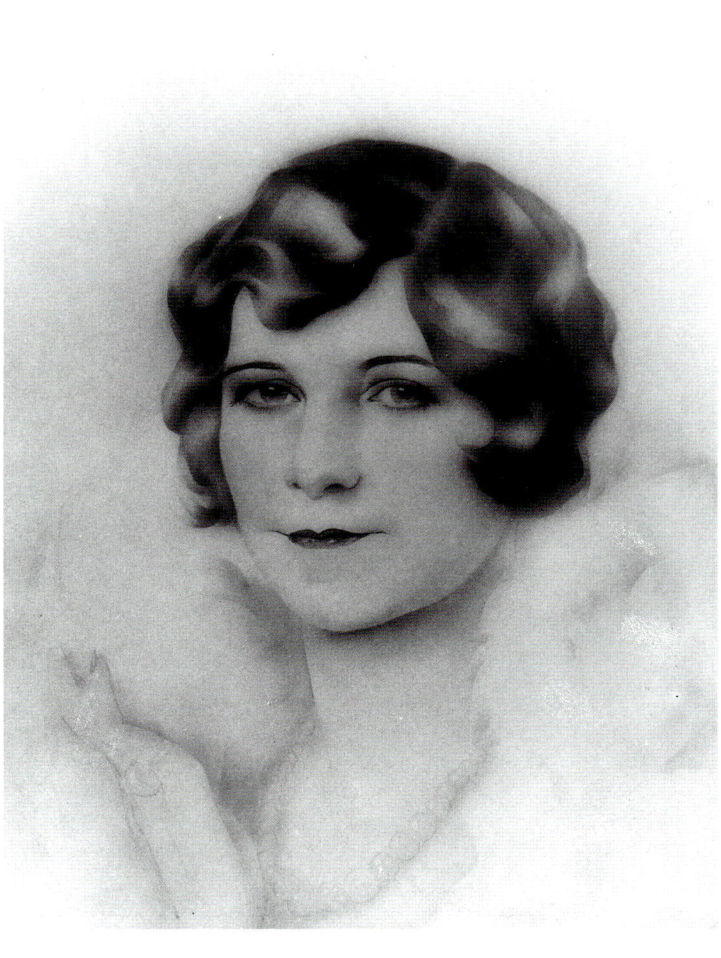

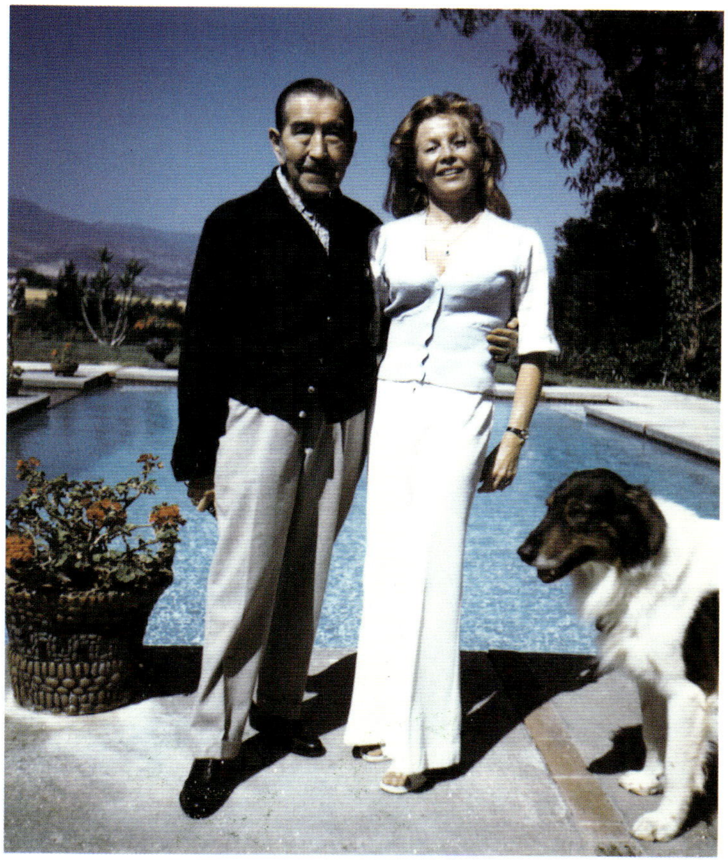

Left: Vargas posing with Jeanne Dean by her pool in 1975.

Below: Vargas taking a break from his work at *Playboy* in the late 1970s.

Bottom: A Vargas painting from the 1940s. © *1991, The Hearst Corporation. All rights reserved.*

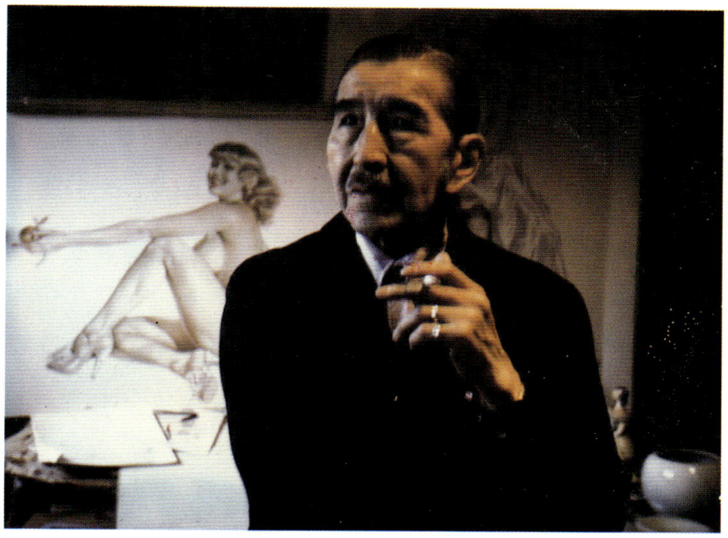

the woman's face is beautifully expressed by an ever-so-slight smile.

Because Vargas's faces are so appealing, it may seem curious that some of his paintings have no faces at all. In some cases, the Varga Girl's back was turned toward the viewer because the artist was rushing to meet a deadline. In a few instances, the fact that we cannot see the face makes the image more alluring. But, for the most part, we should be grateful for Vargas's early training in his father's photography studio. It was undoubtedly there that he first gained an appreciation of the beauty of the human face, and throughout his later career he expressed that appreciation in his paintings.

Vargas is also popular today, of course, because of the nostalgic feelings that his paintings evoke. Even those of us who were not yet born at the time of World War II can feel as if we are being transported back to the 1940s when we gaze at these images. This is especially true of the images with overt military themes. The uniformed Varga Girls were a direct attempt to support military recruiting, and many officers believed that they were effective. In December 1942, for example, Vargas received a letter from the U.S. Coast Guard praising his paintings of women in uniform: "This is really going to be of great help to us, since recruiting is getting away to a very slow start," it said.

Ultimately, however, Vargas did not create the Varga Girls out of a sense of patriotic duty. Nor was his painting primarily a means of making a living. He painted because he passionately loved doing so. His work, even during the 1940s, is uneven in quality, probably because of the intense deadline pressures he faced. But in his best works his artistic passion shines through. And when we come upon these works, we cannot escape the conclusion that Vargas was an artist of brilliant, if limited, vision. The pages that follow are the evidence of that brilliance.

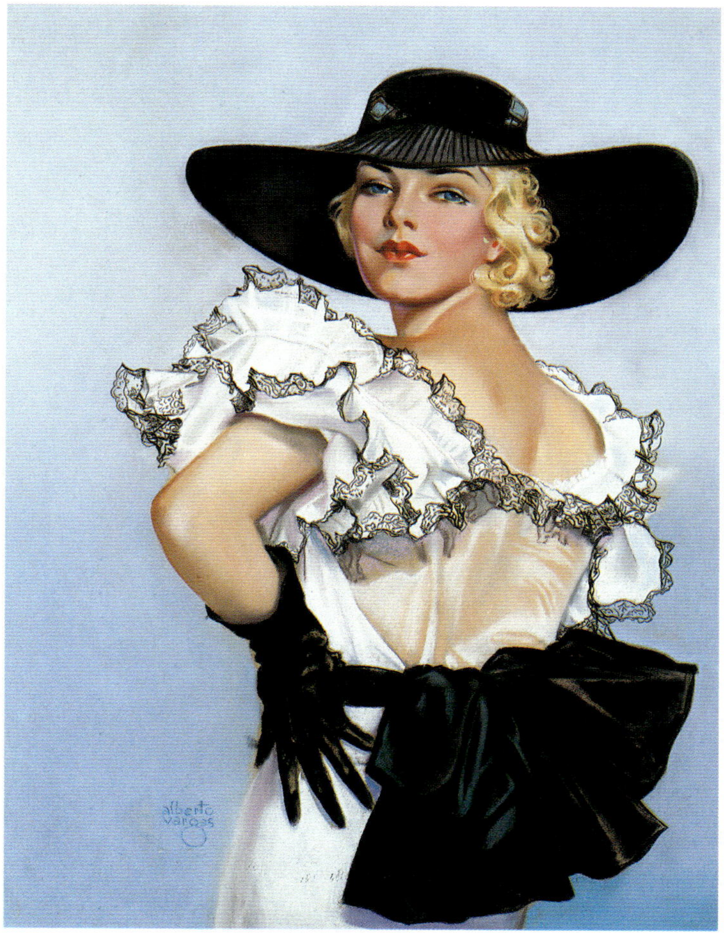

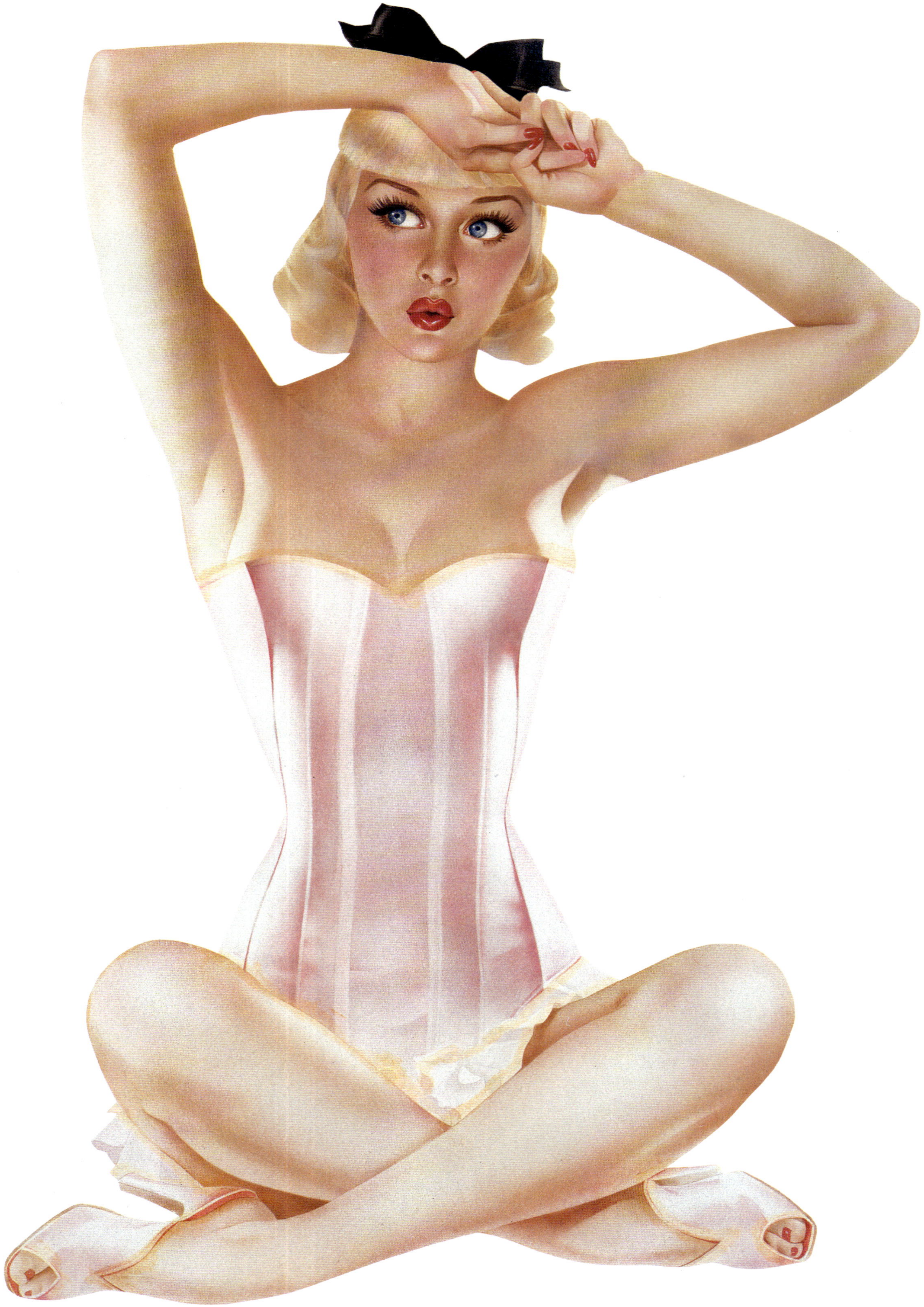

Sweet Innocence

Left: November 1943 Foldout

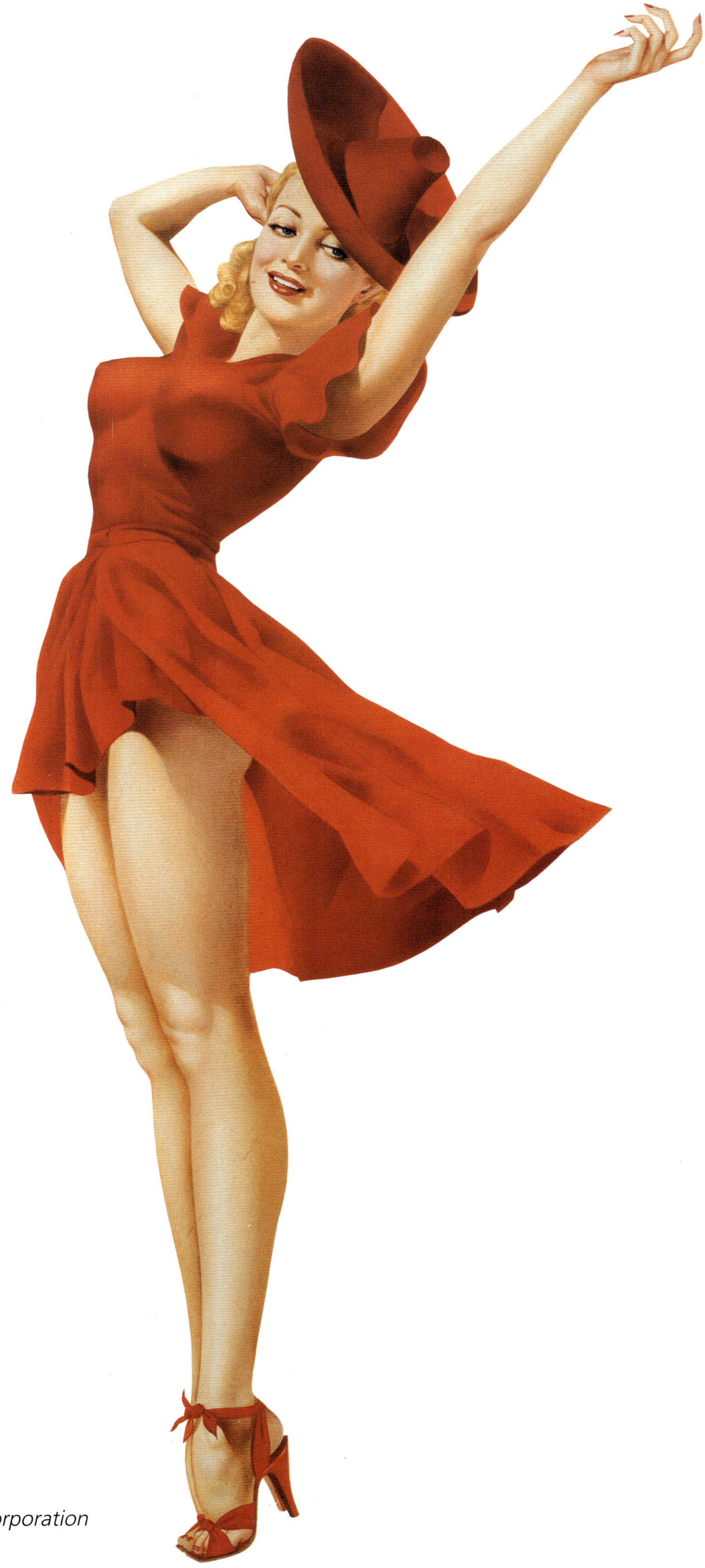

September 1941

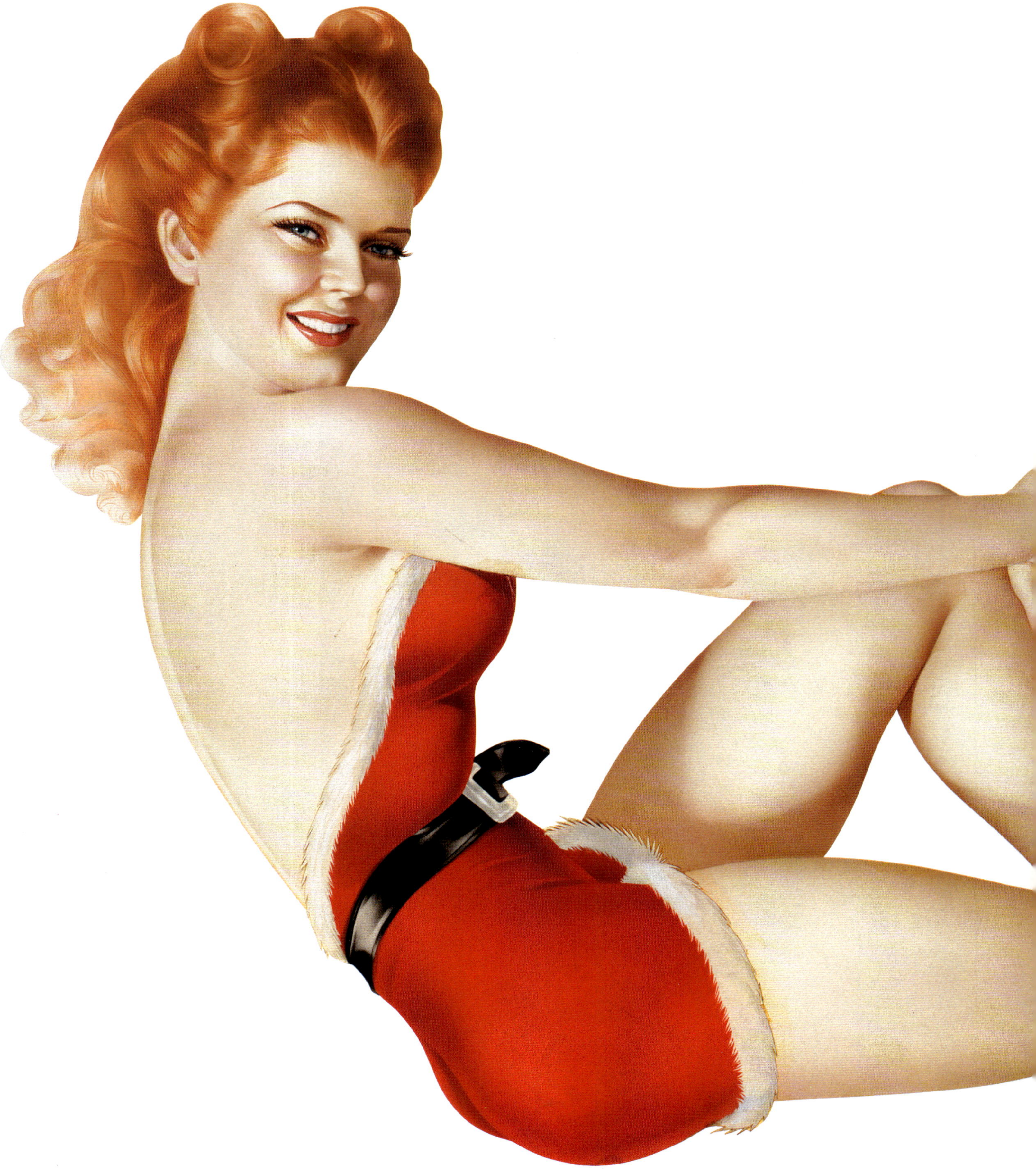

December 1942

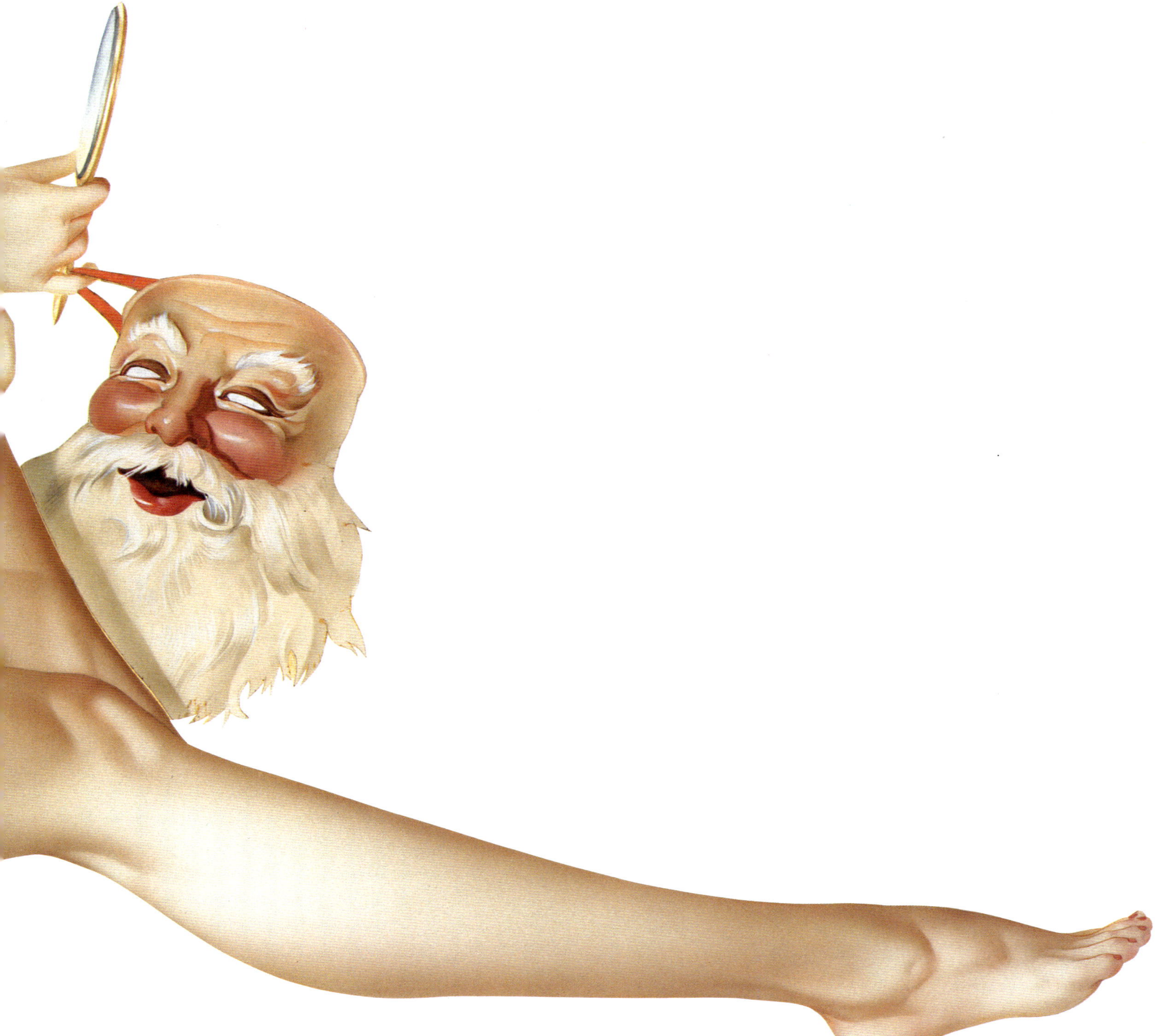

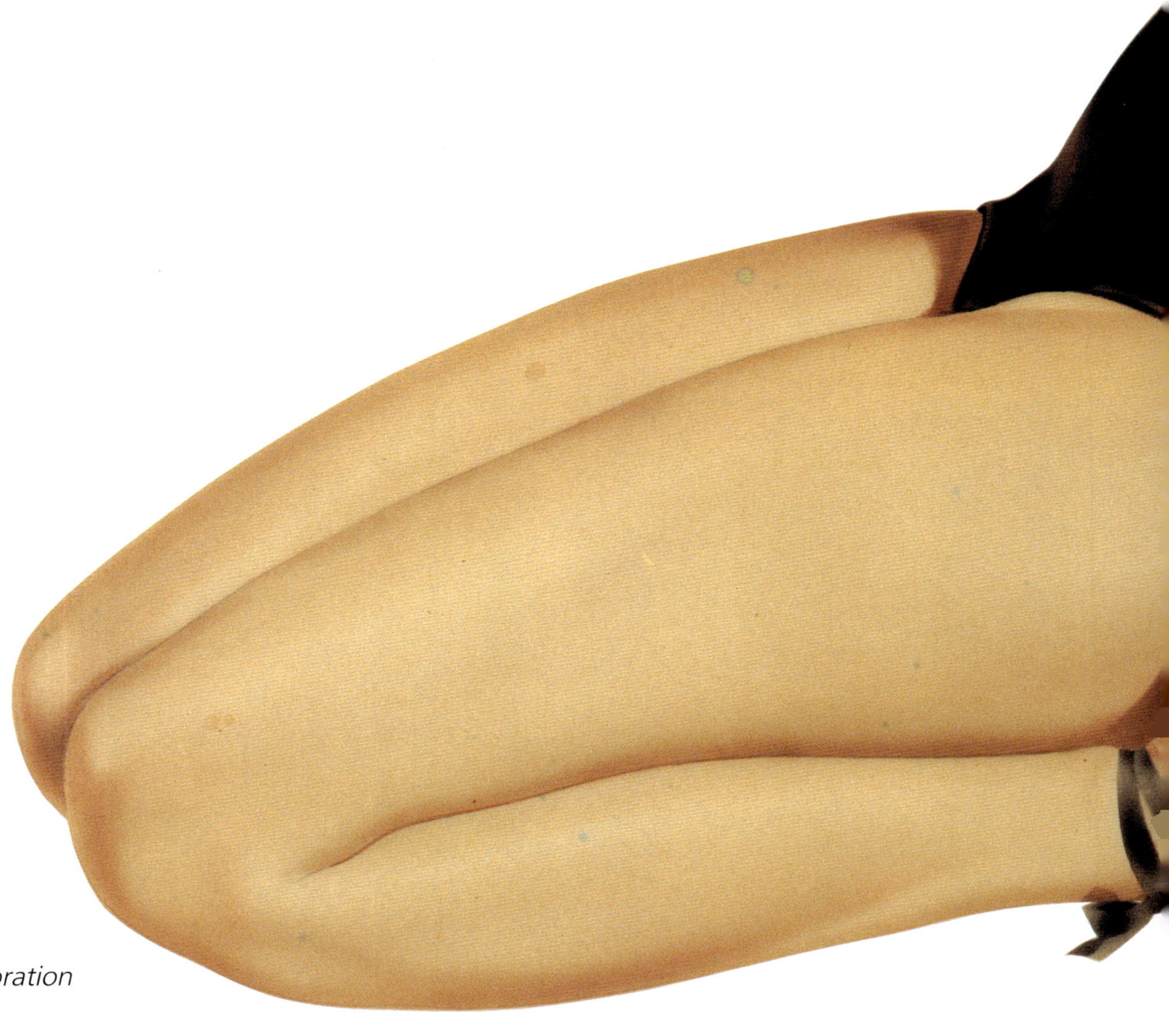

June 1943

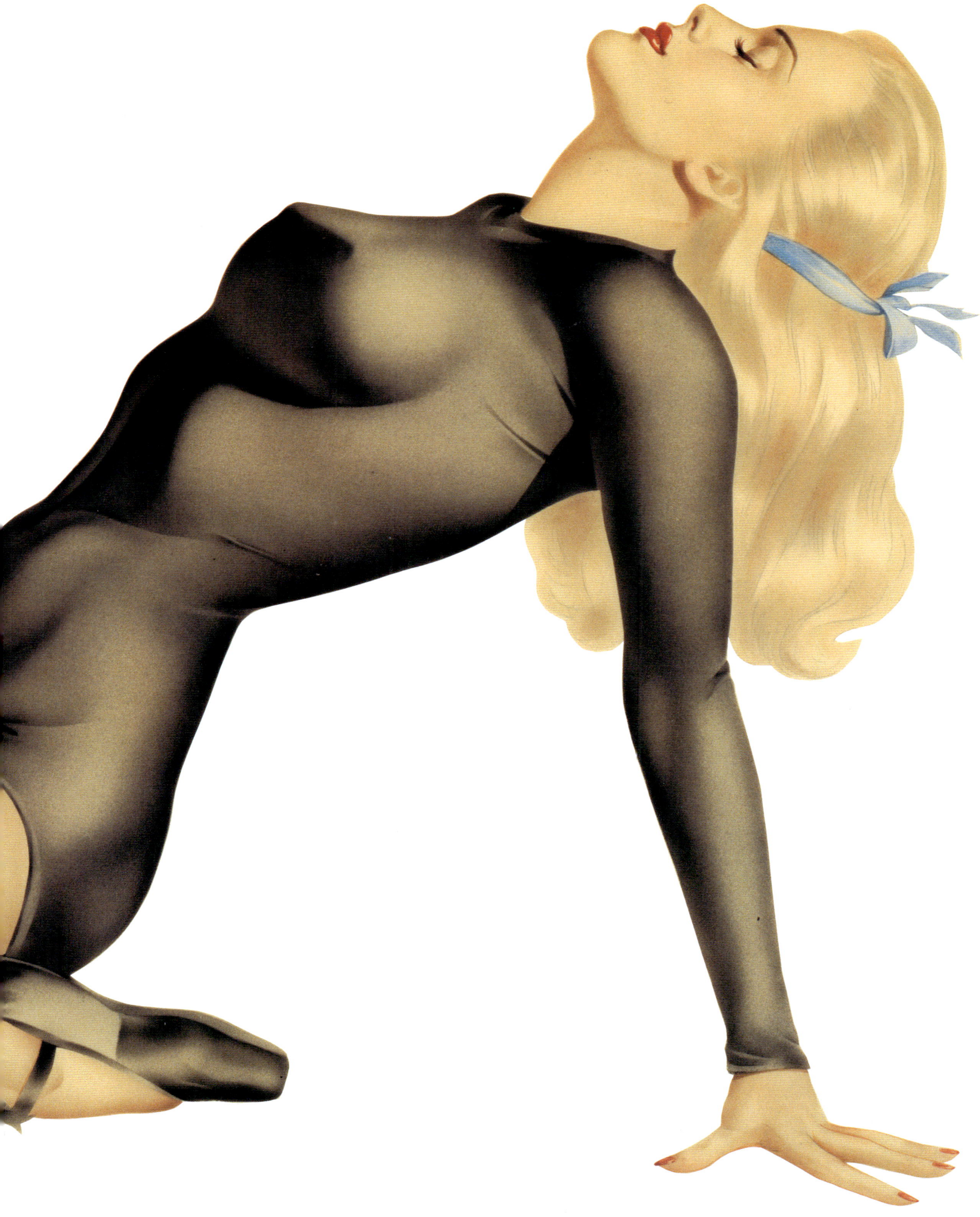

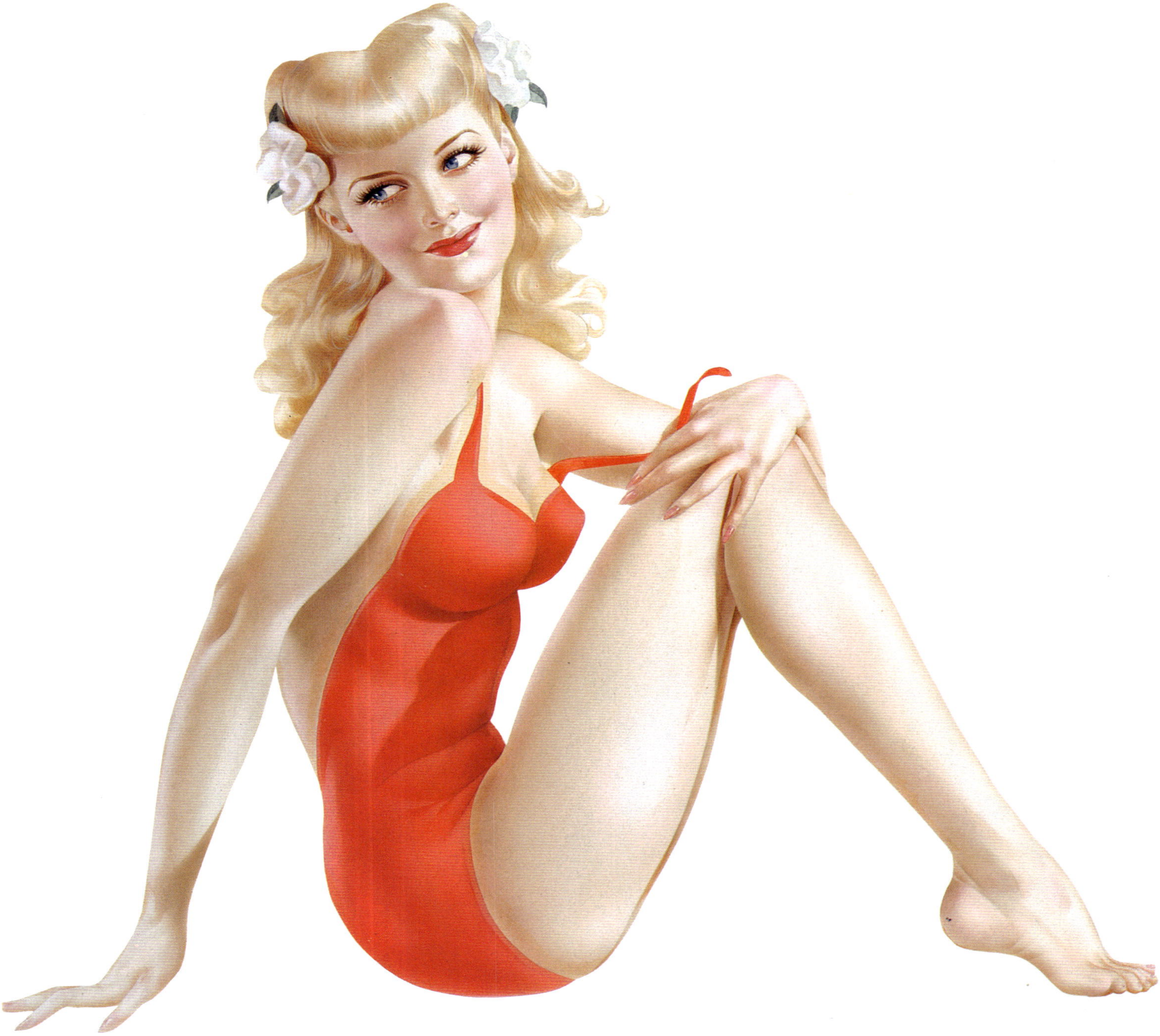

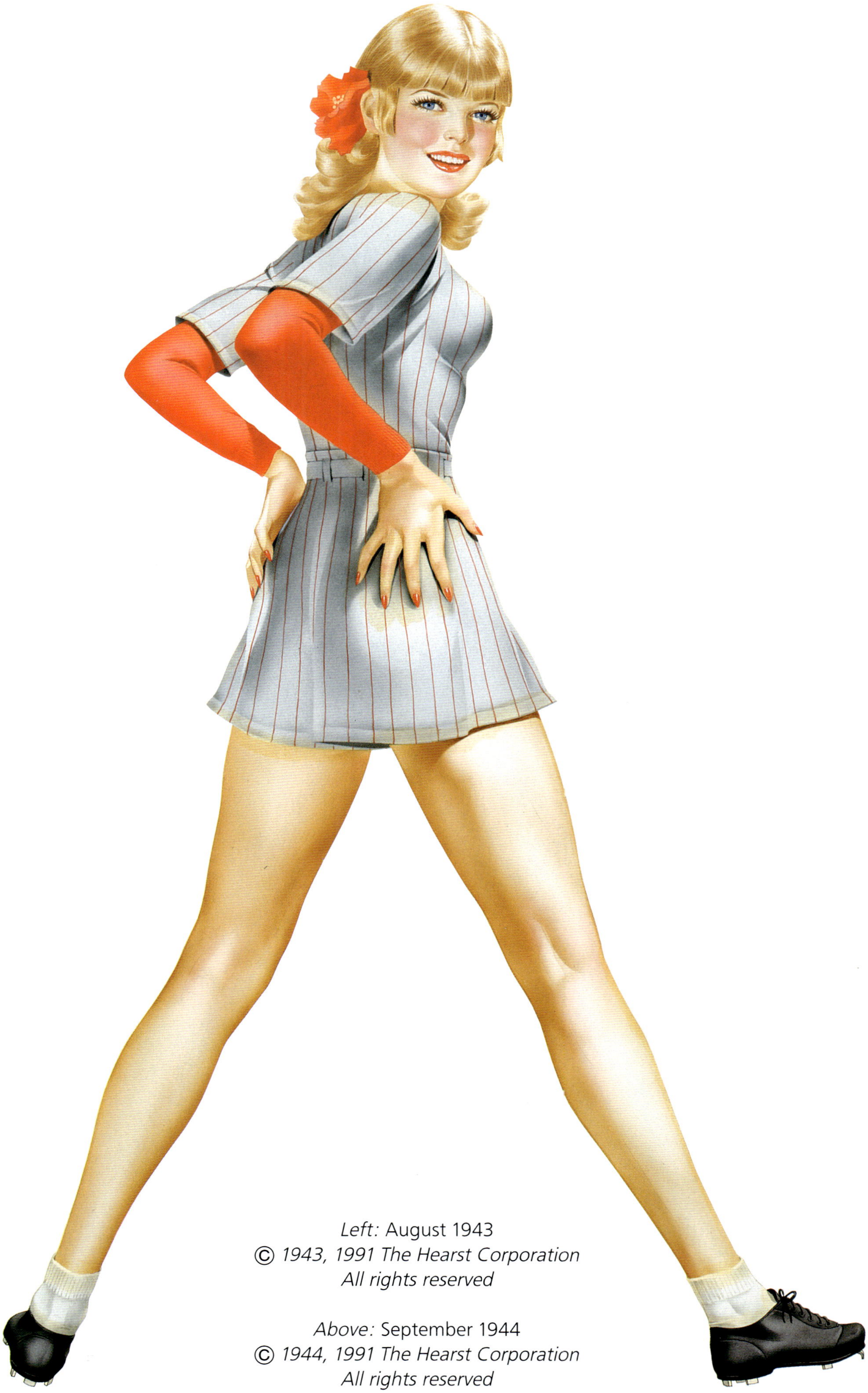

Left: August 1943

Above: September 1944

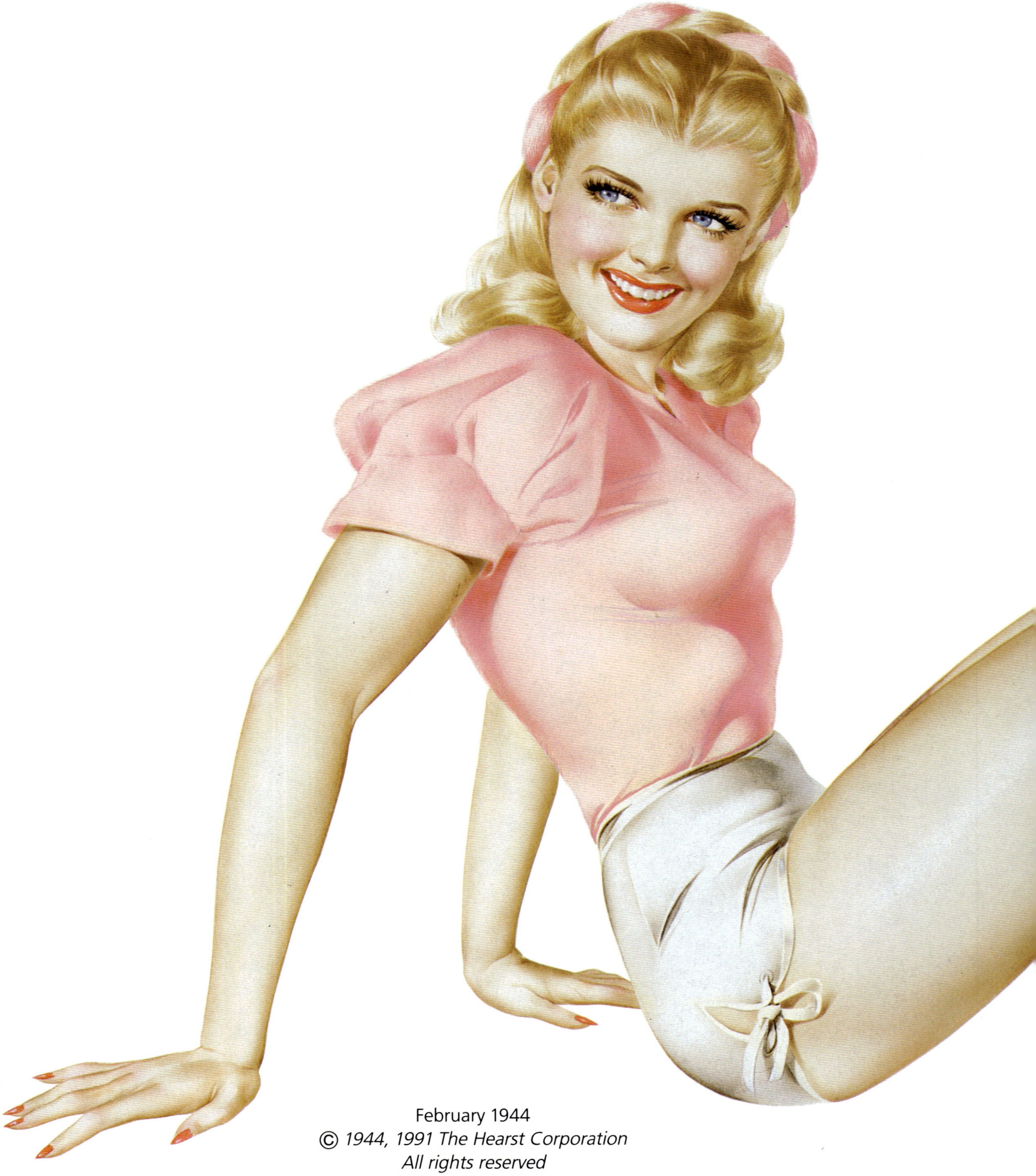

February 1944

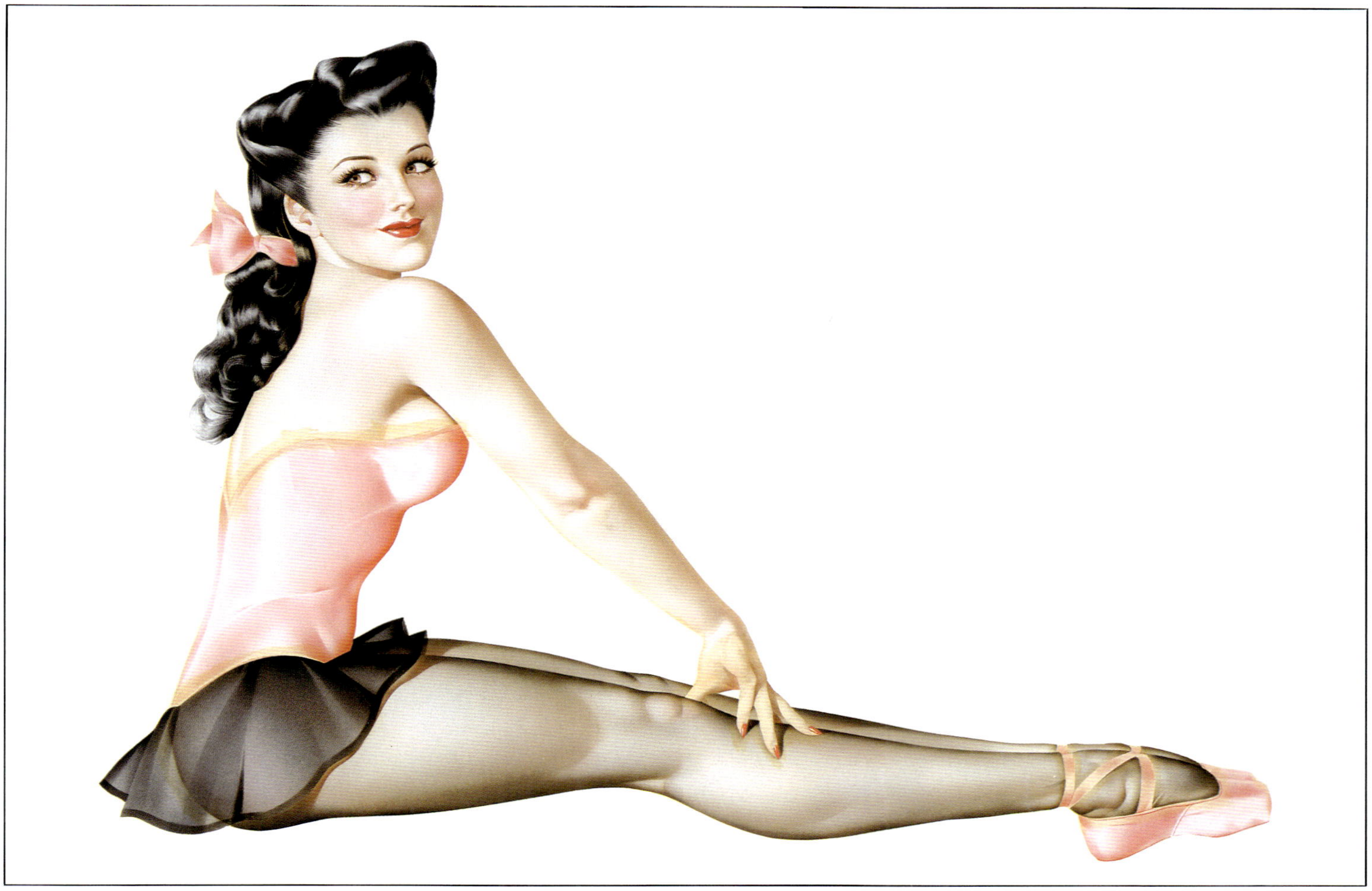

Above: June 1944

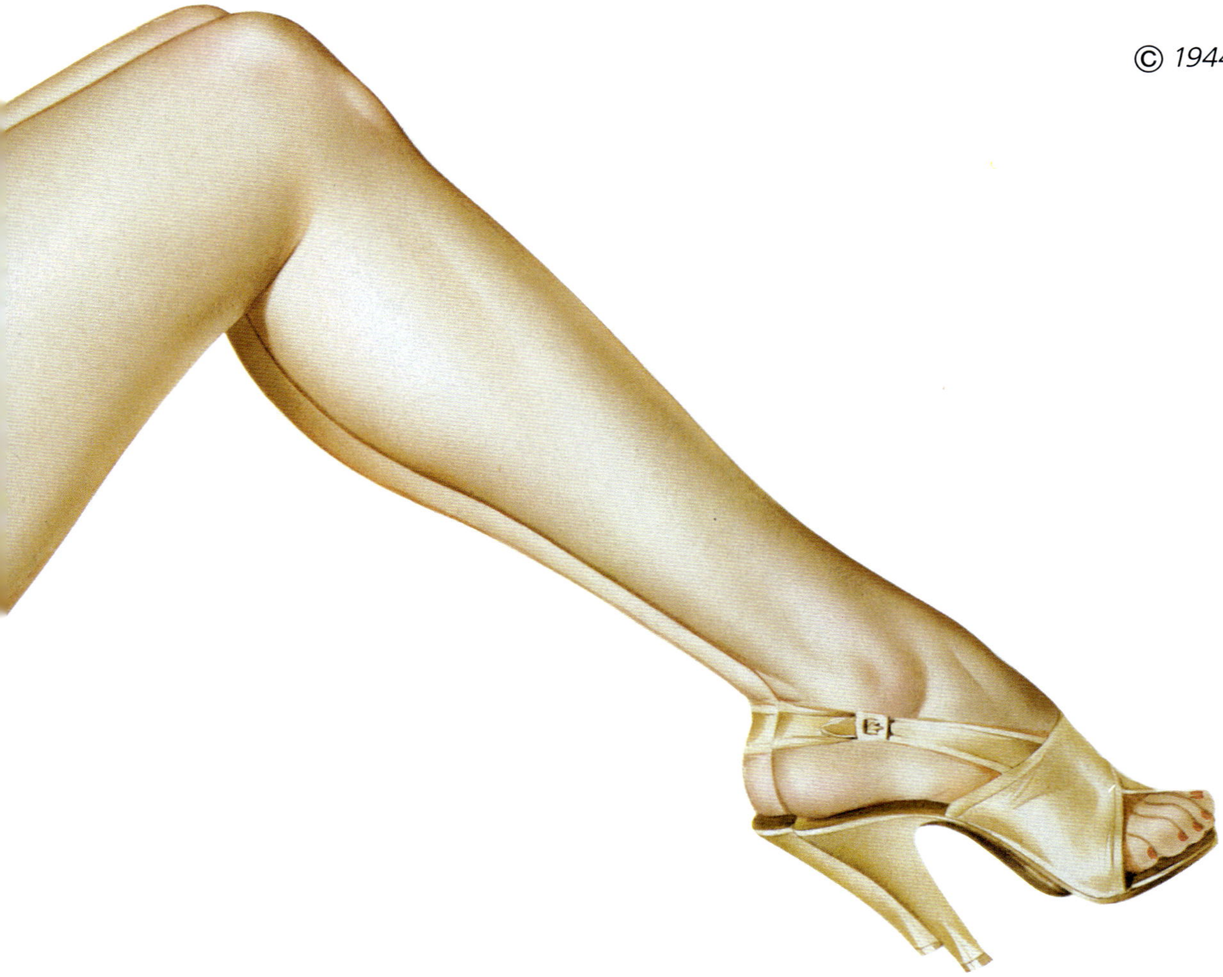

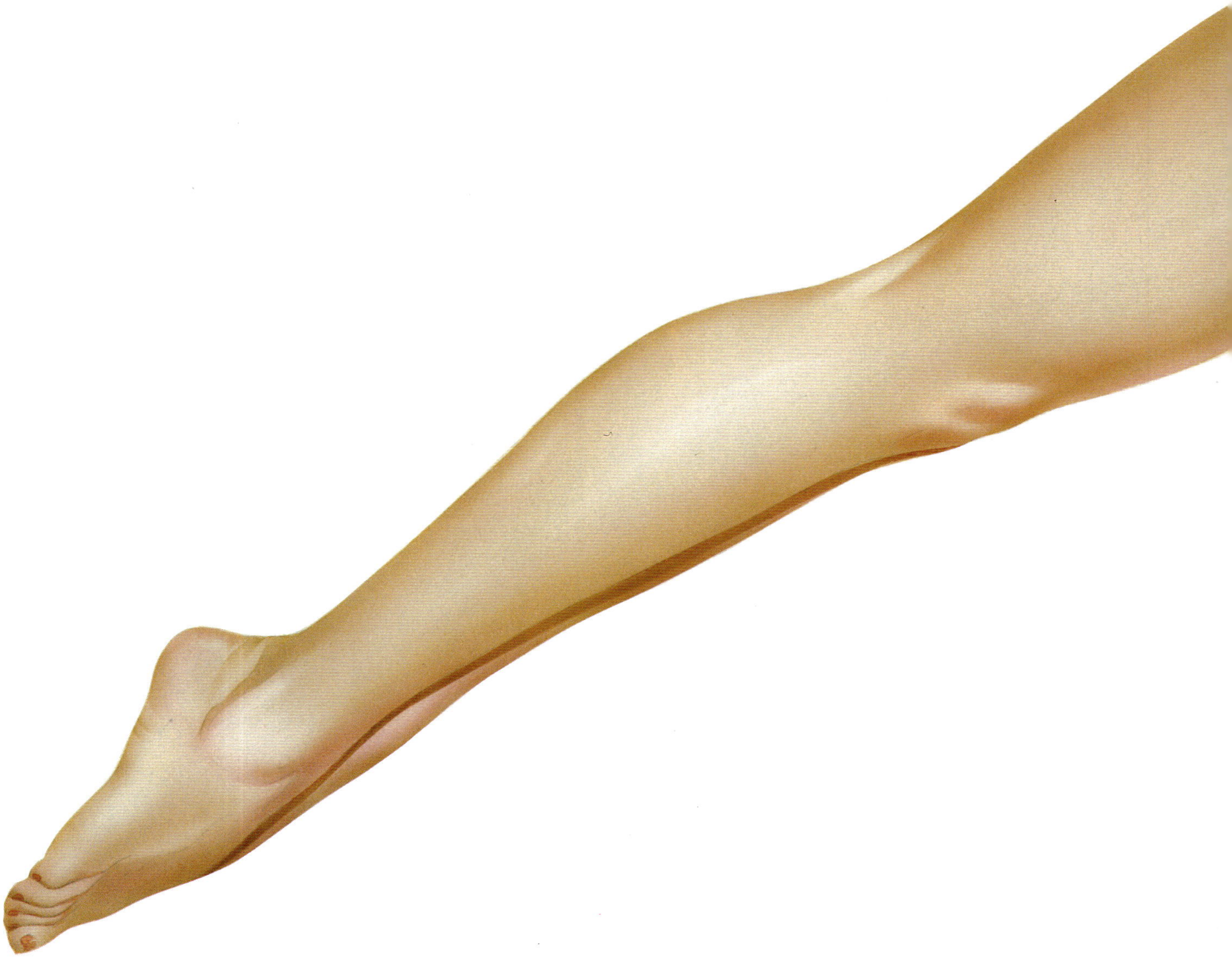

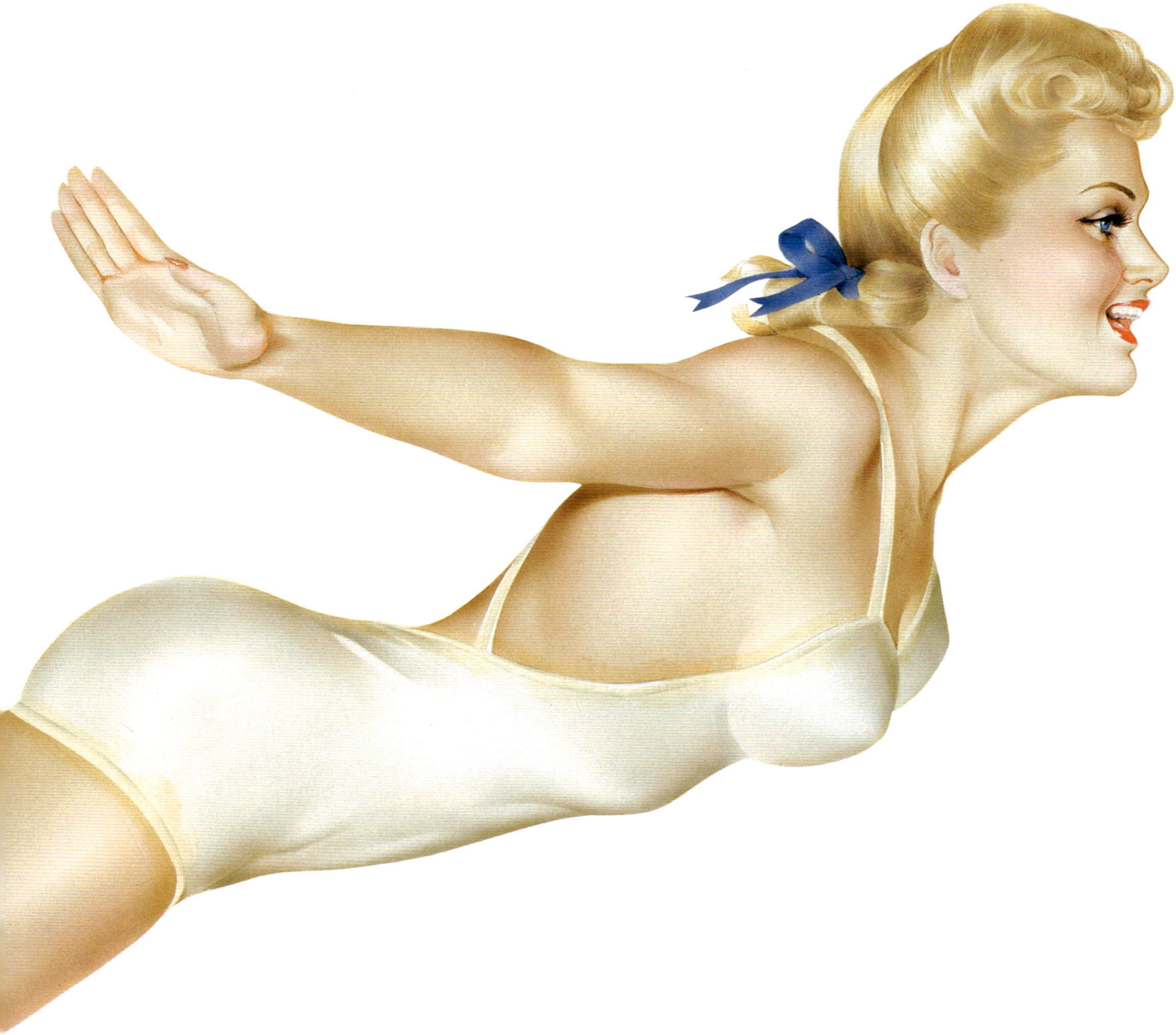

August 1944 Calendar

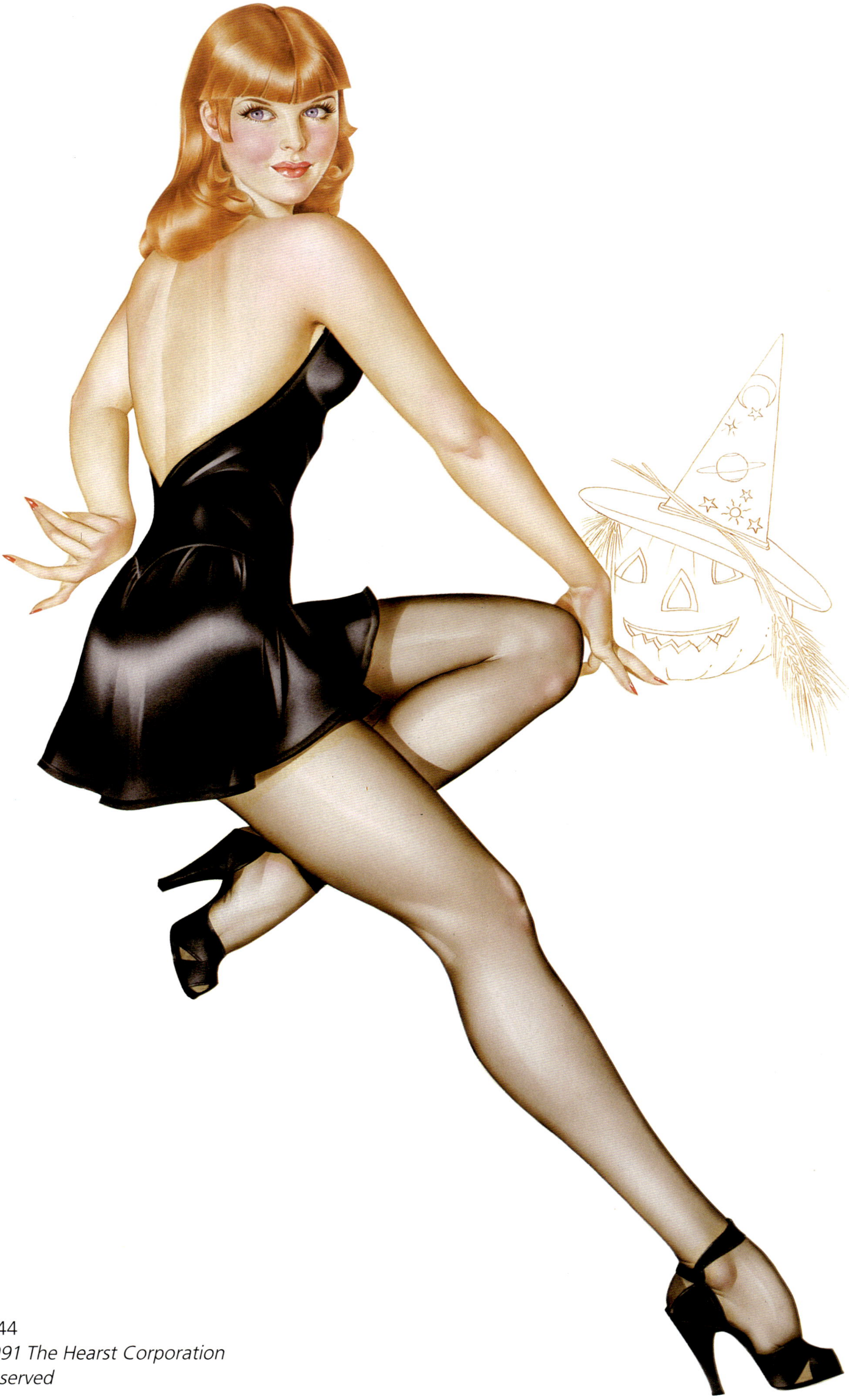

October 1944

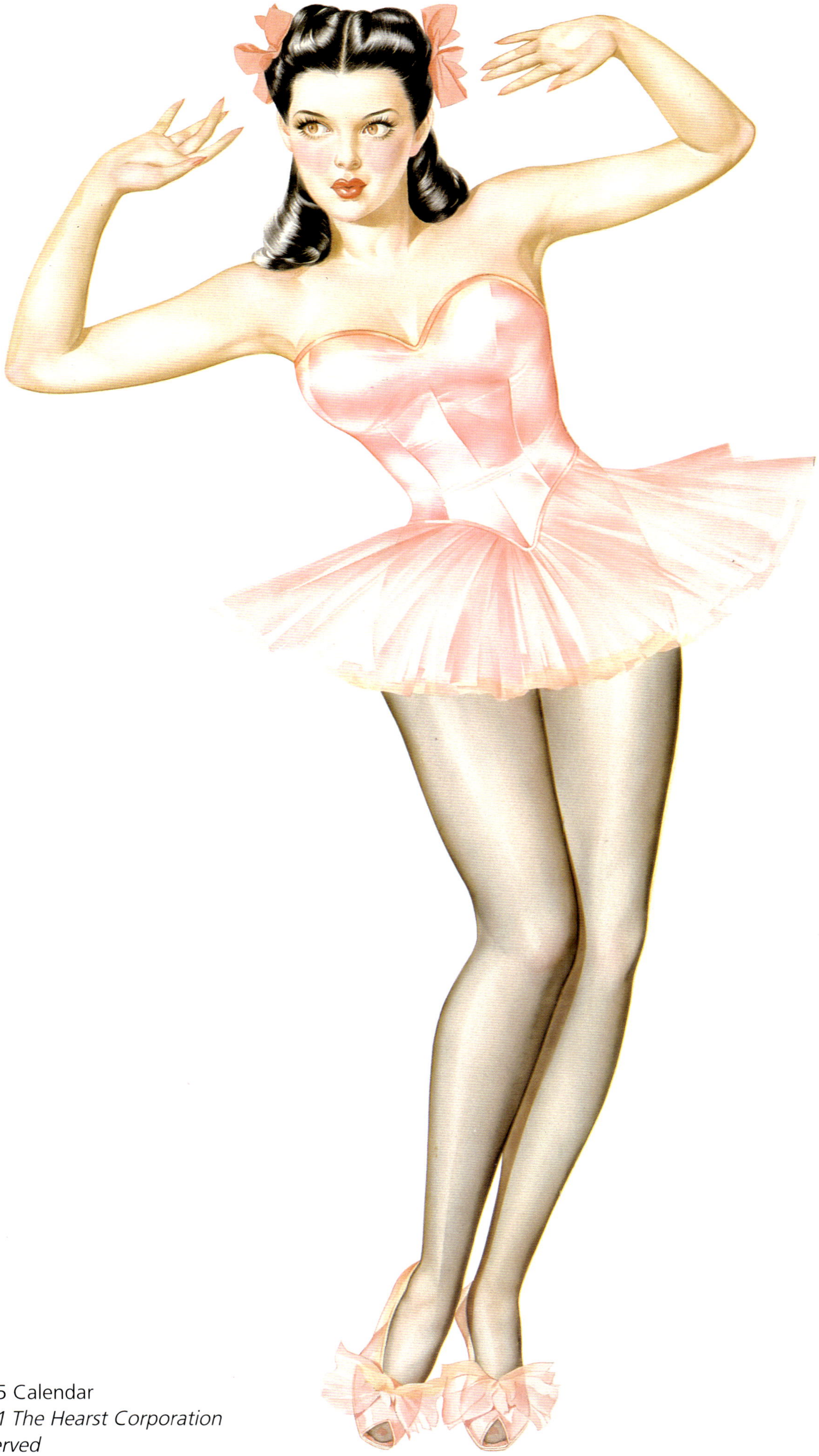

February 1945 Calendar

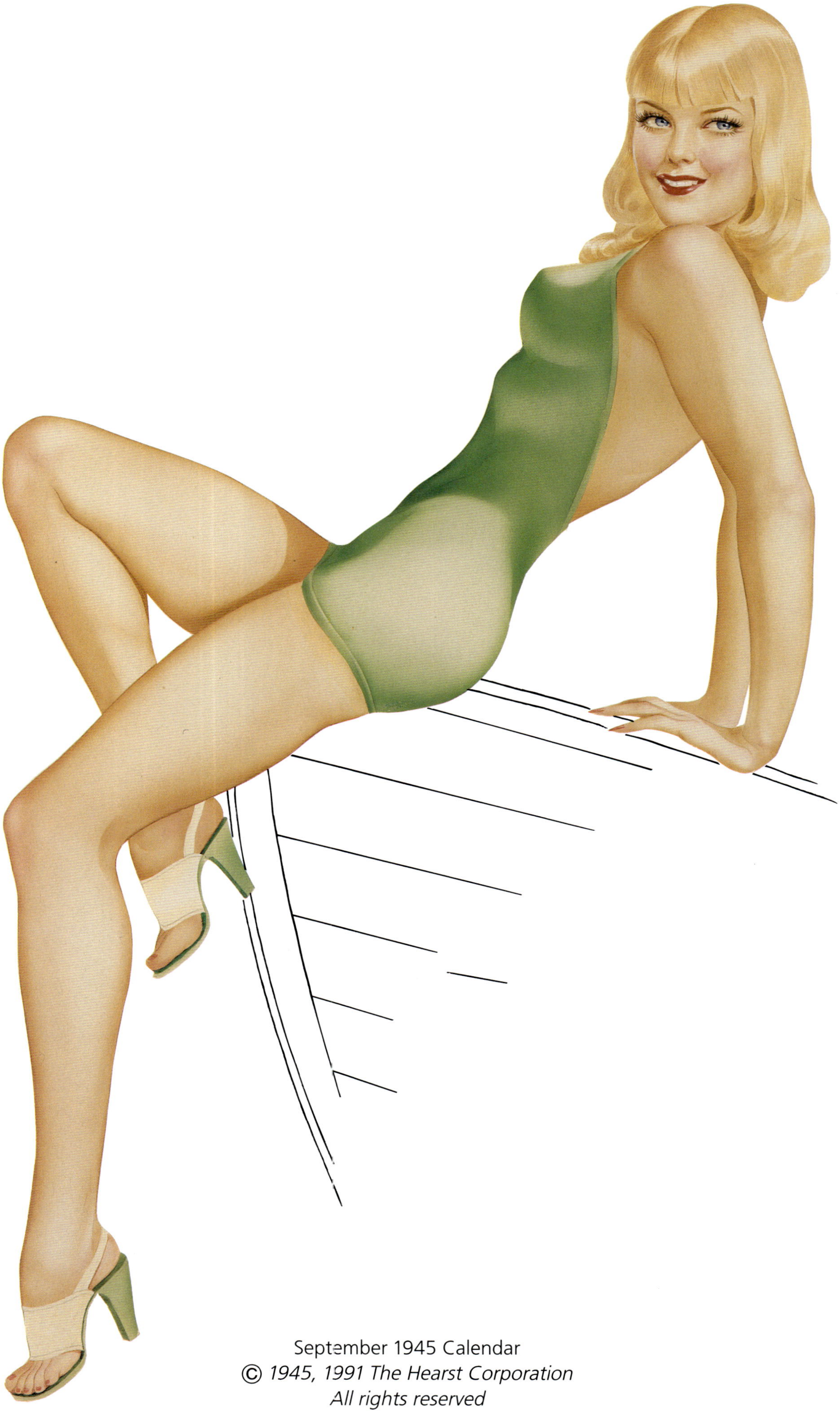

September 1945 Calendar

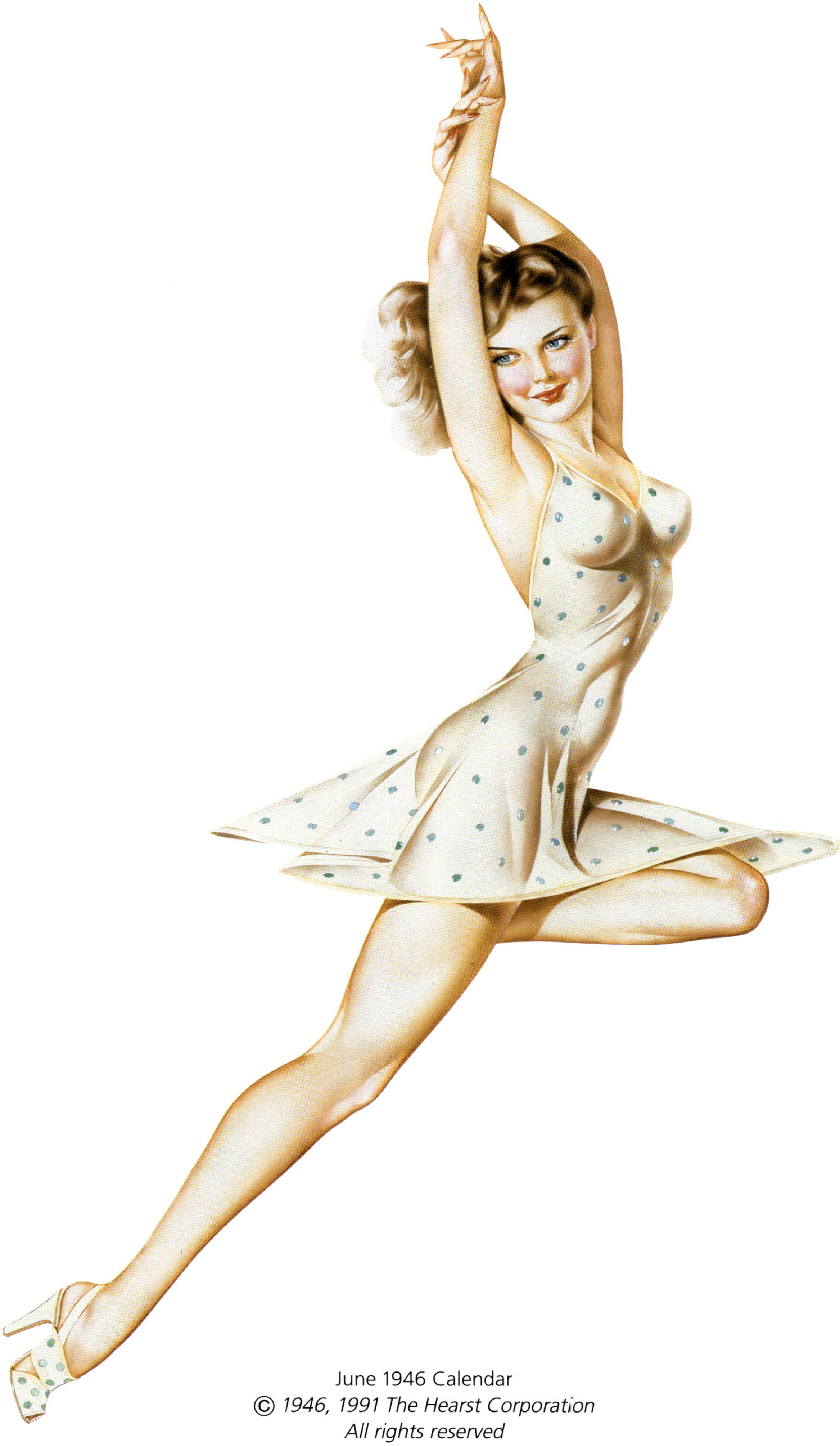

June 1946 Calendar

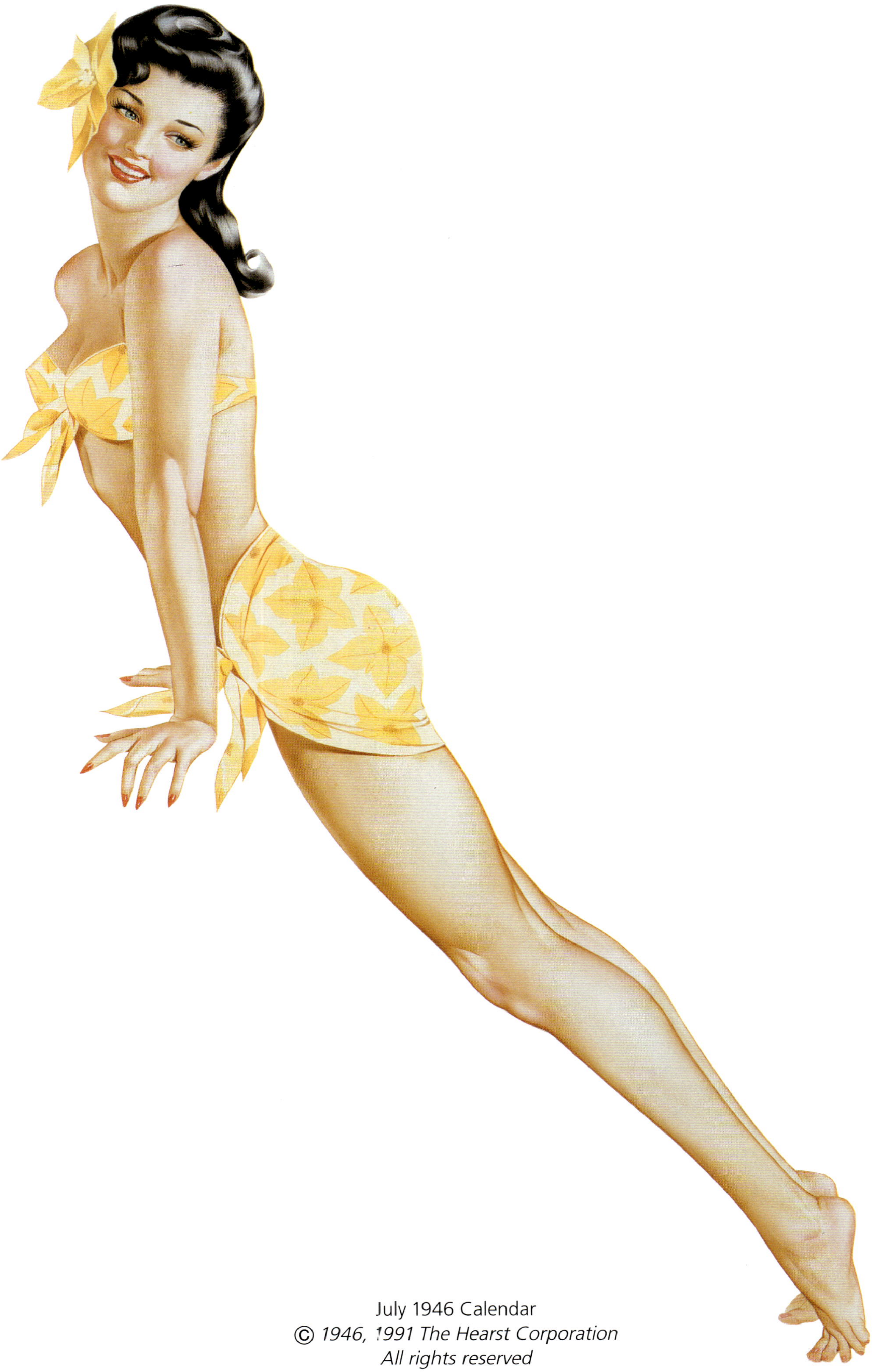

July 1946 Calendar

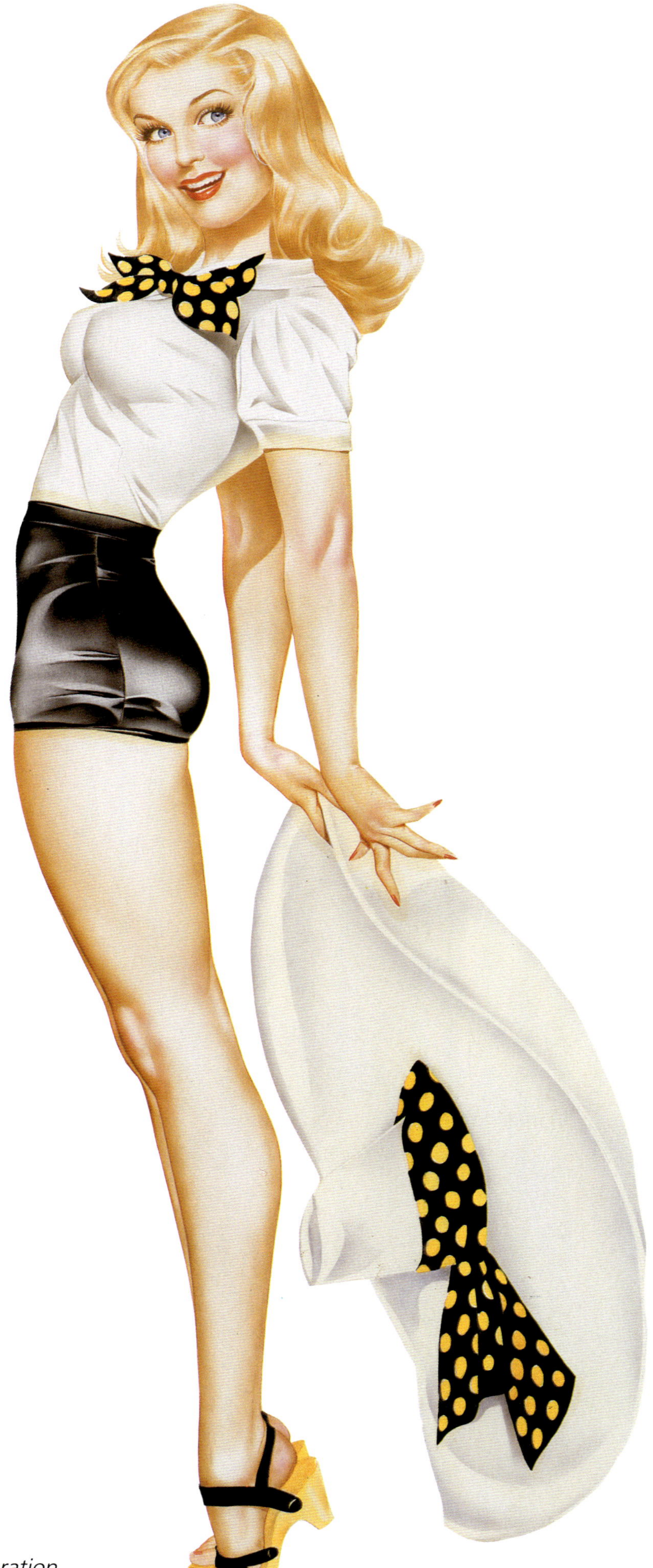

September 1946 Calendar

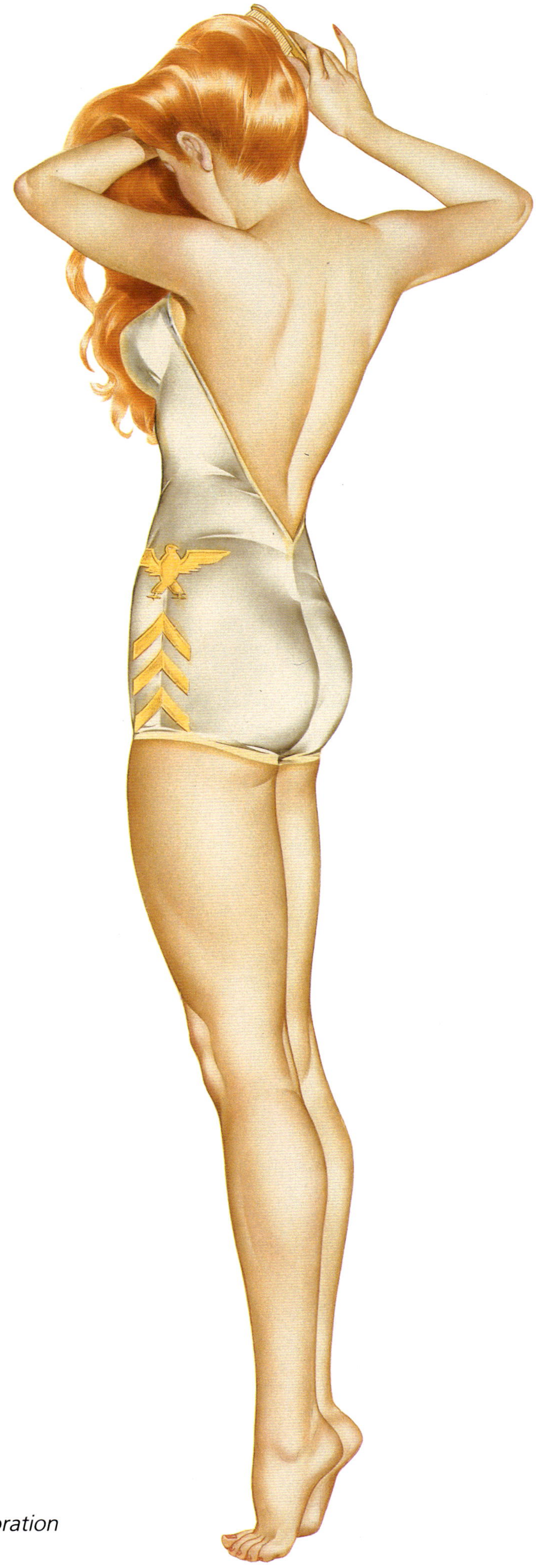

October 1946 Calendar

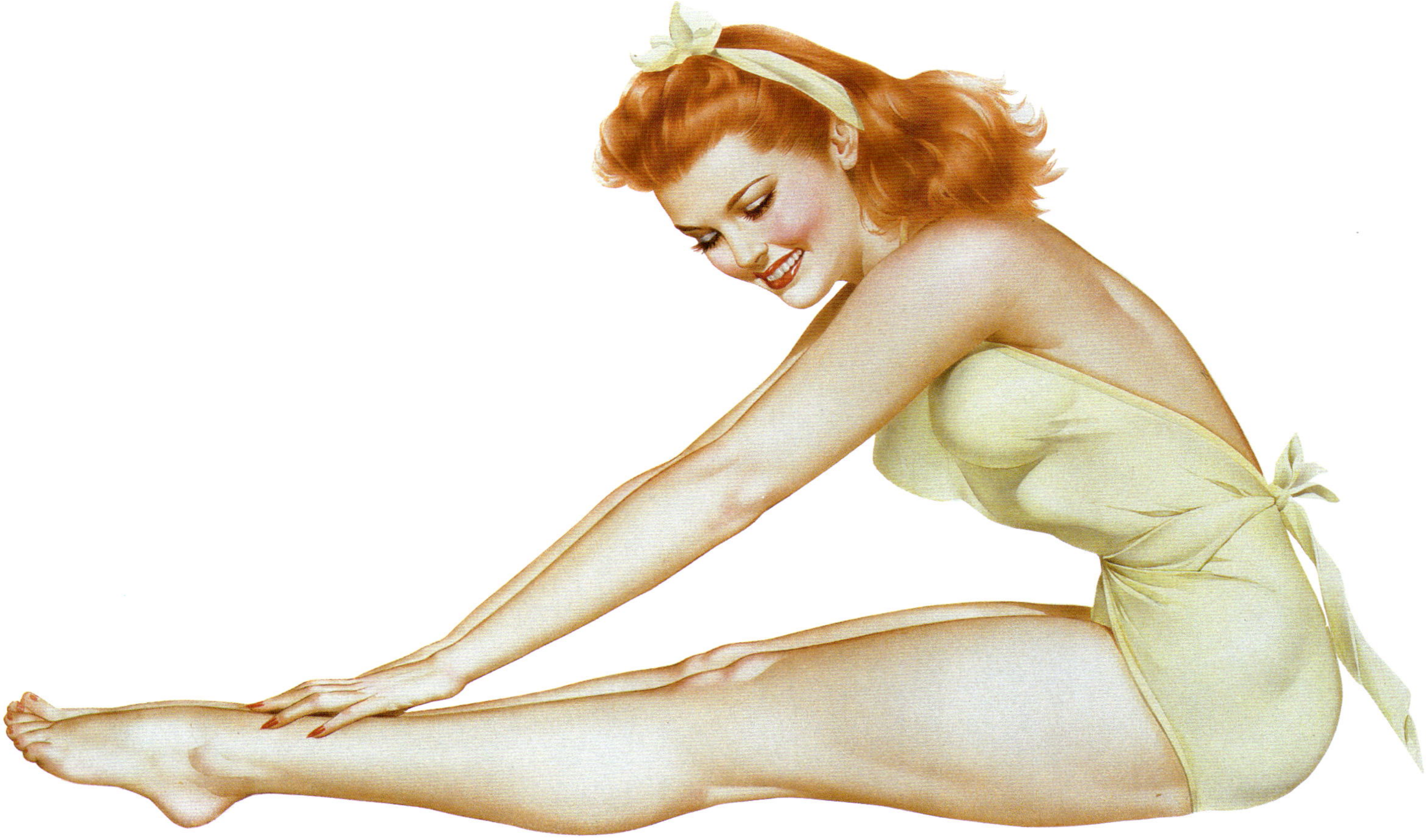

March 1947 Calendar

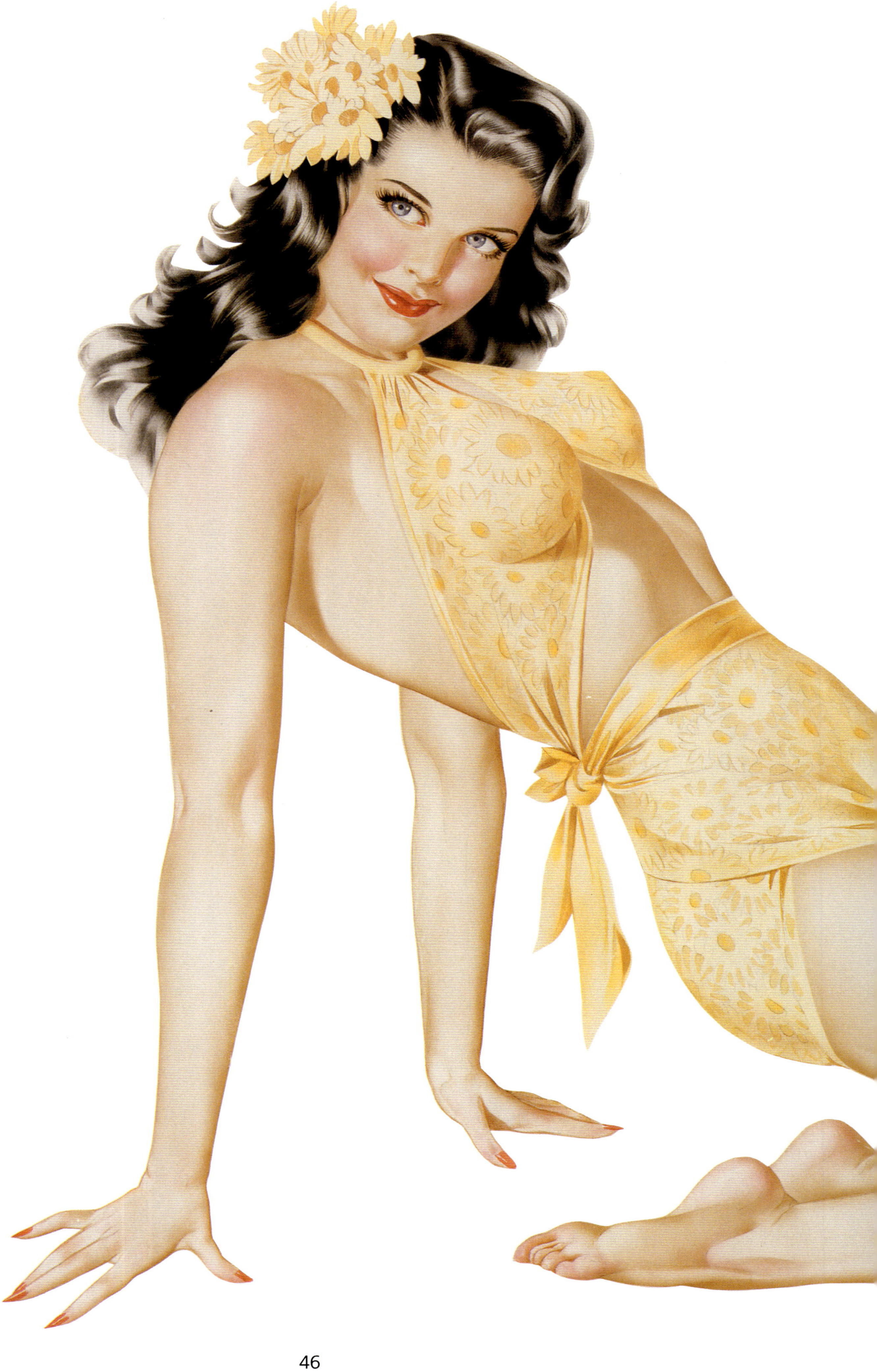

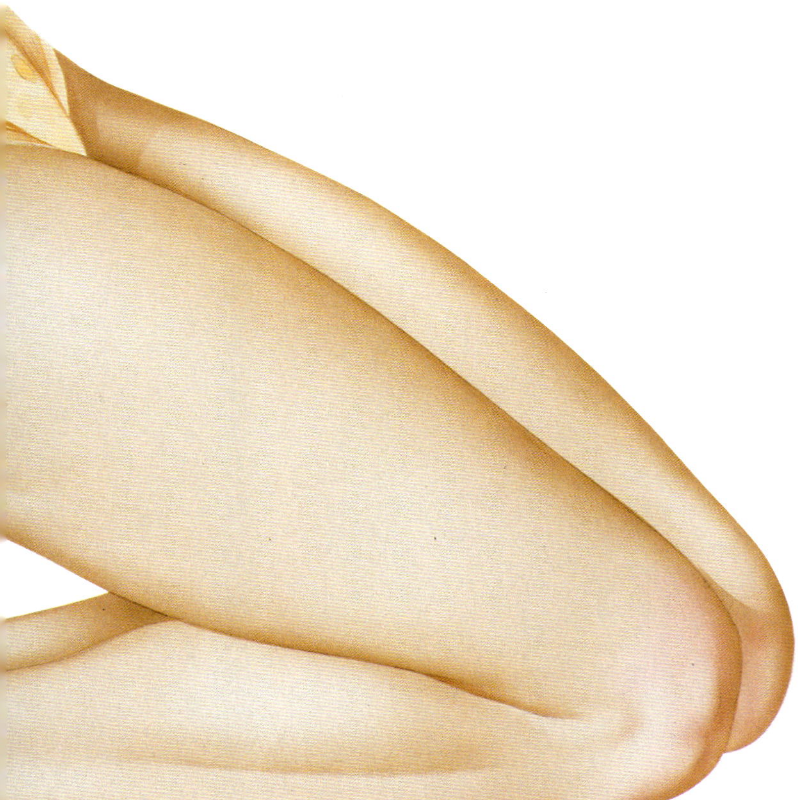

June 1947 Calendar

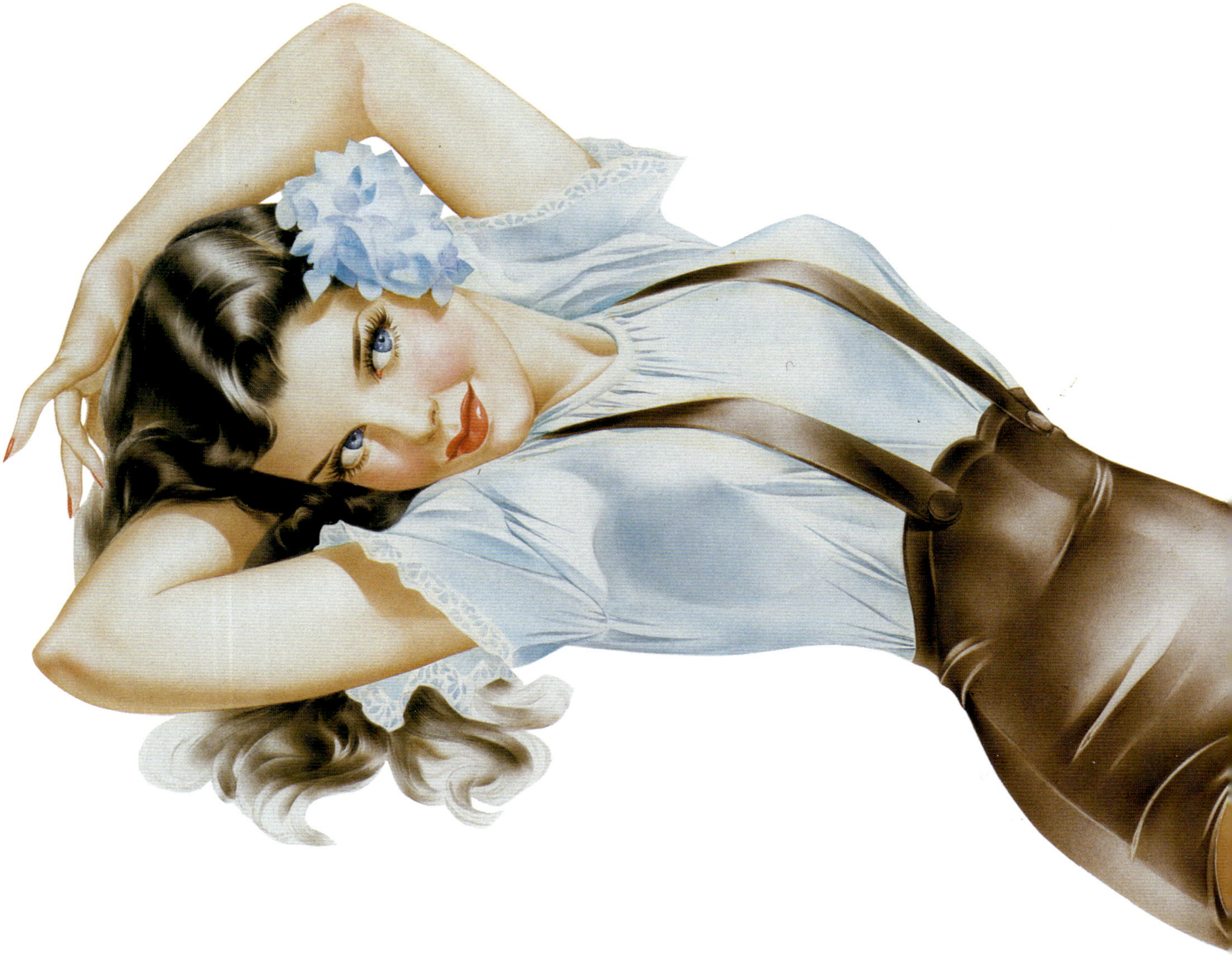

October 1947 Calendar

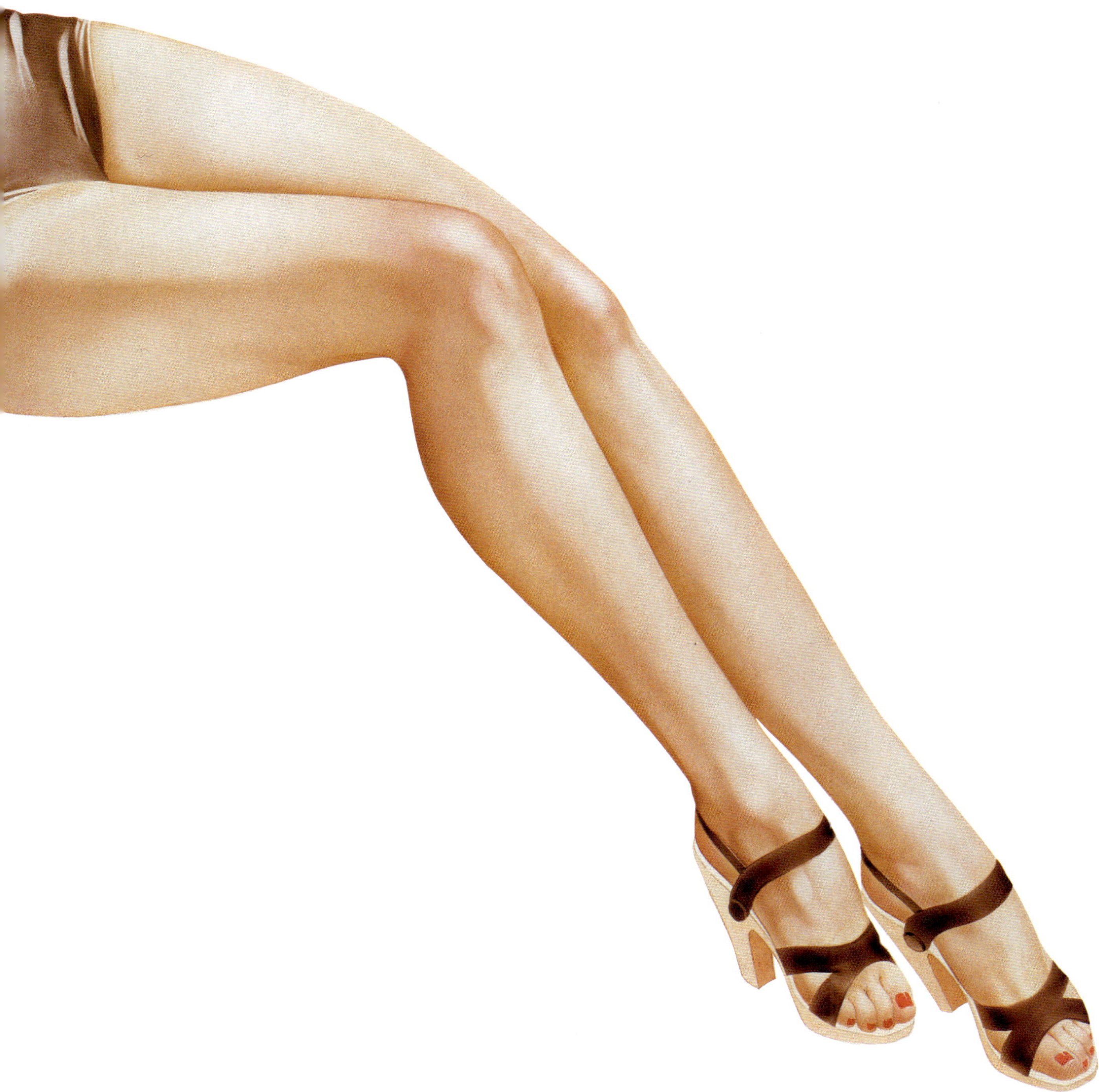

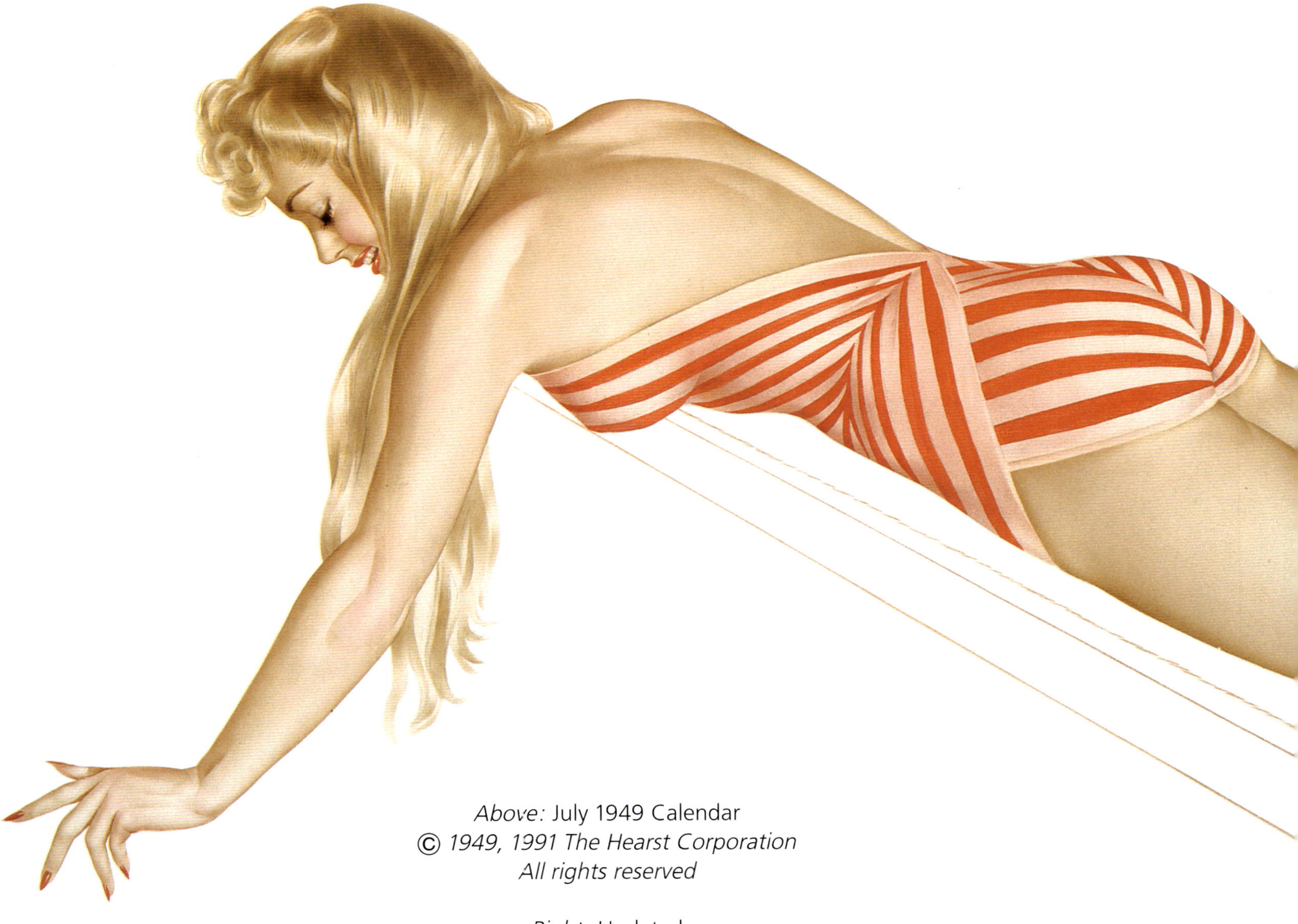

Above: July 1949 Calendar

Right: Undated

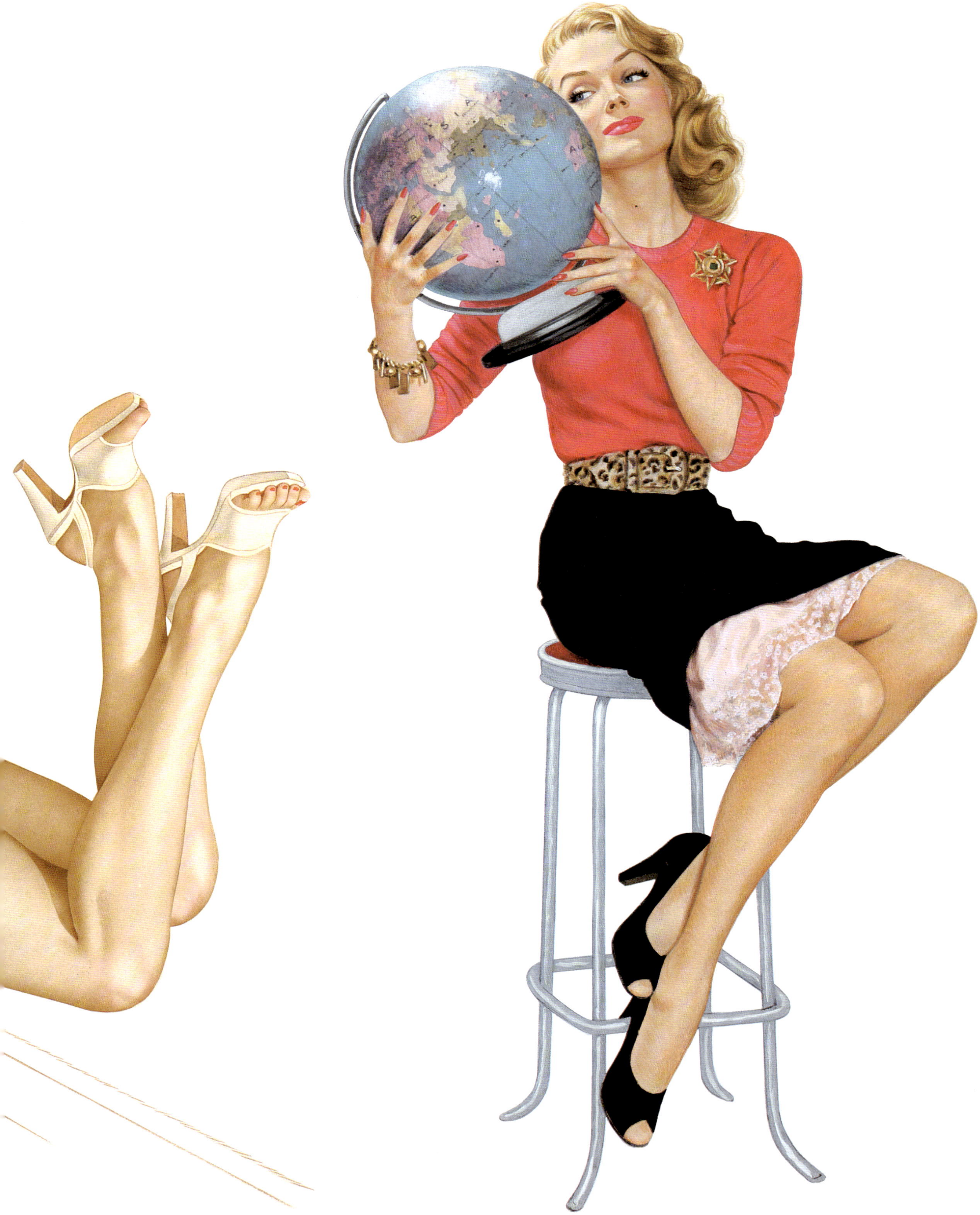

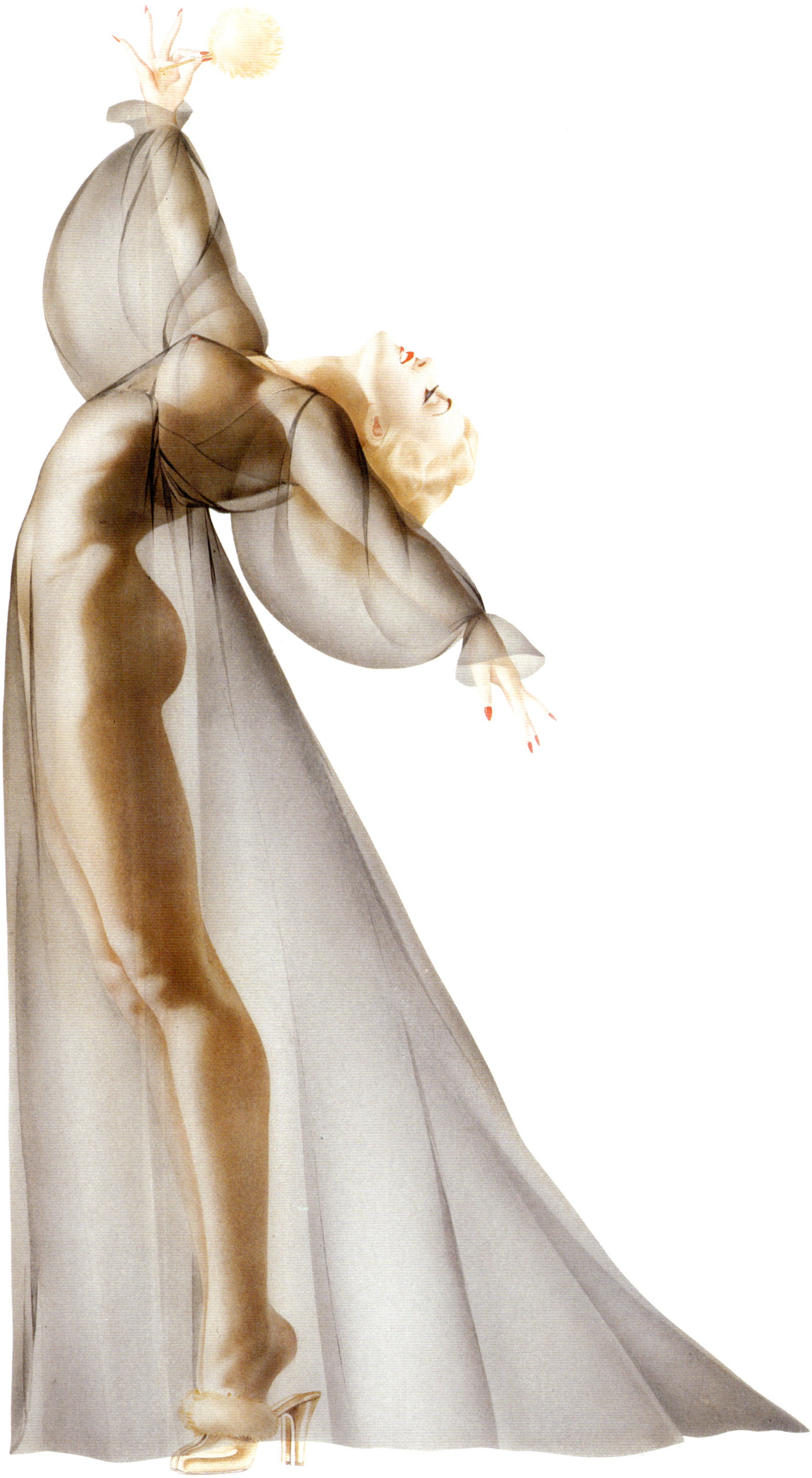

The Art of Seduction

September 1941

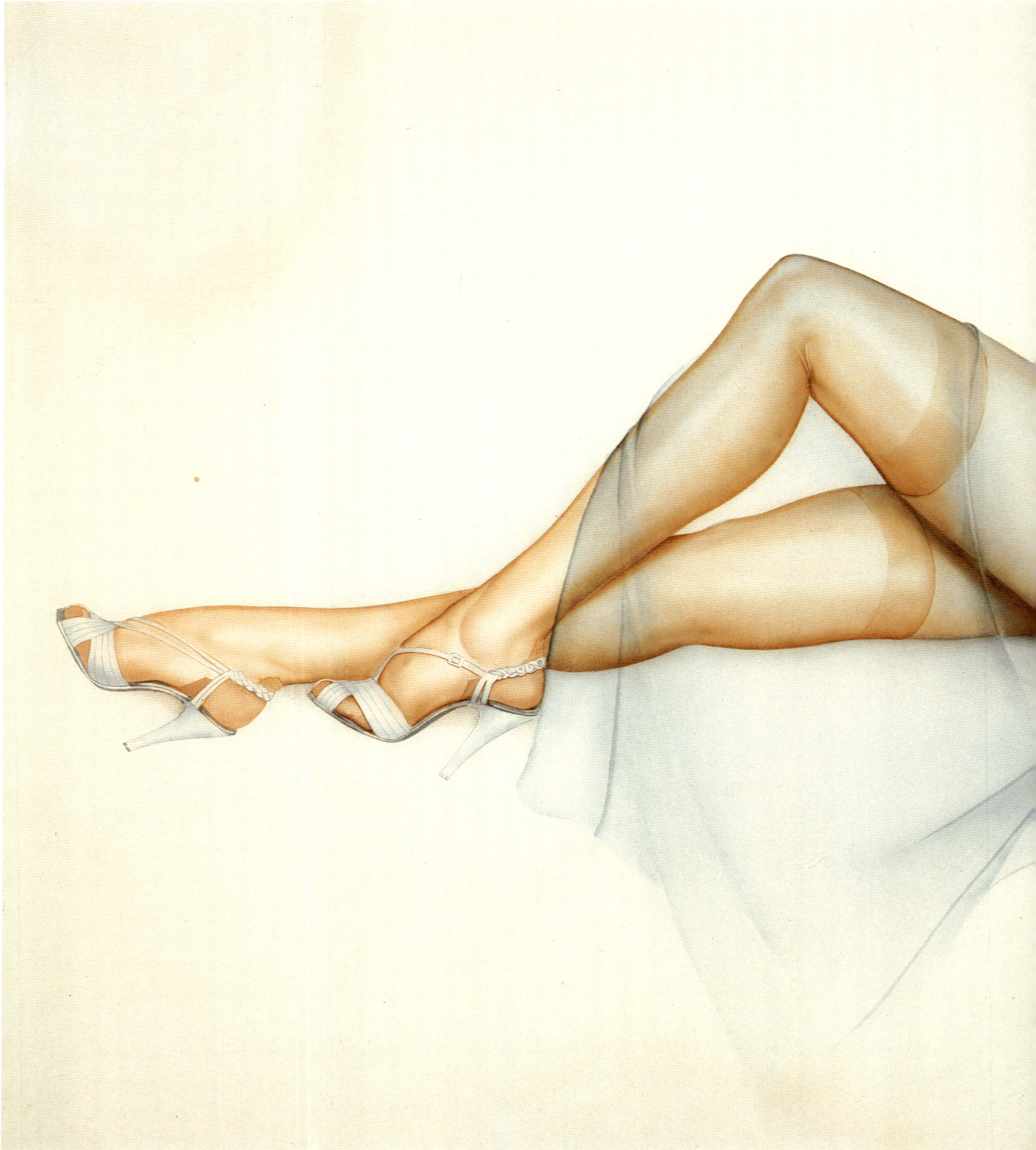

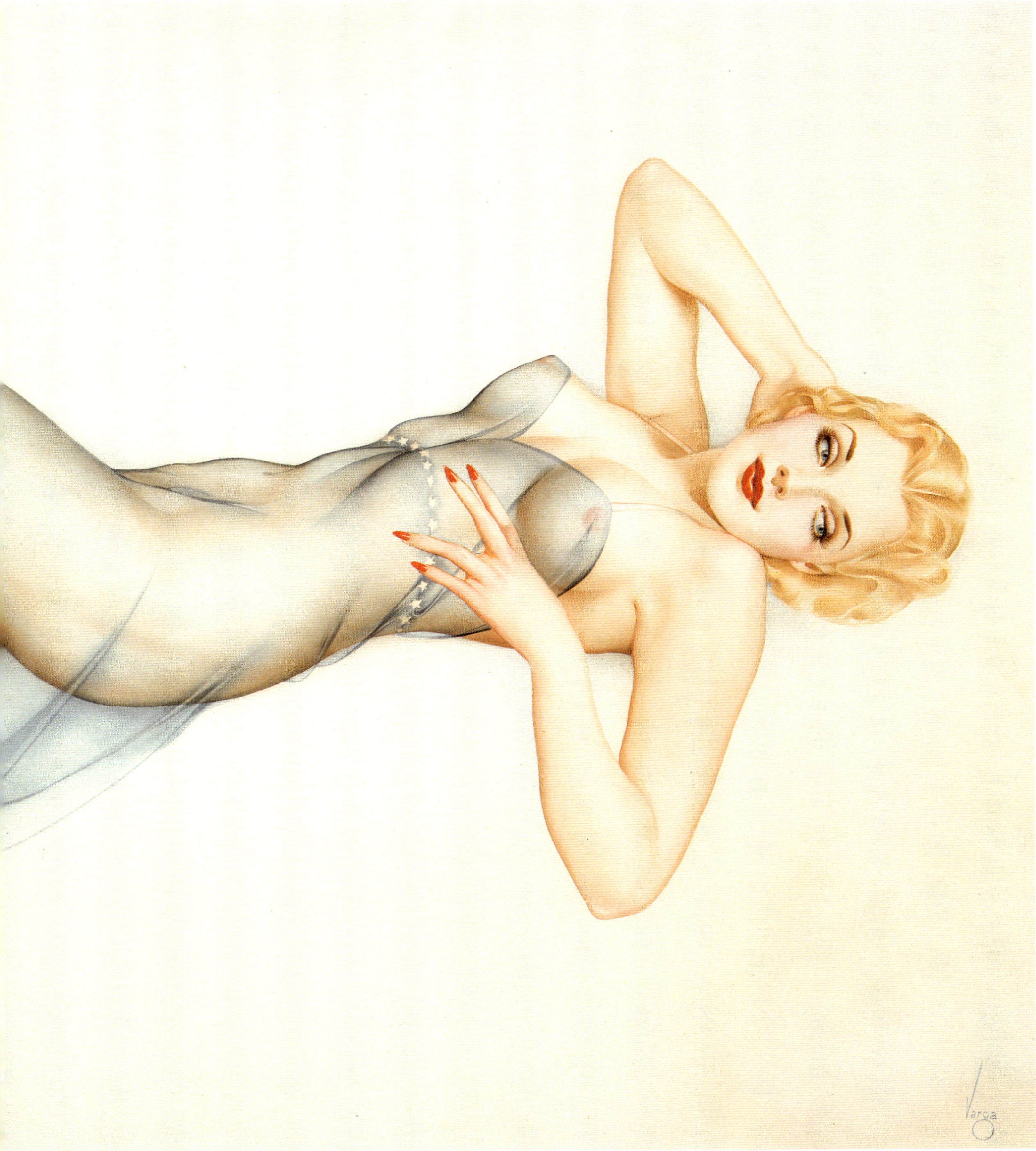

November 1940

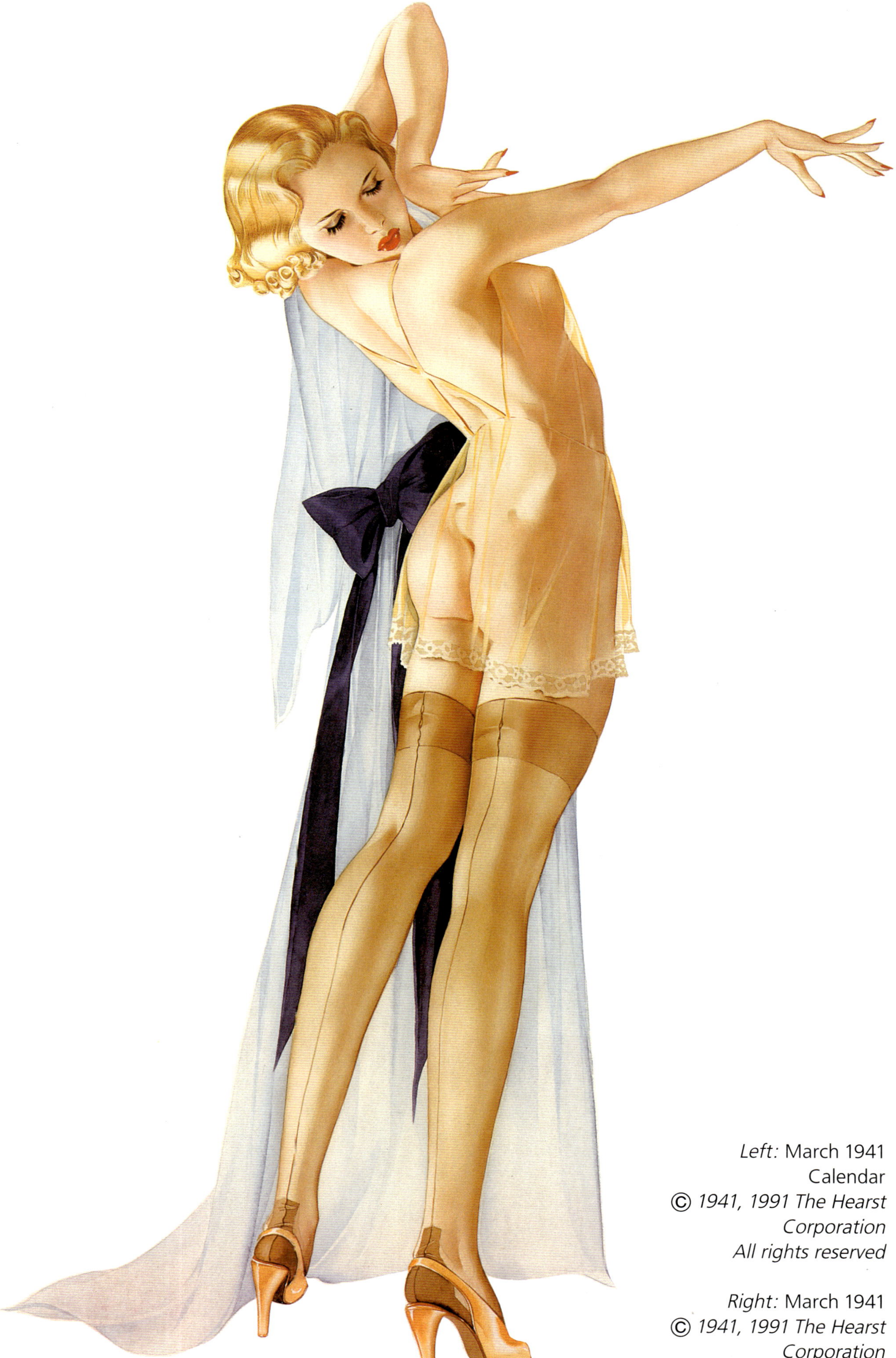

Left: March 1941
Calendar

Right: March 1941

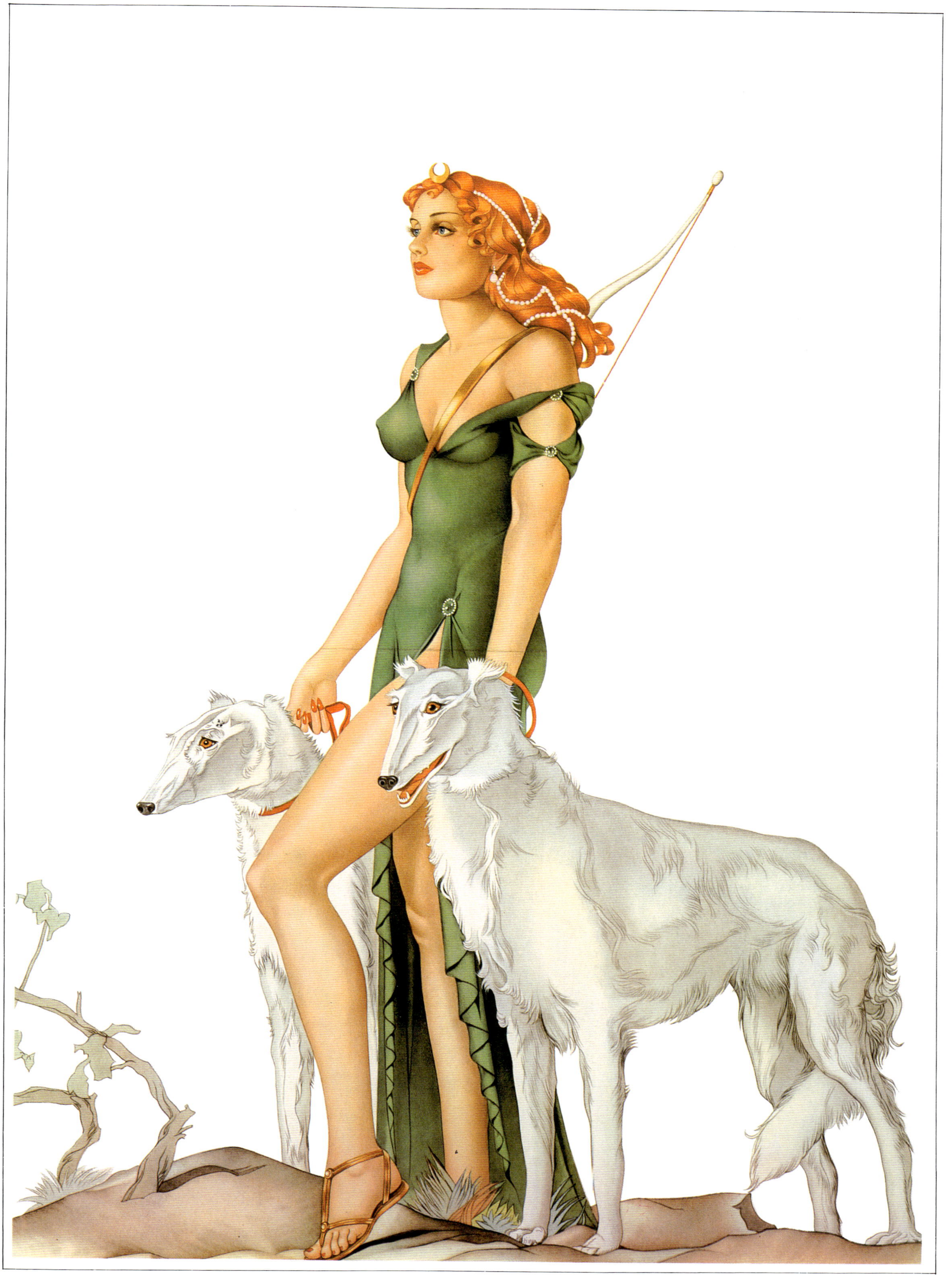

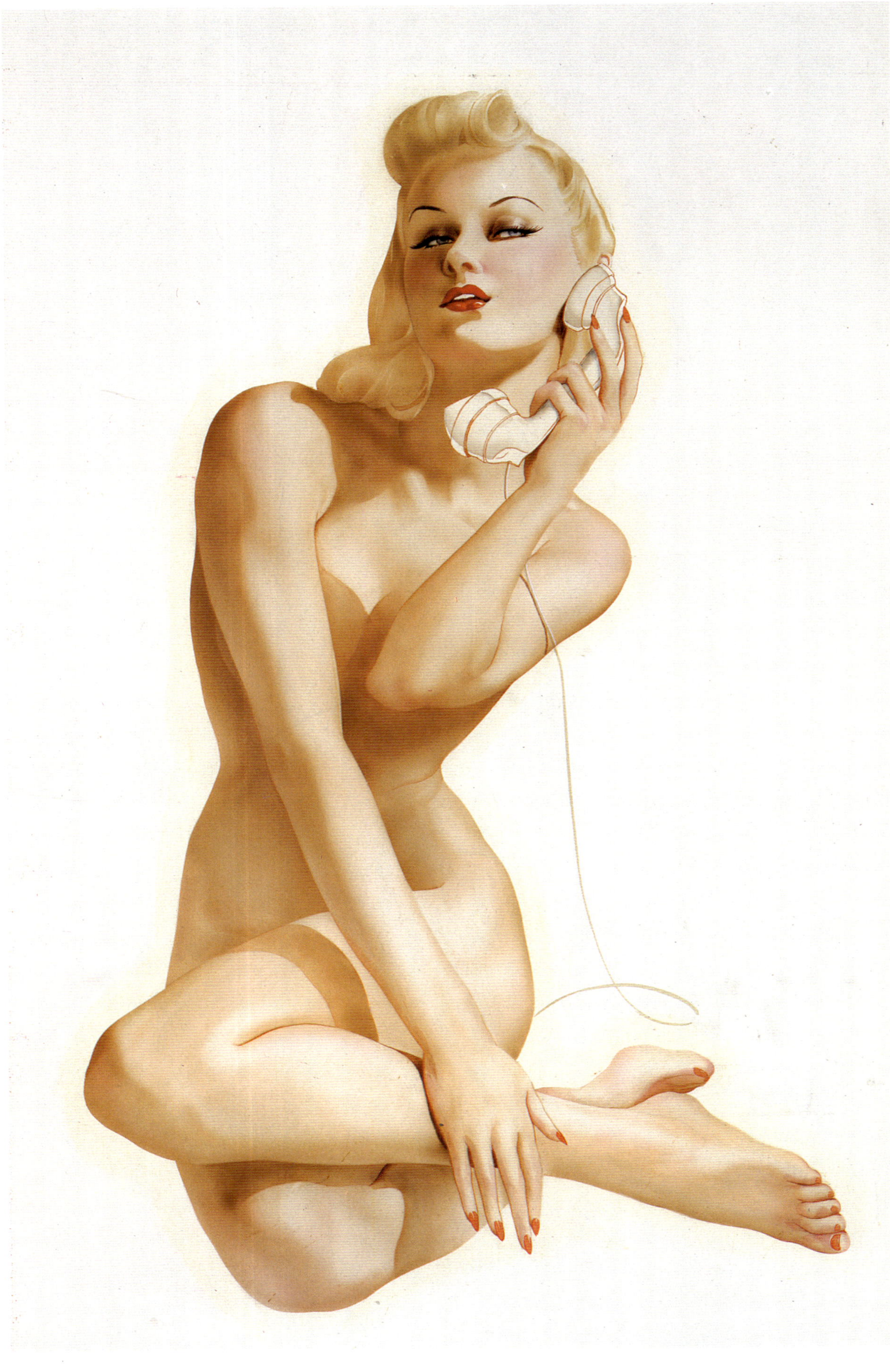

April 1941 Calendar

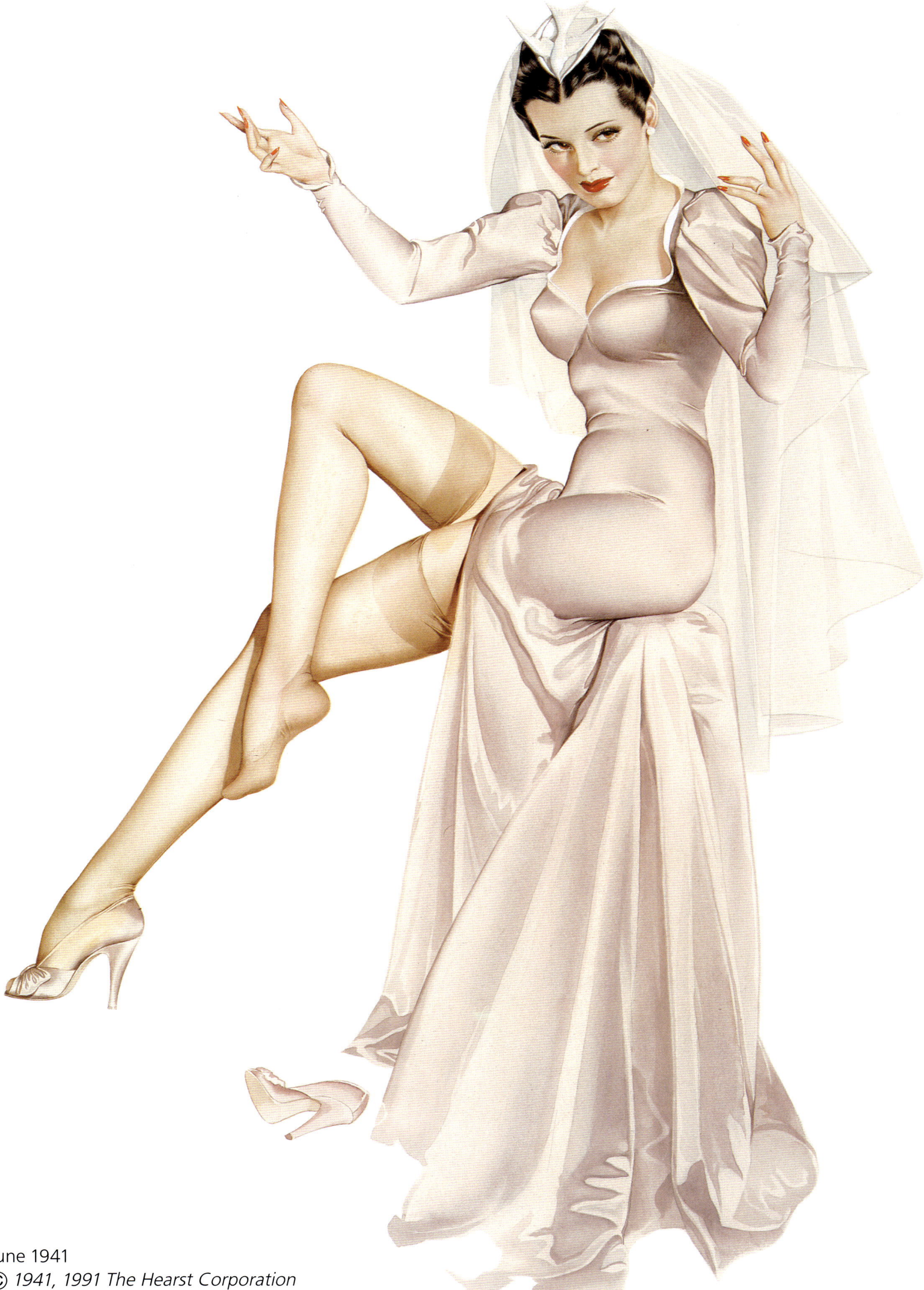

June 1941

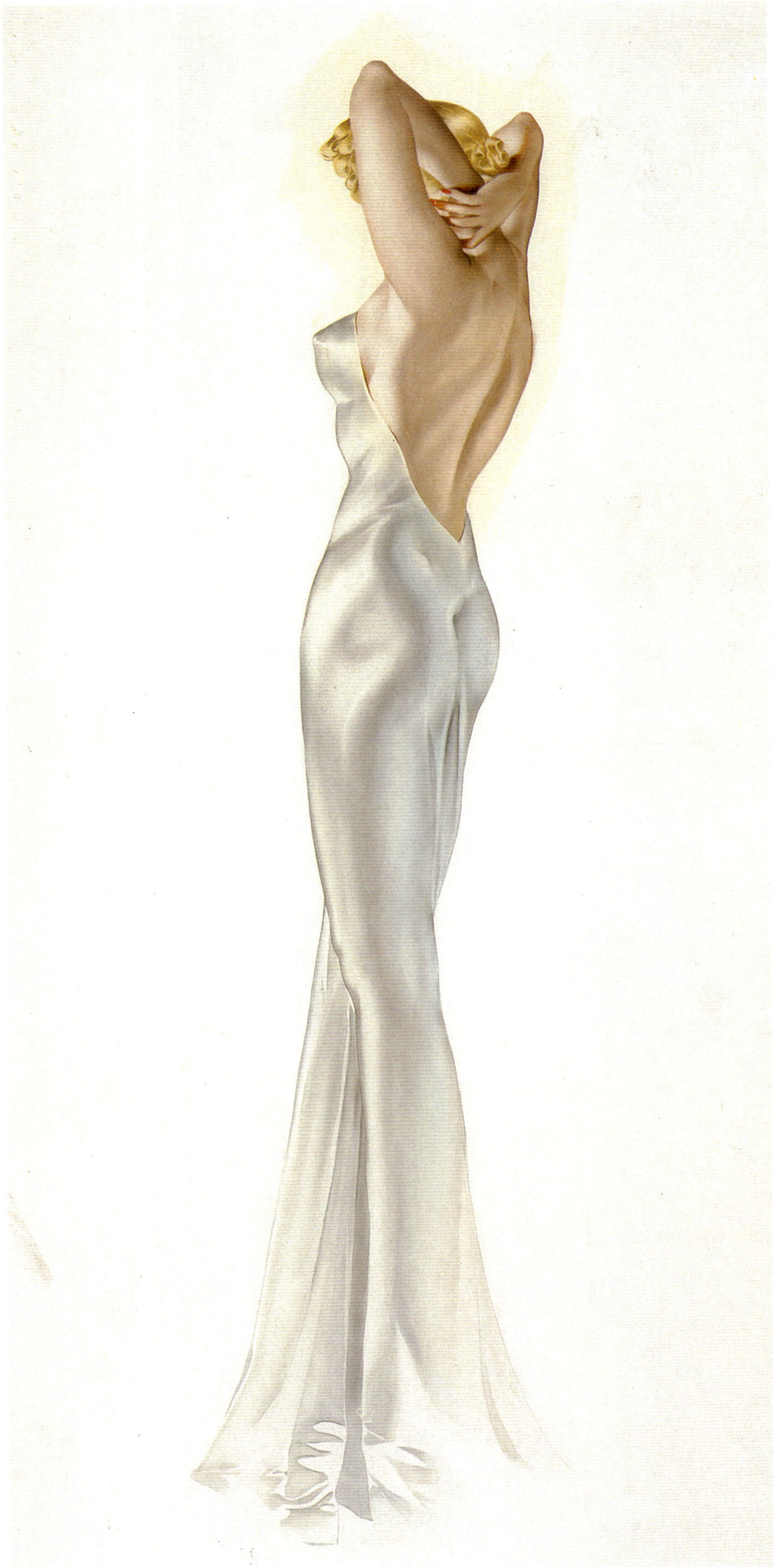

Above: November 1941 Calendar

Right: November 1941 Gatefold

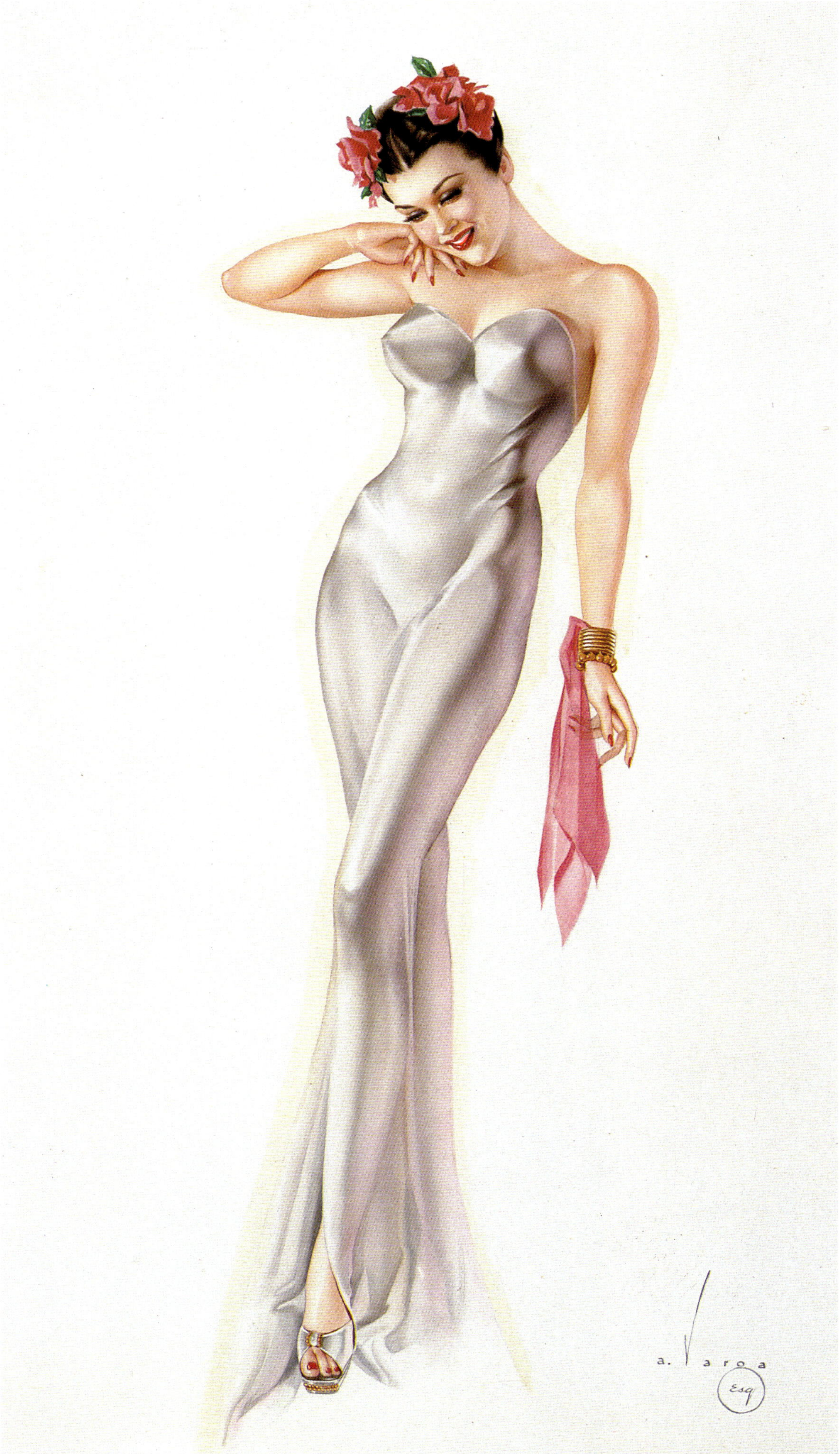
a. Varga
Esq

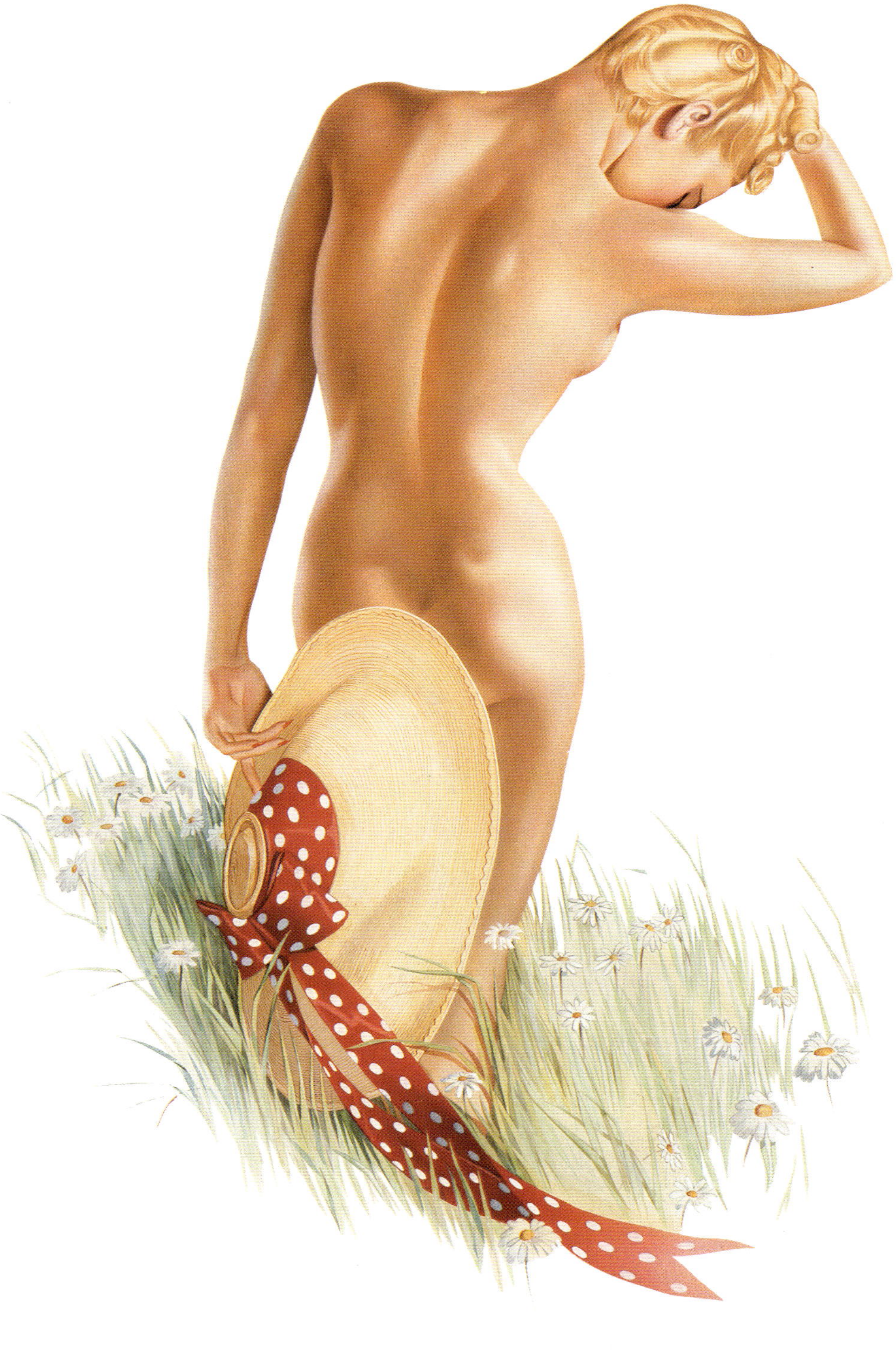

Above: June 1942 Calendar

Right: September 1942 Calendar

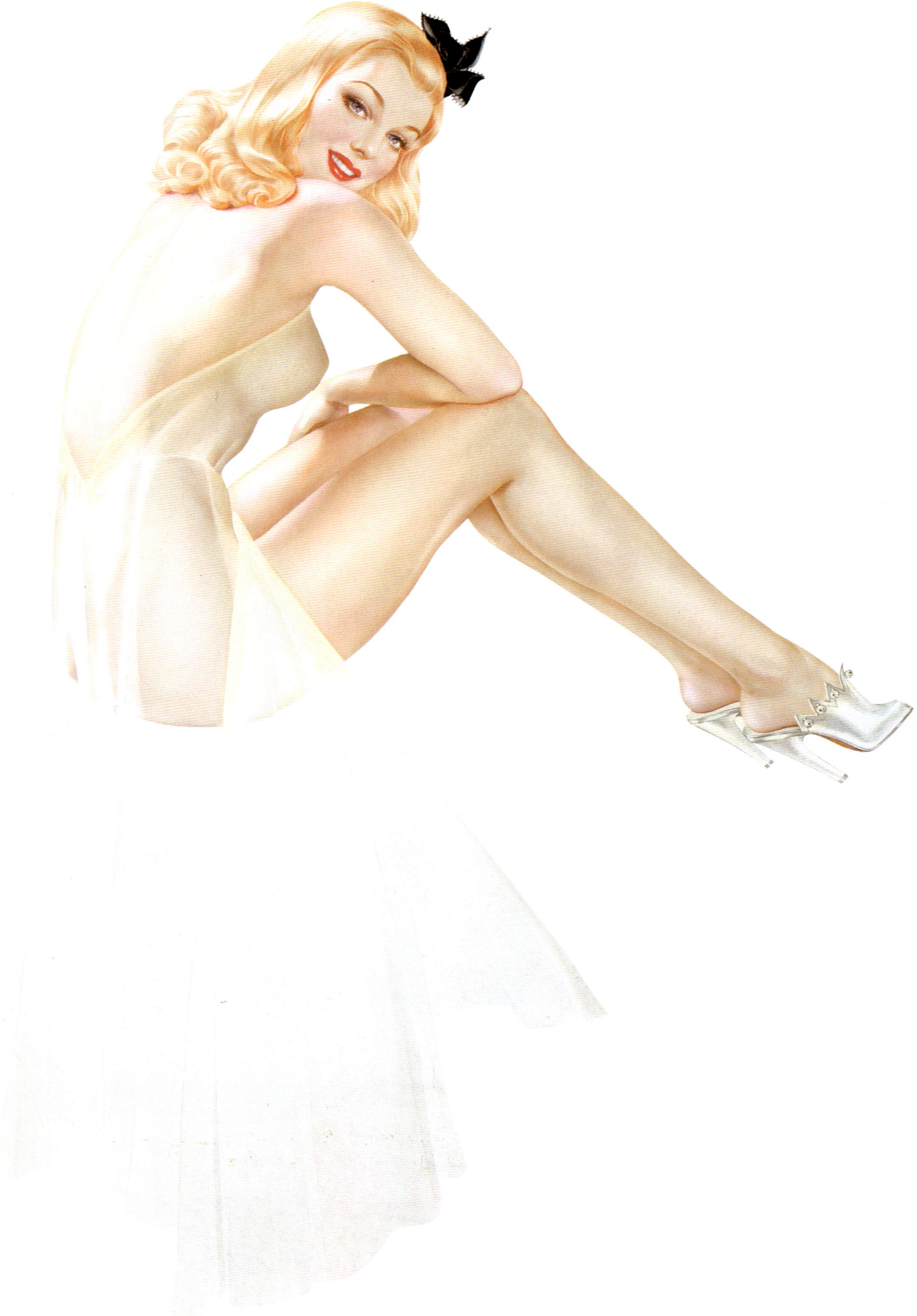

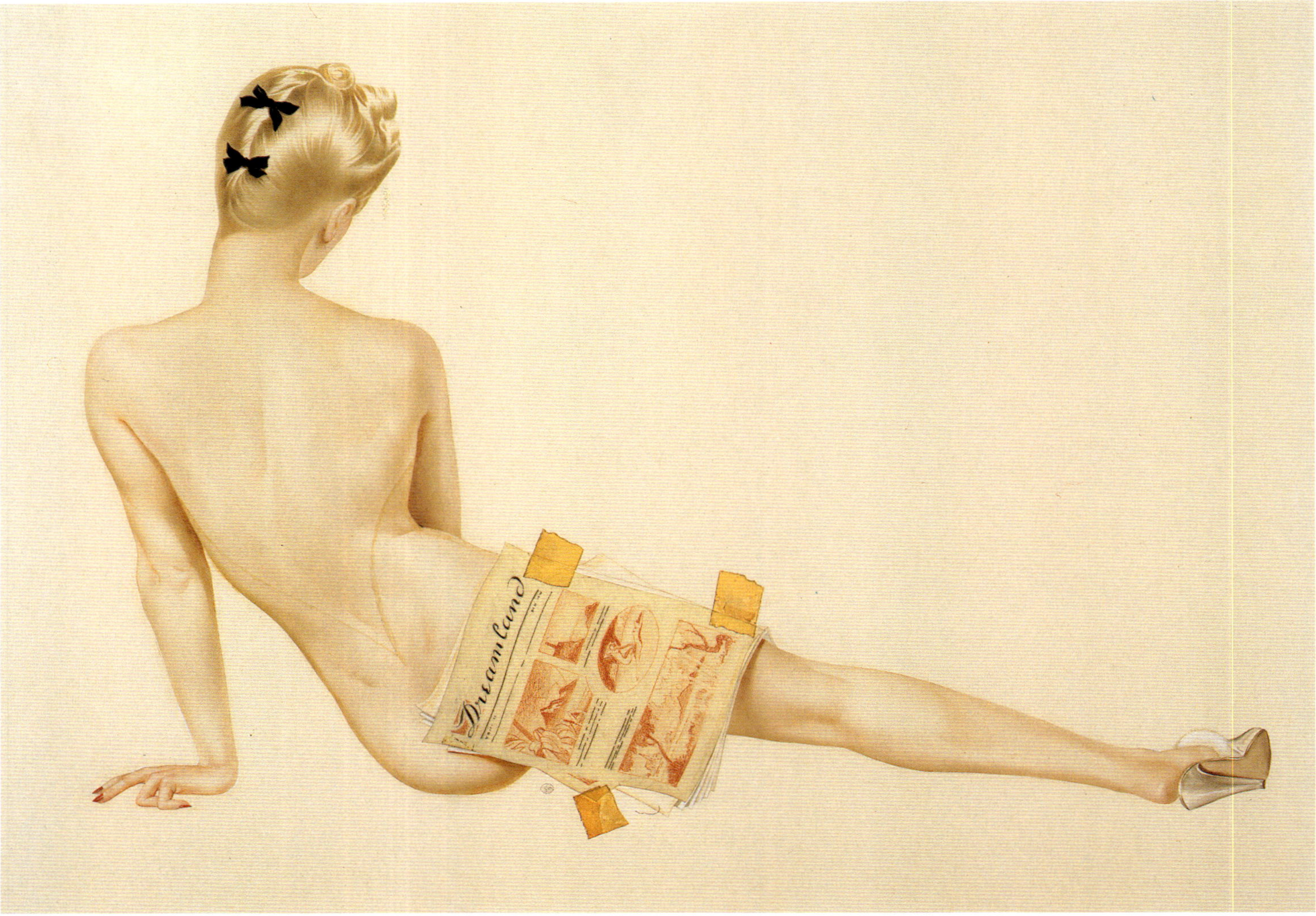

Above: February 1943 Calendar

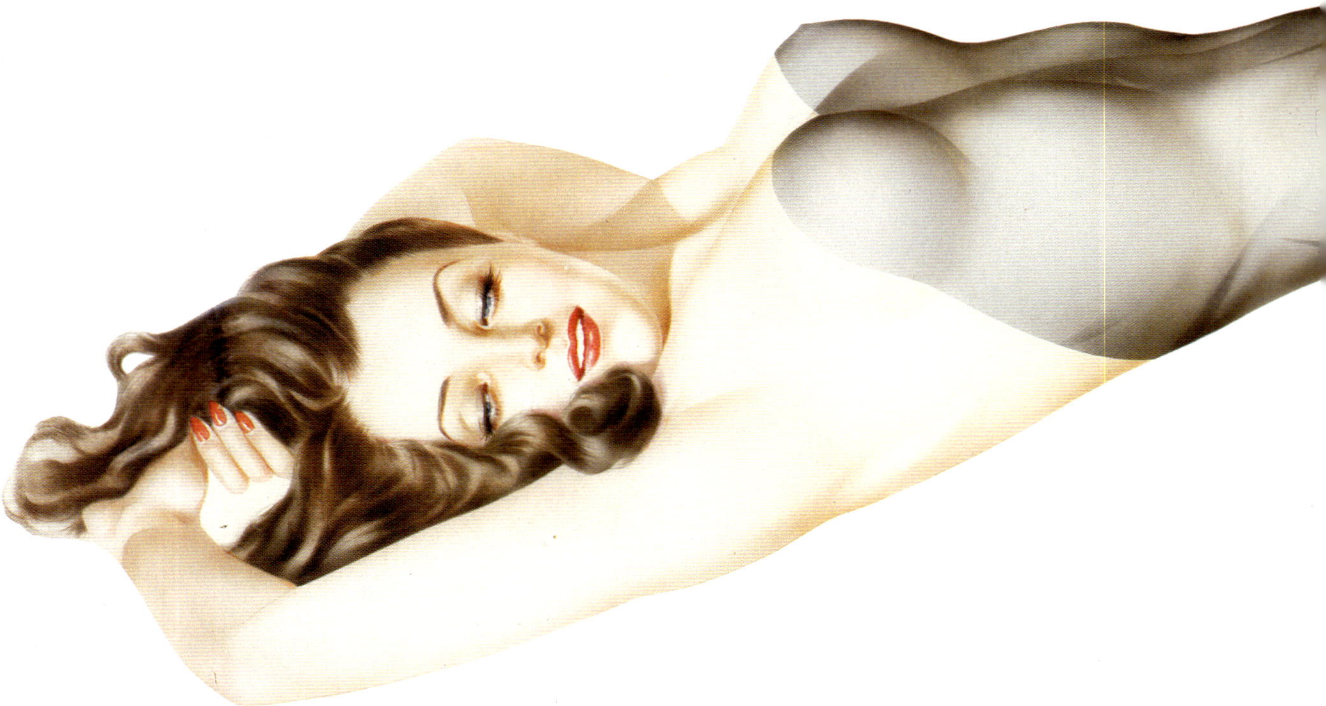

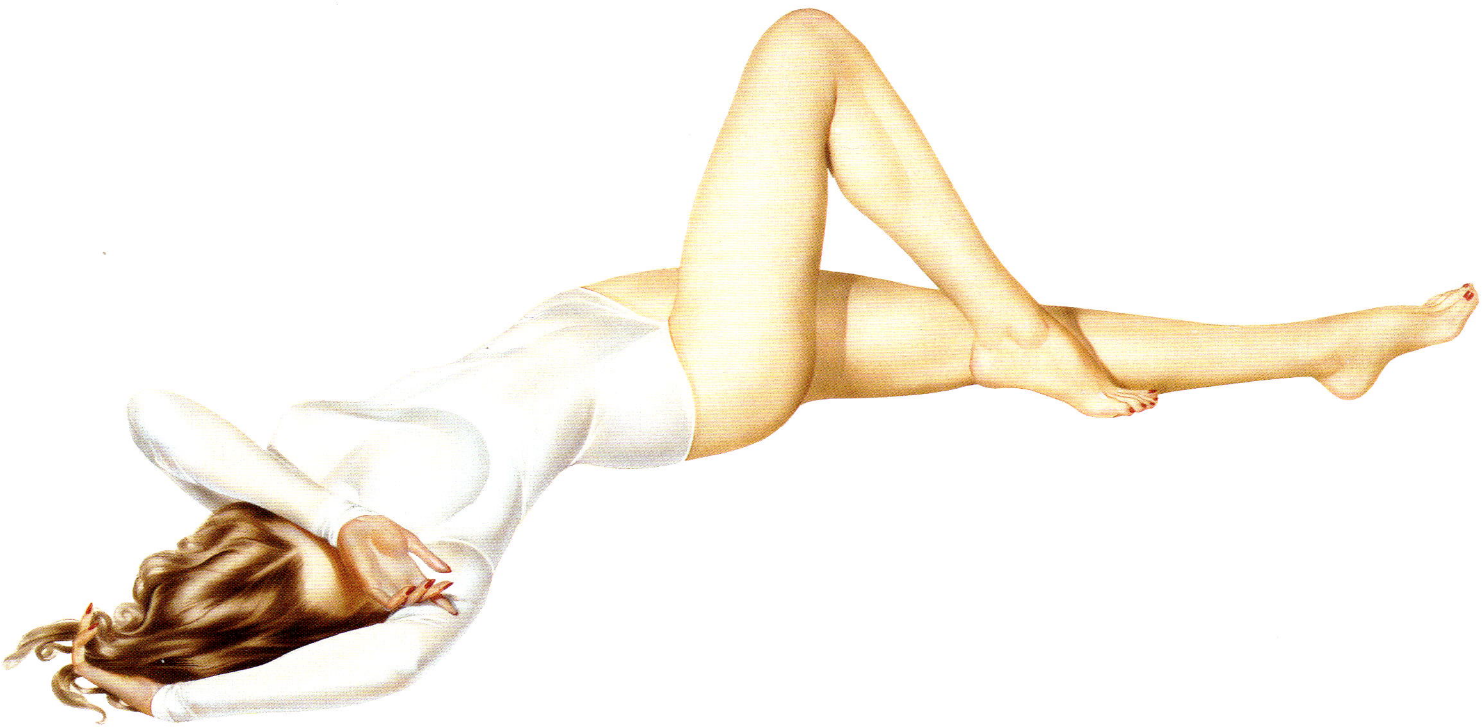

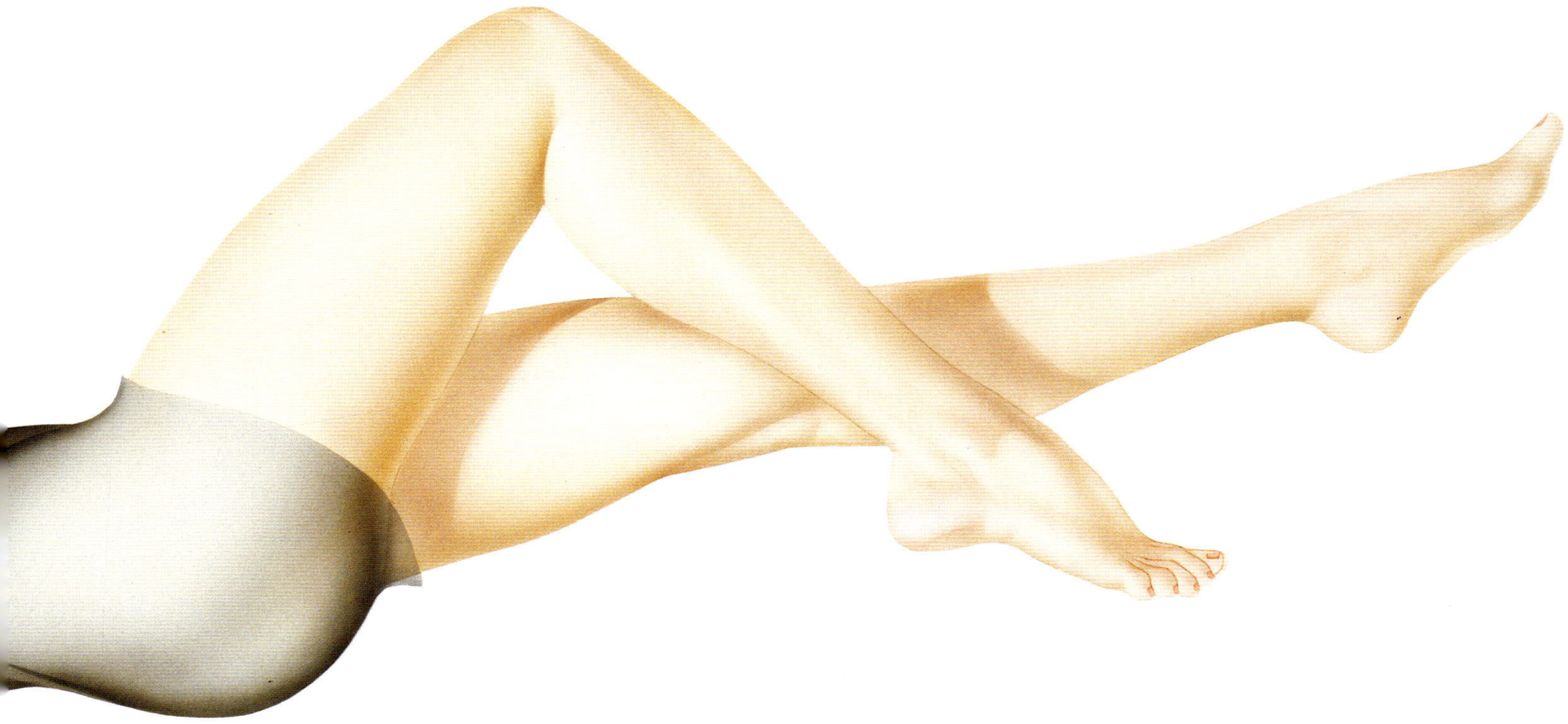

Top: September 1943

Above: August 1943 Calendar

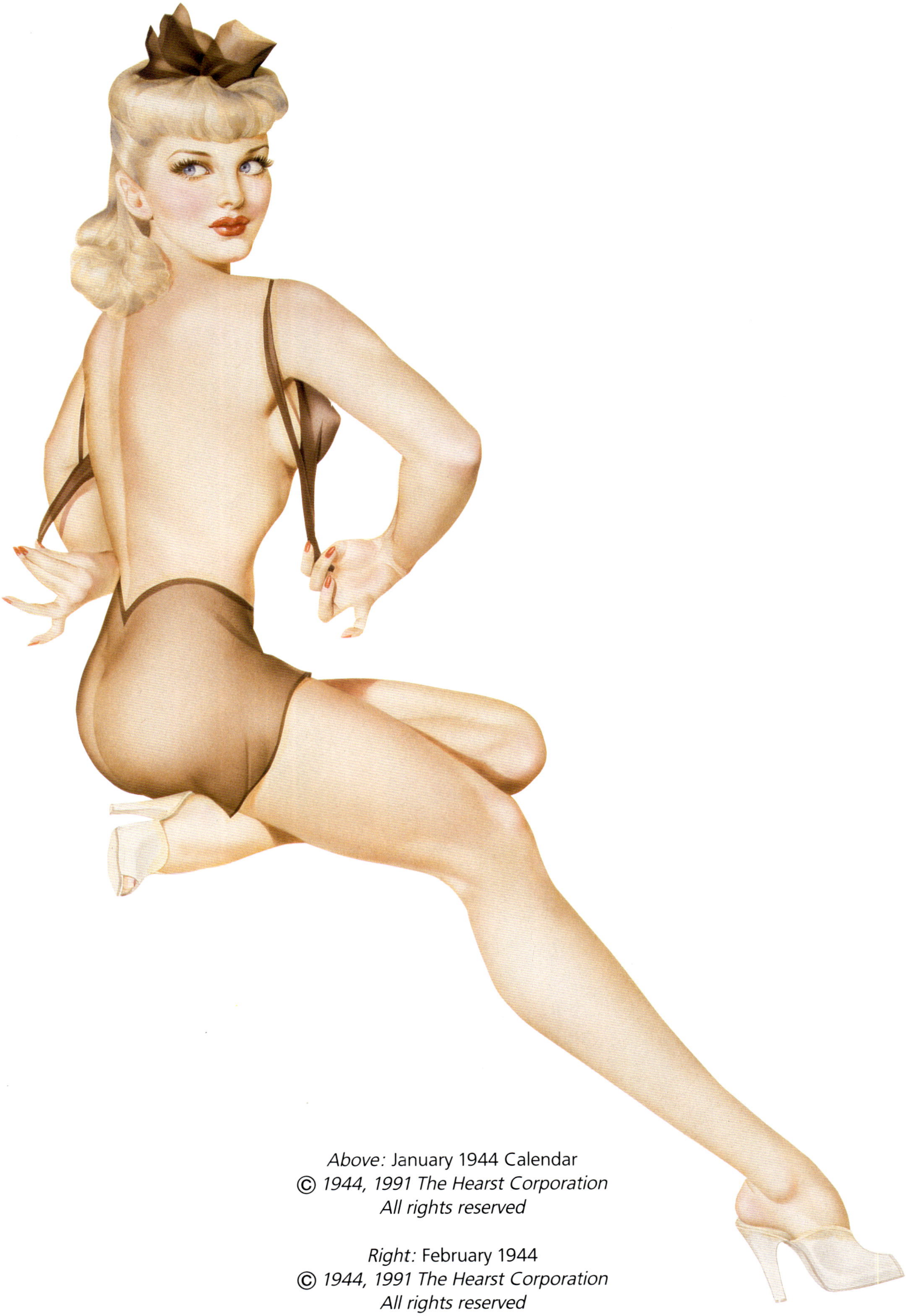

Above: January 1944 Calendar

Right: February 1944

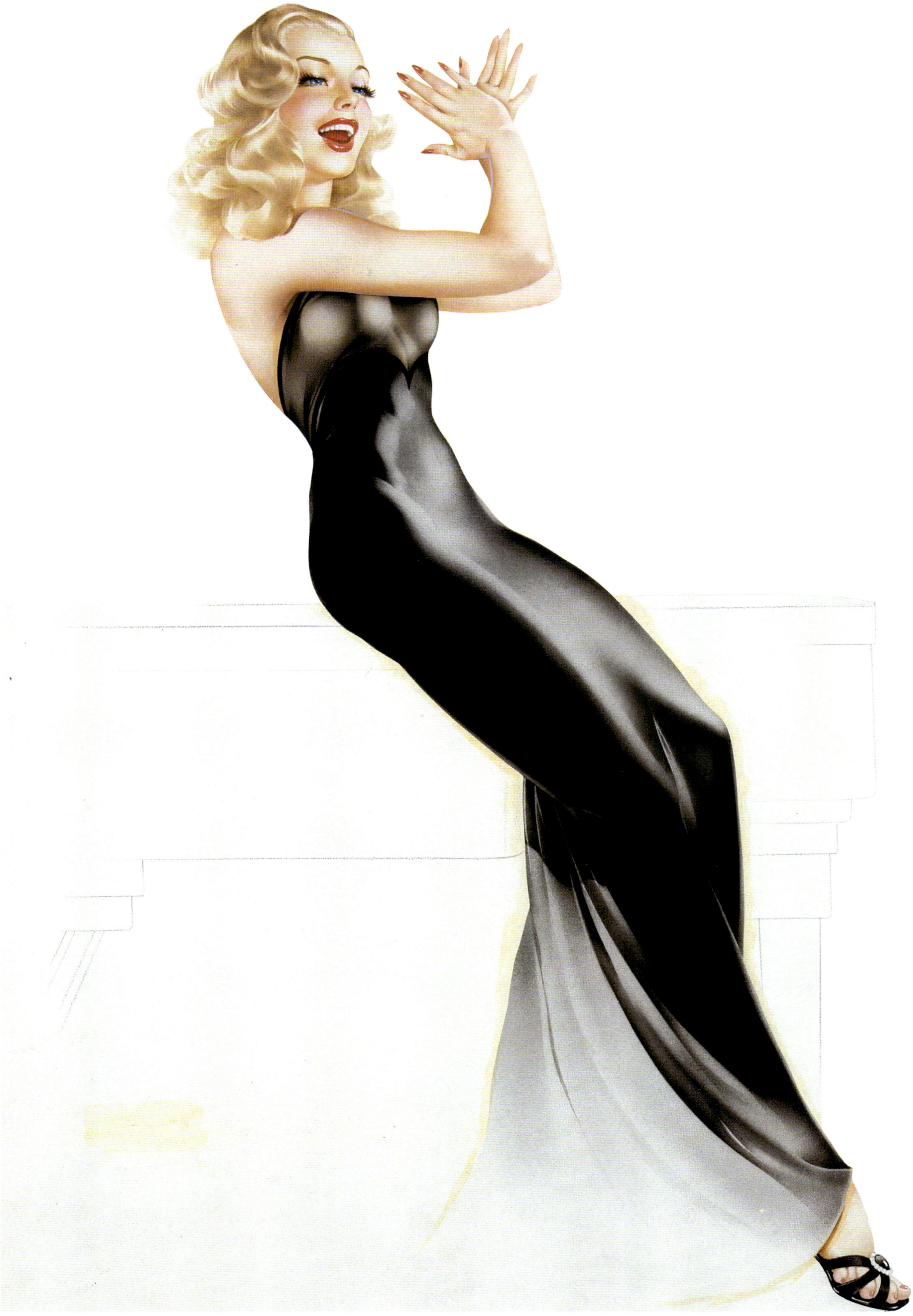

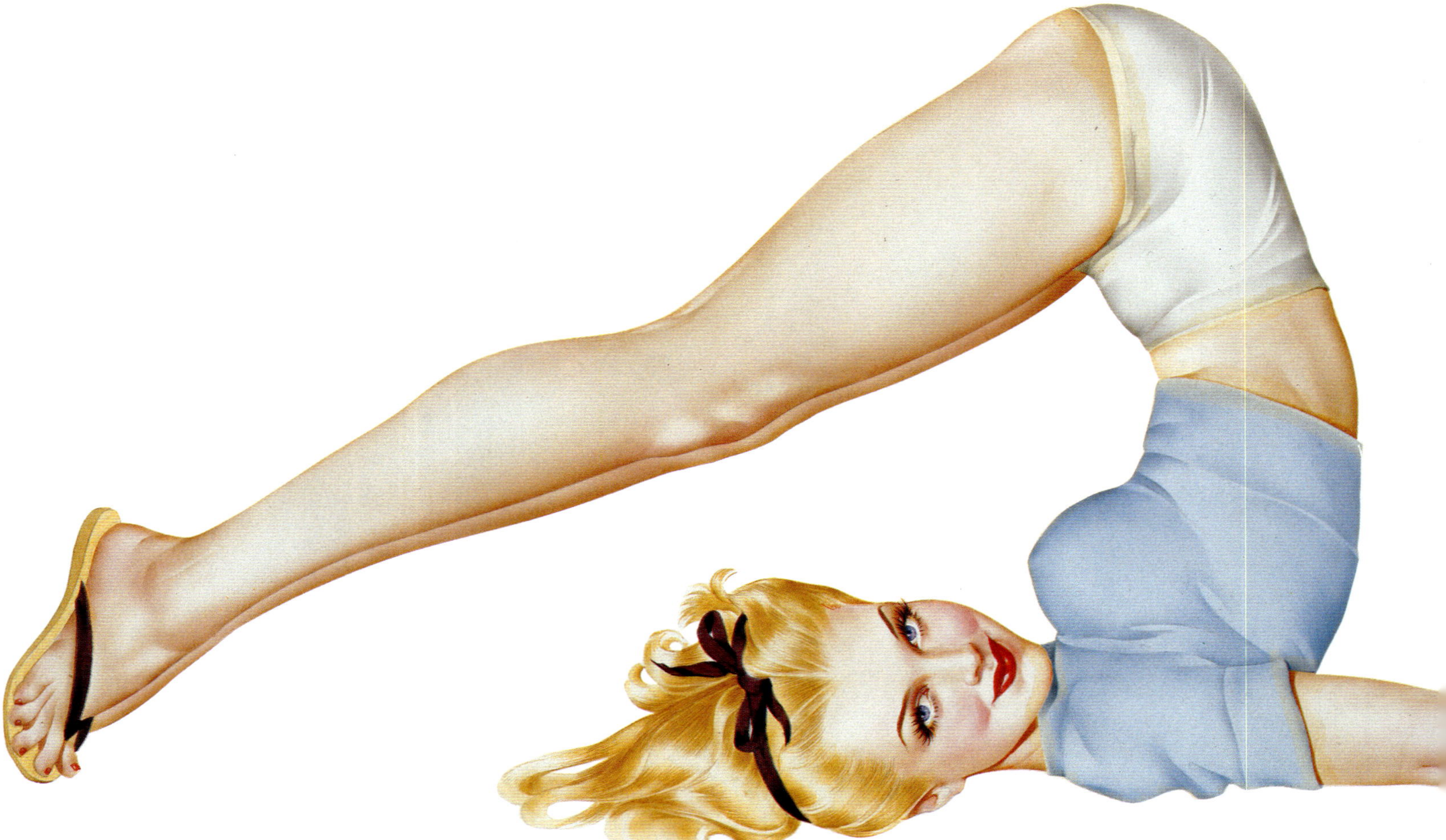

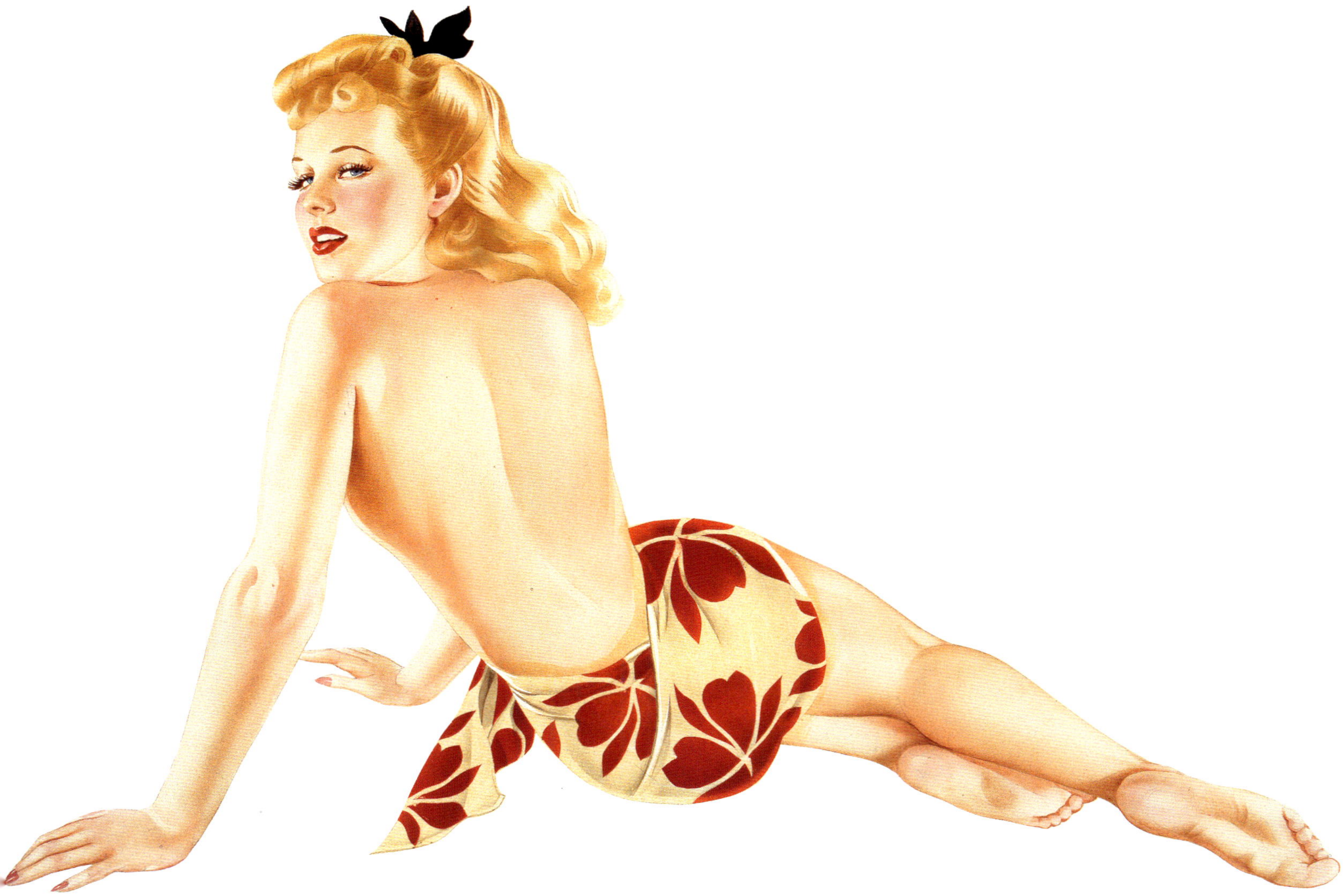

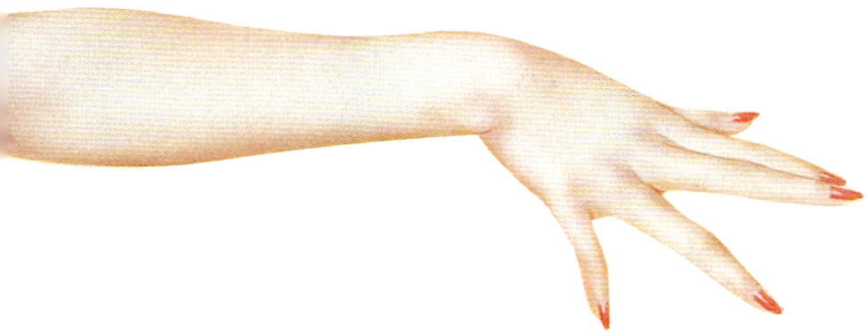

Above: April 1944 Military Edition

Left: February 1944 Calendar

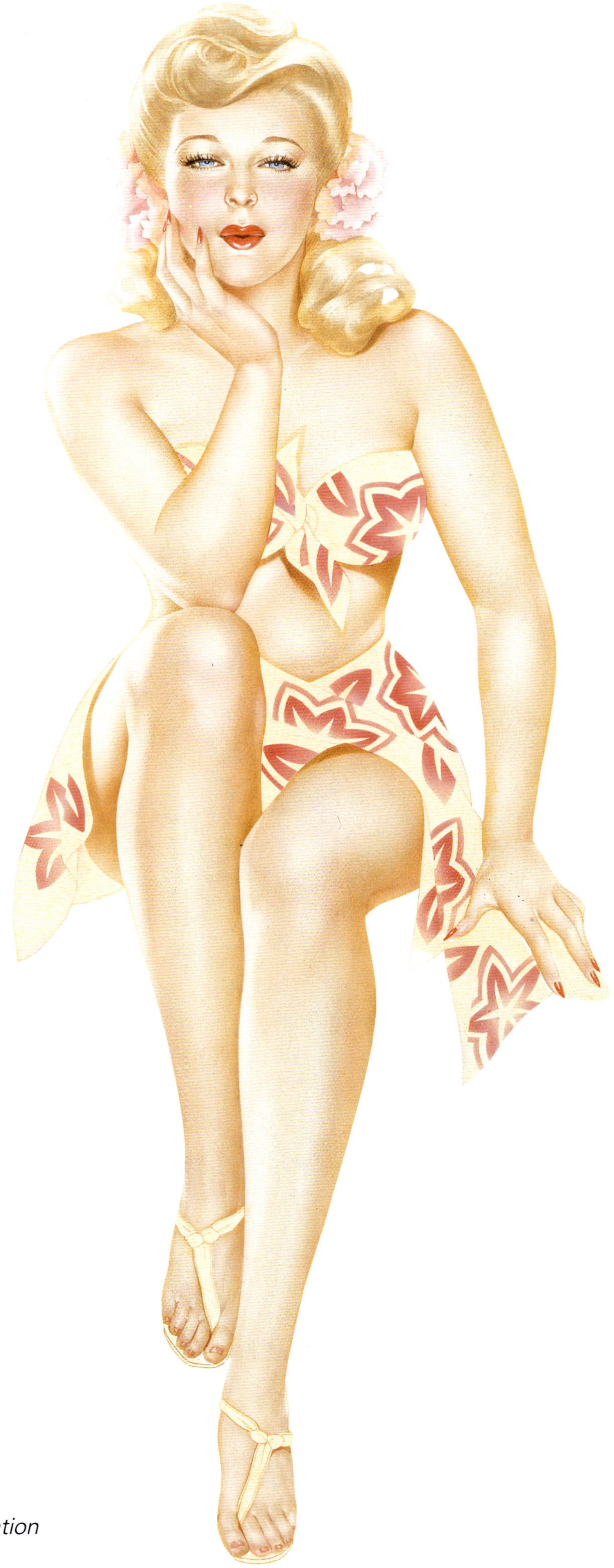

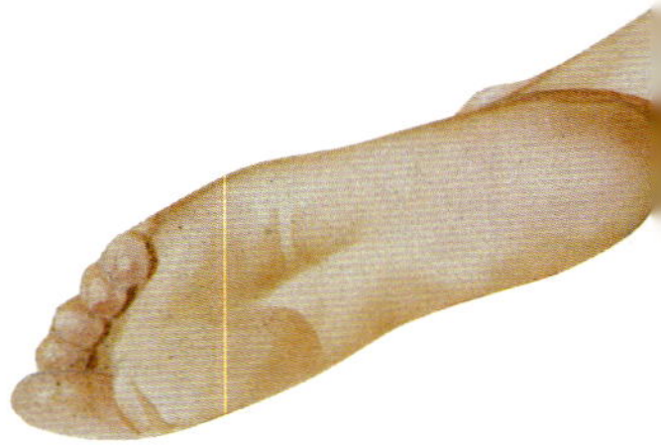

May 1944

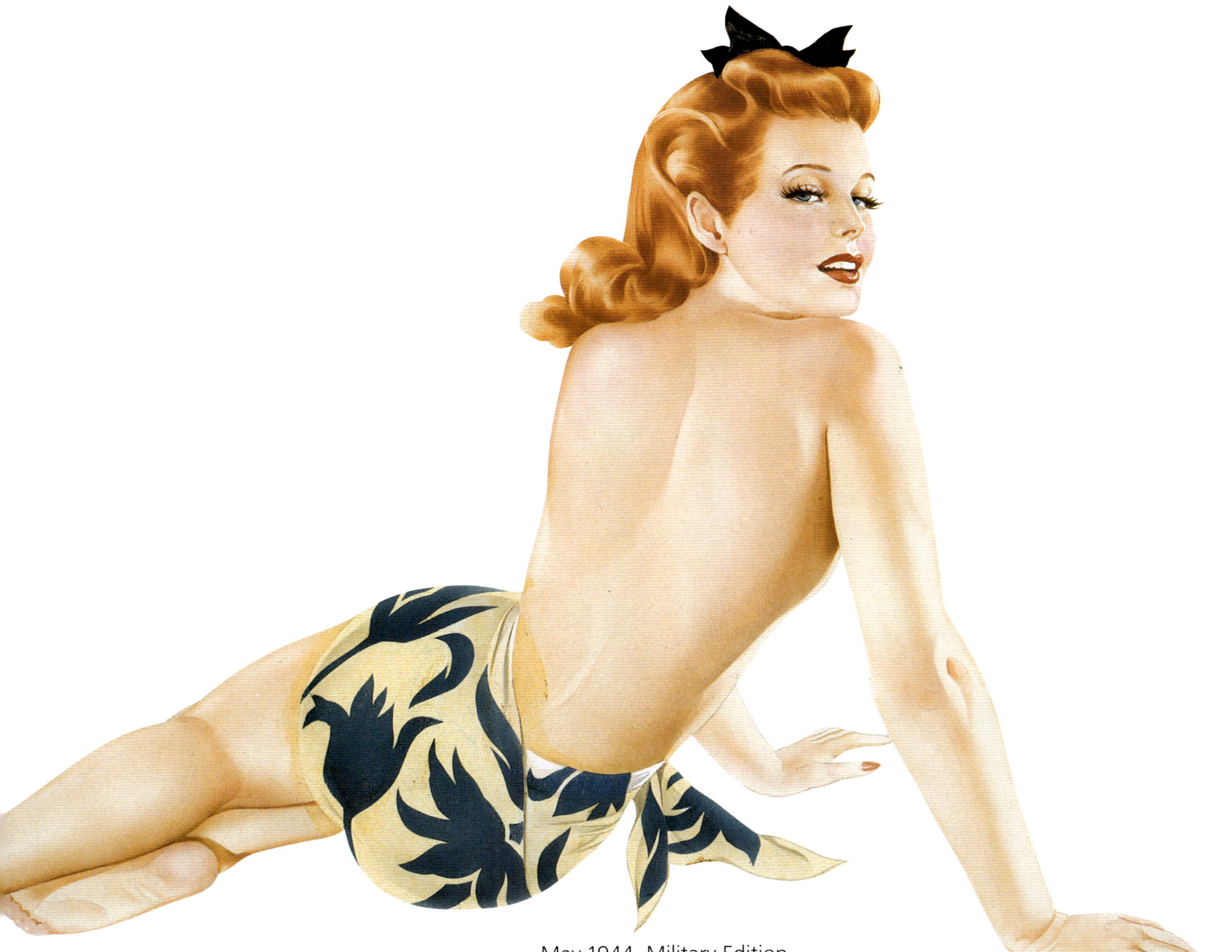

May 1944, Military Edition

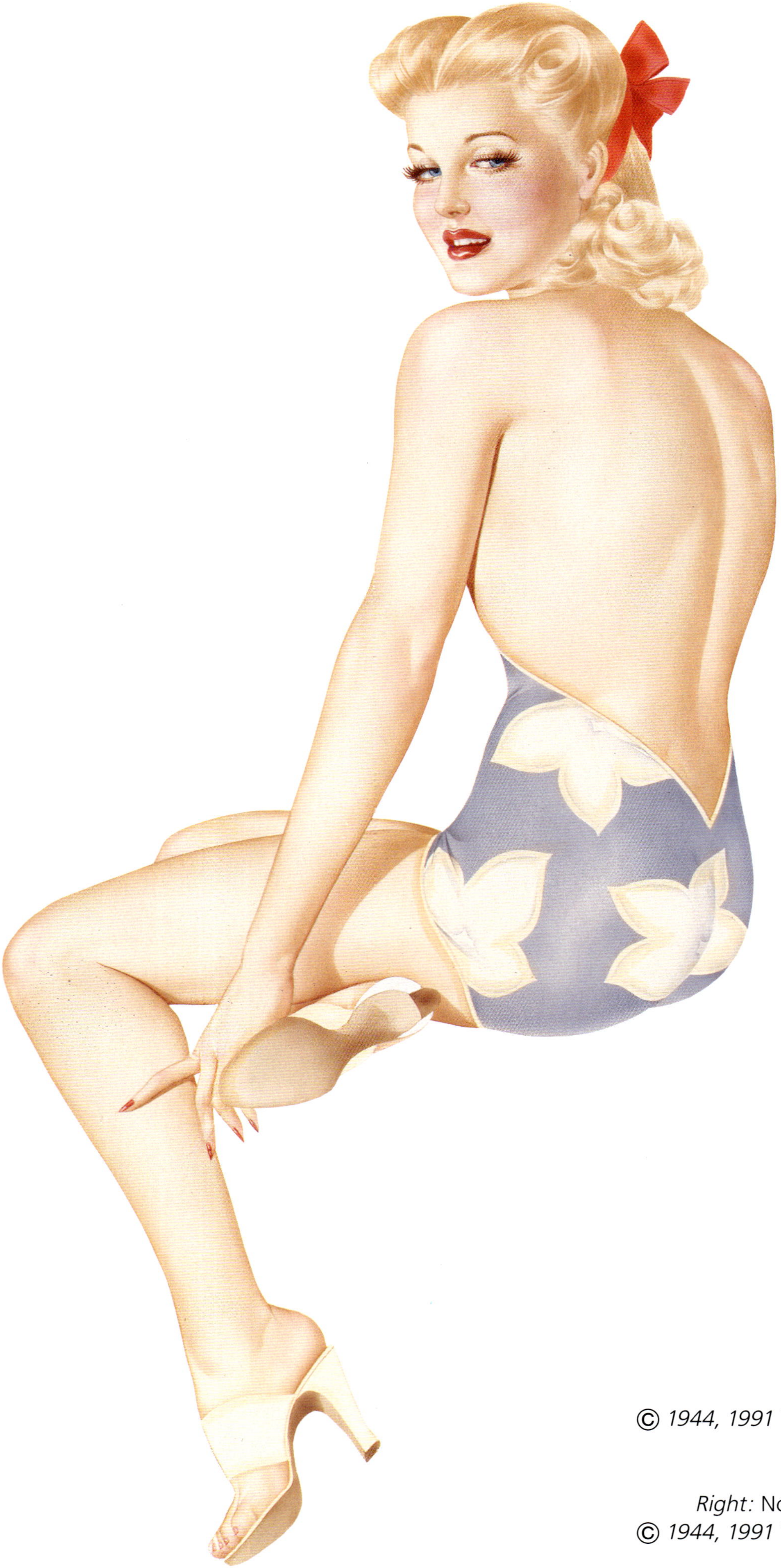

Above: July 1944

Right: November 1944 Gatefold

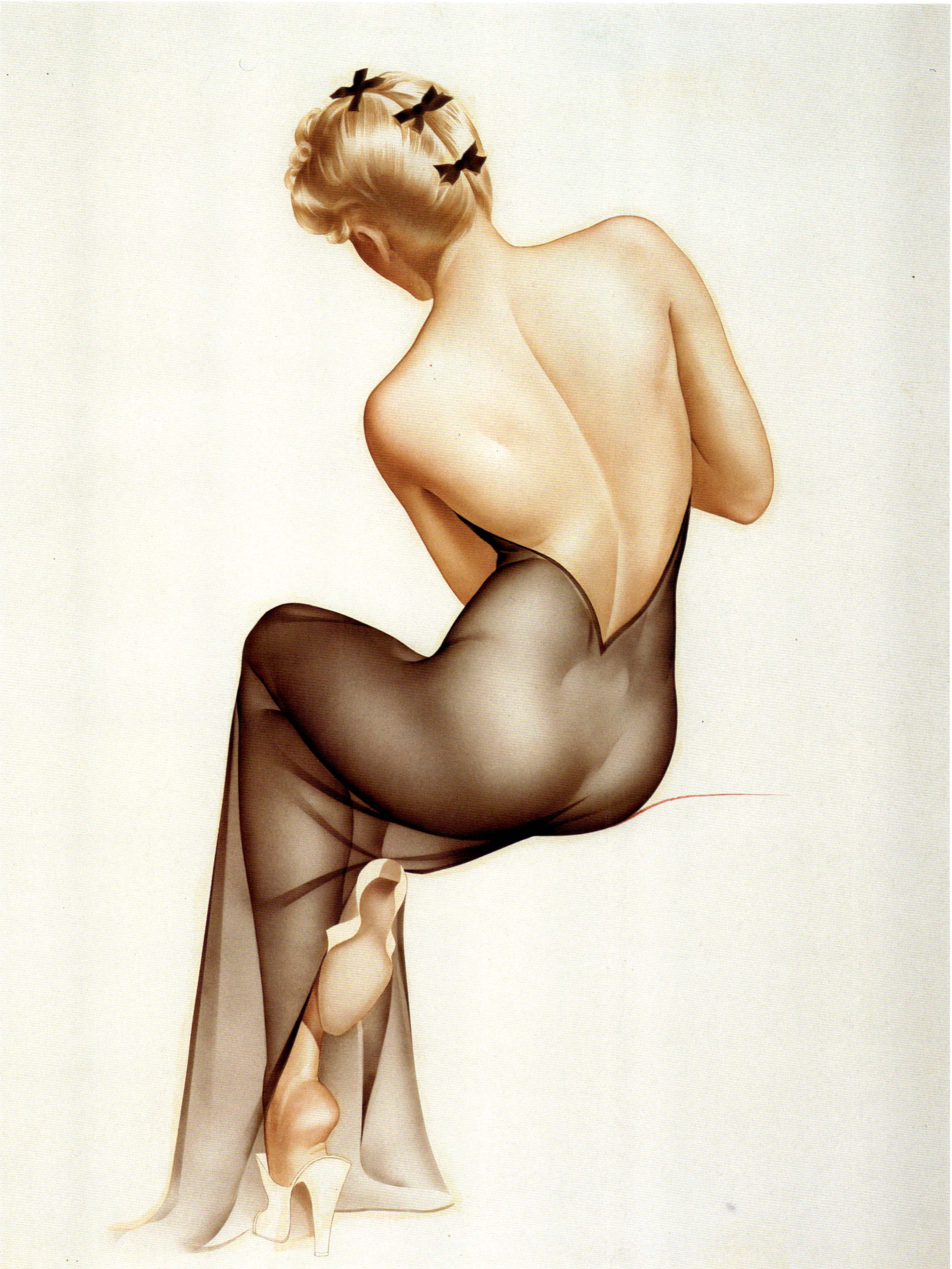

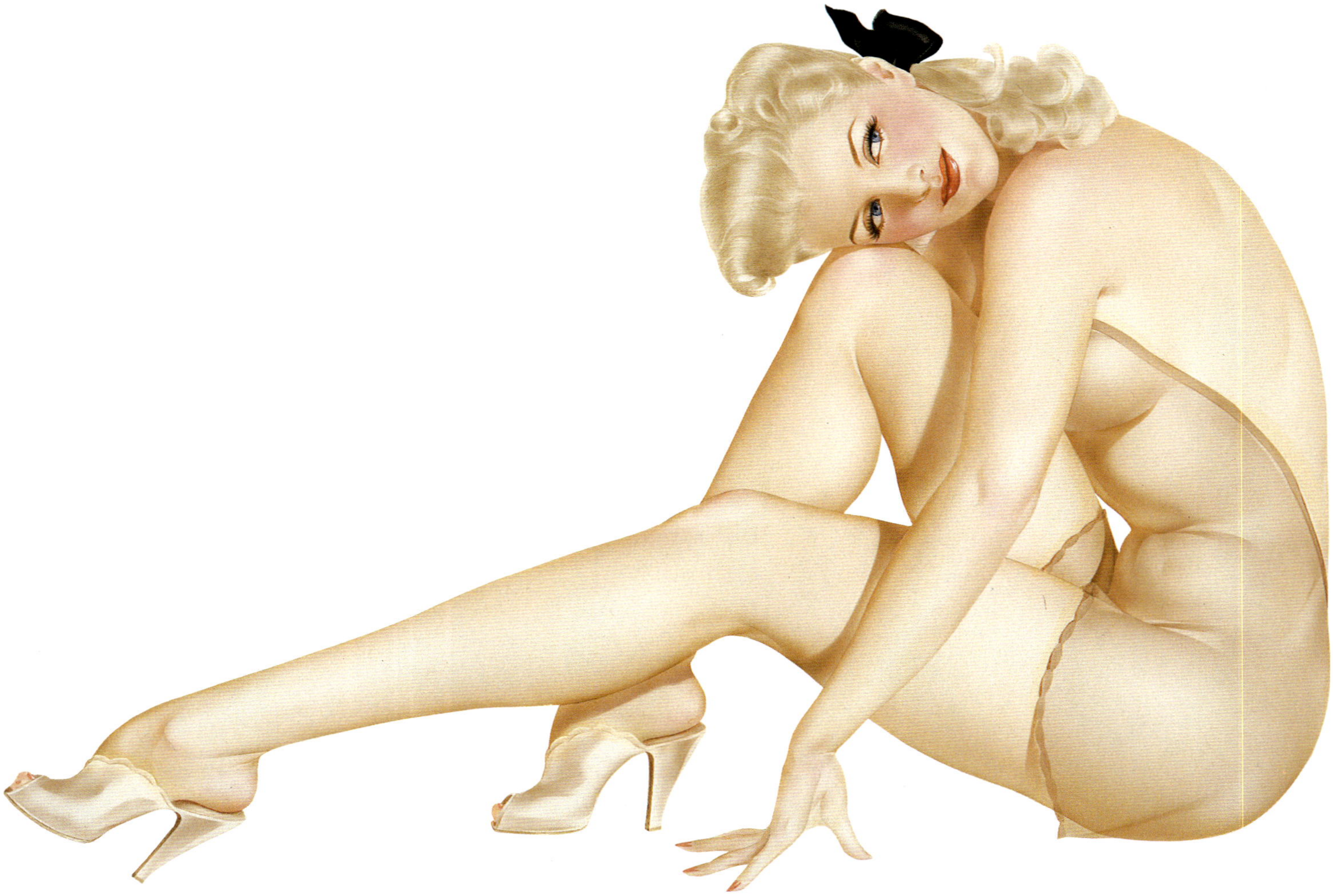

November 1944 Calendar

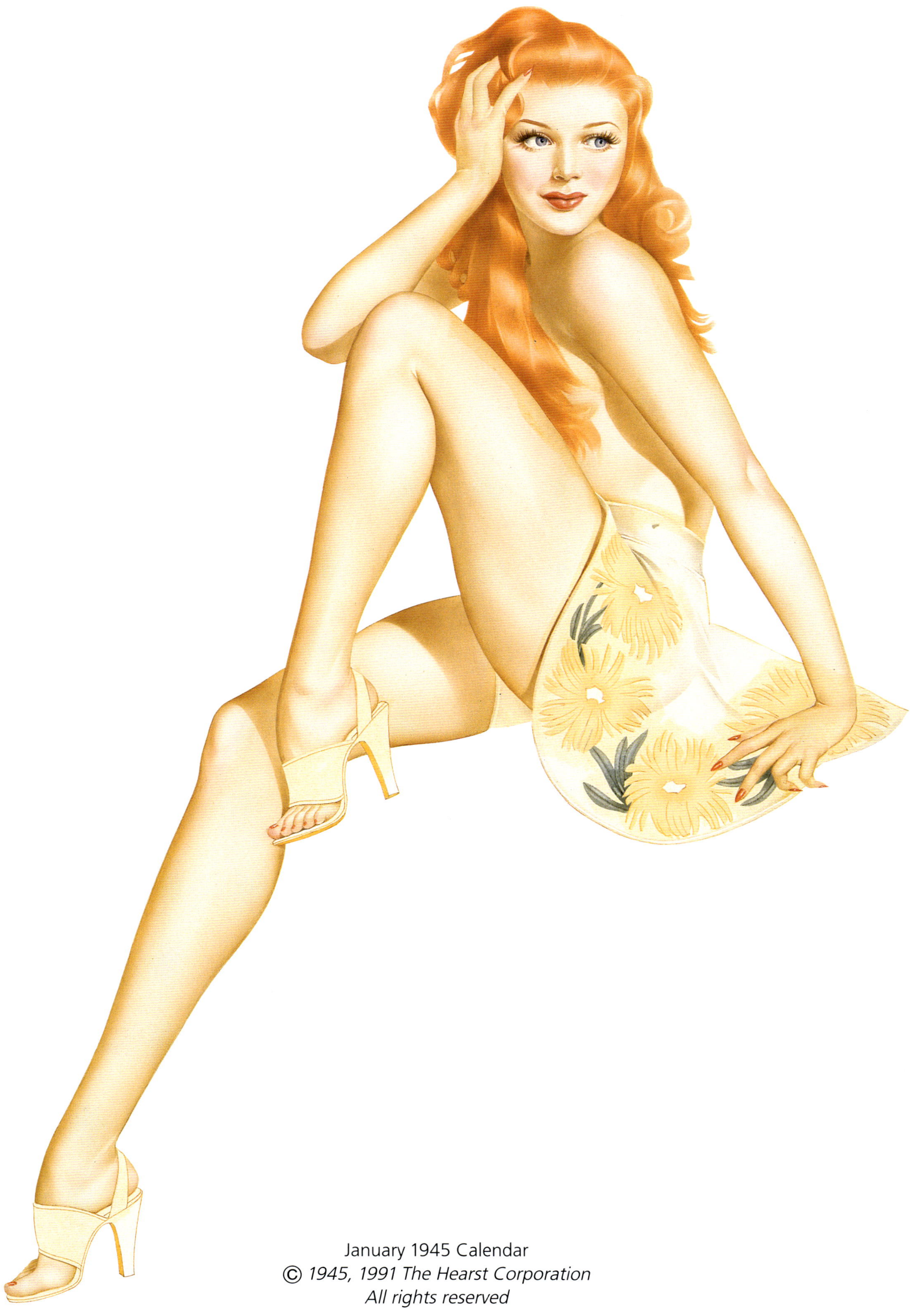

January 1945 Calendar

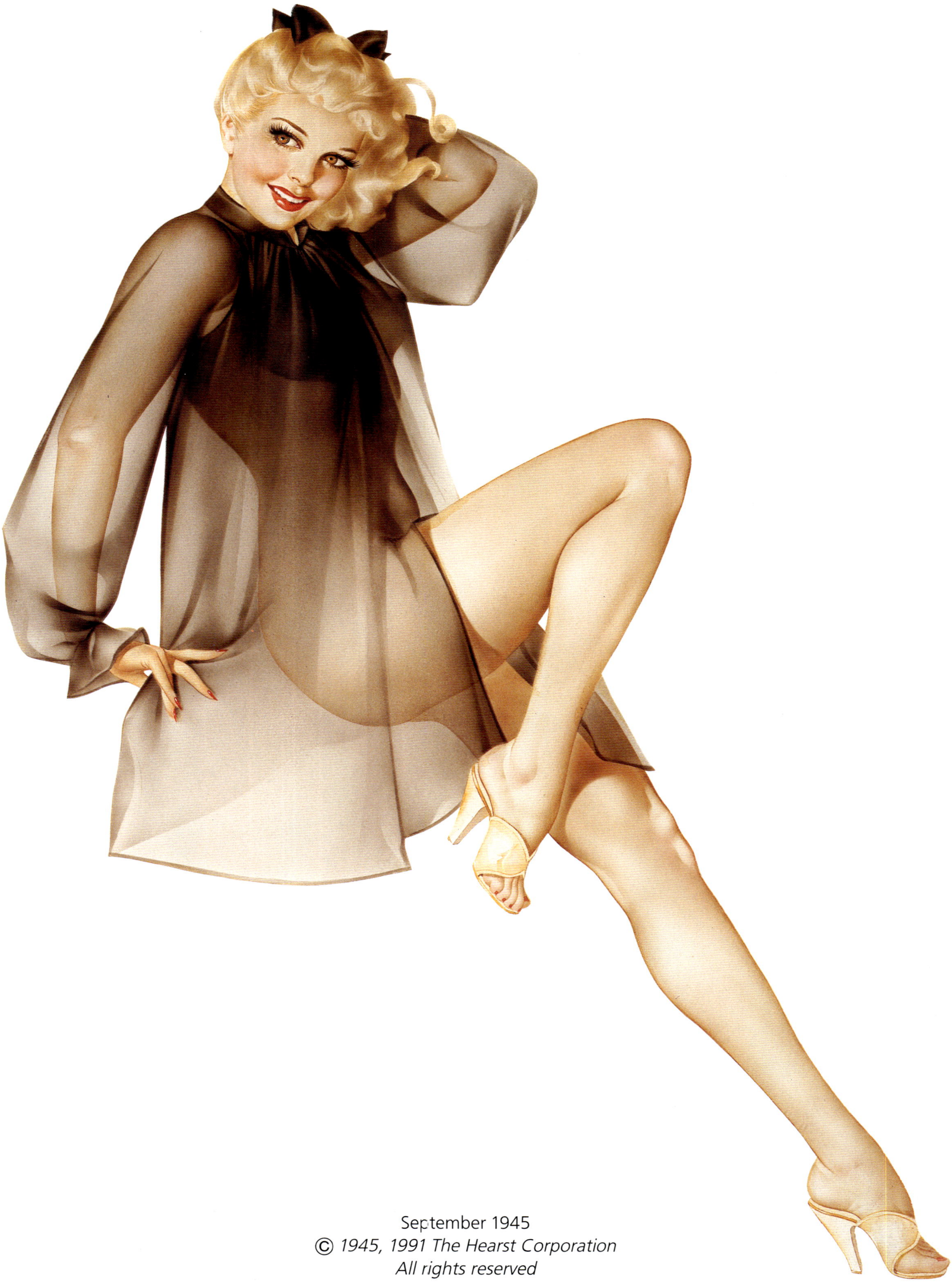

September 1945

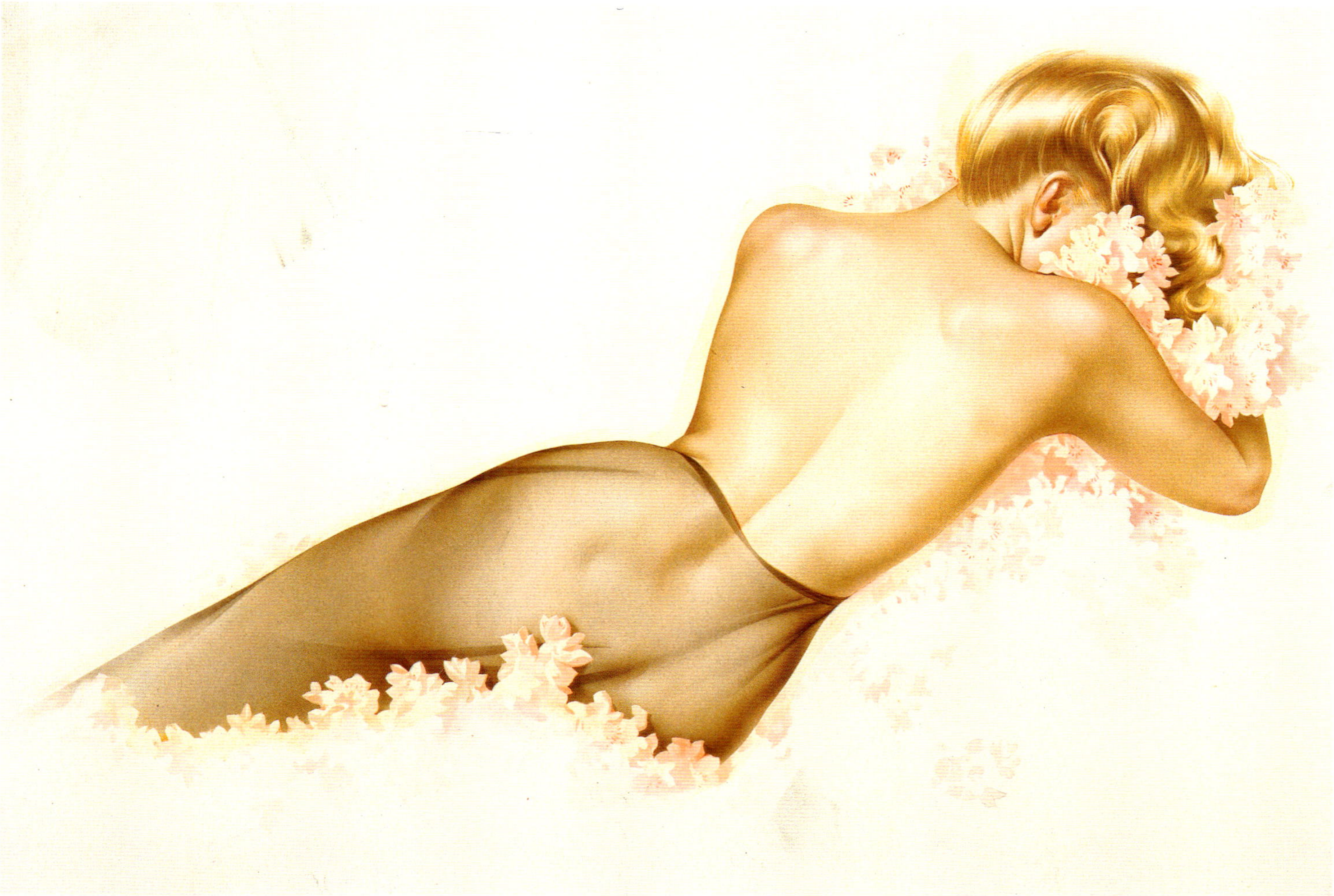

April 1946

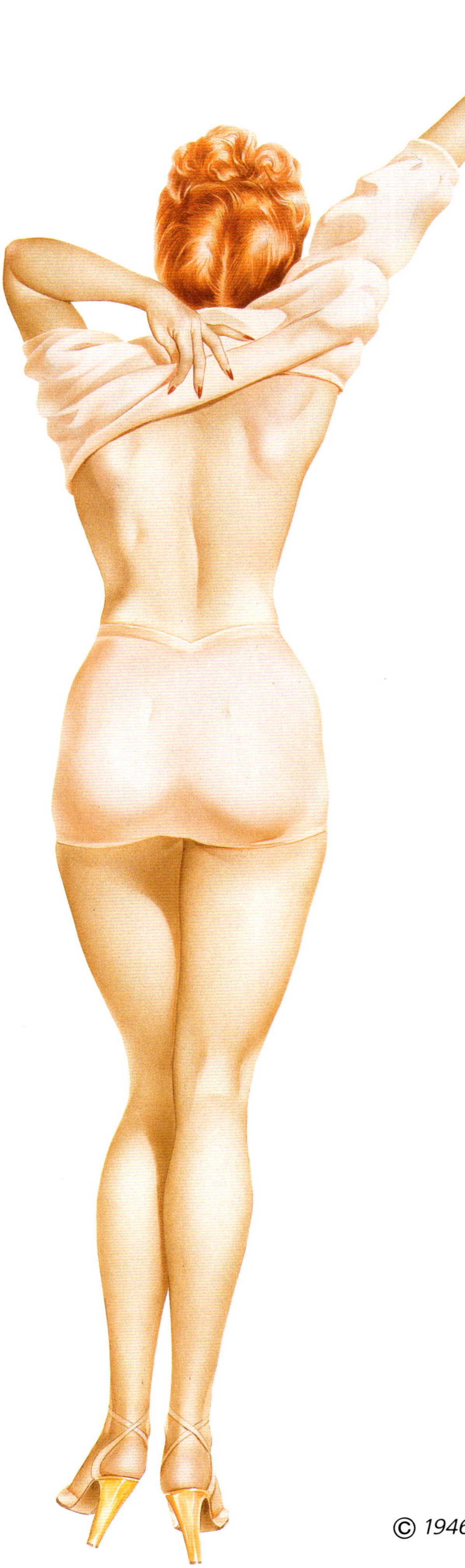

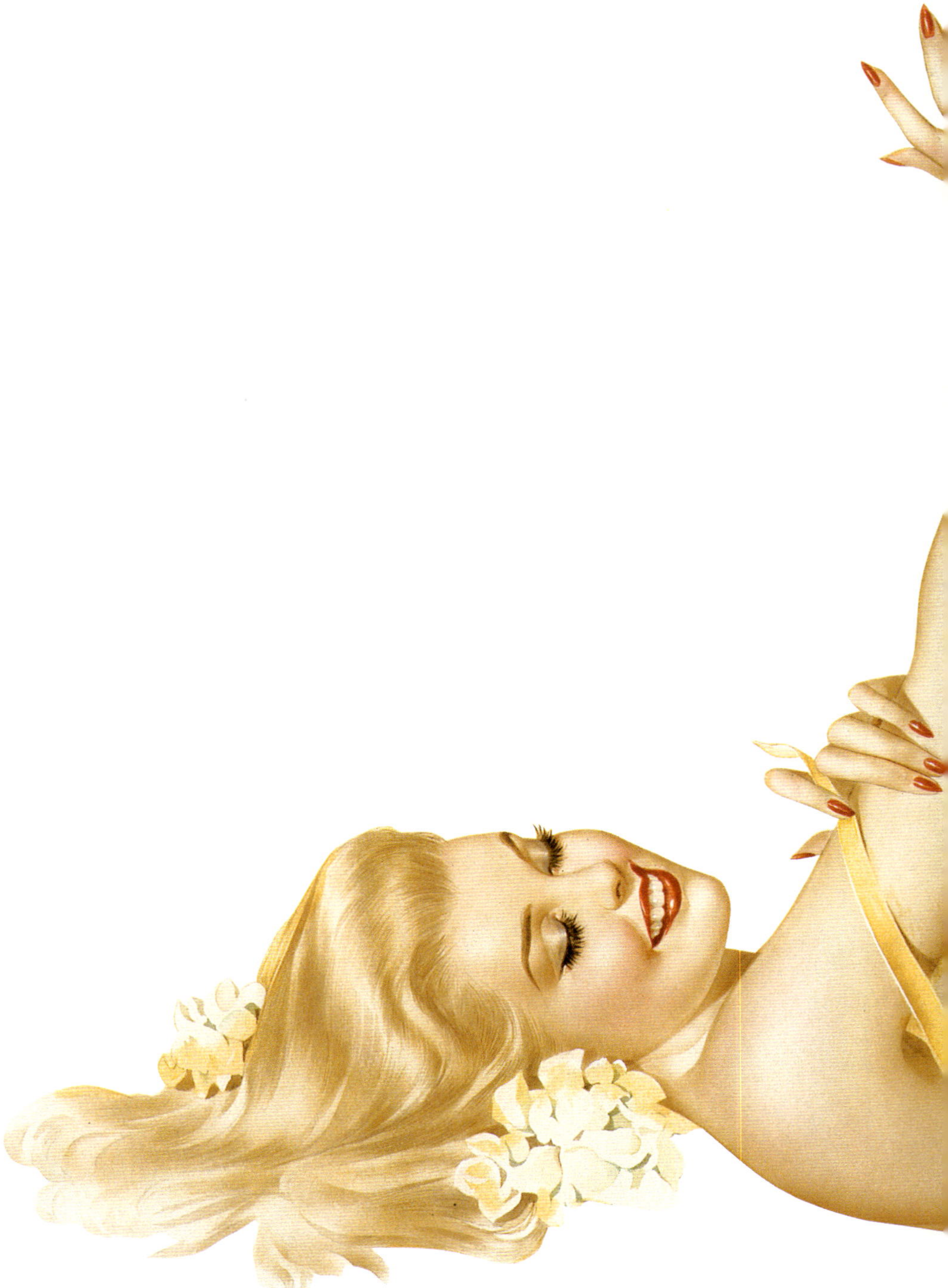

Left: May 1946

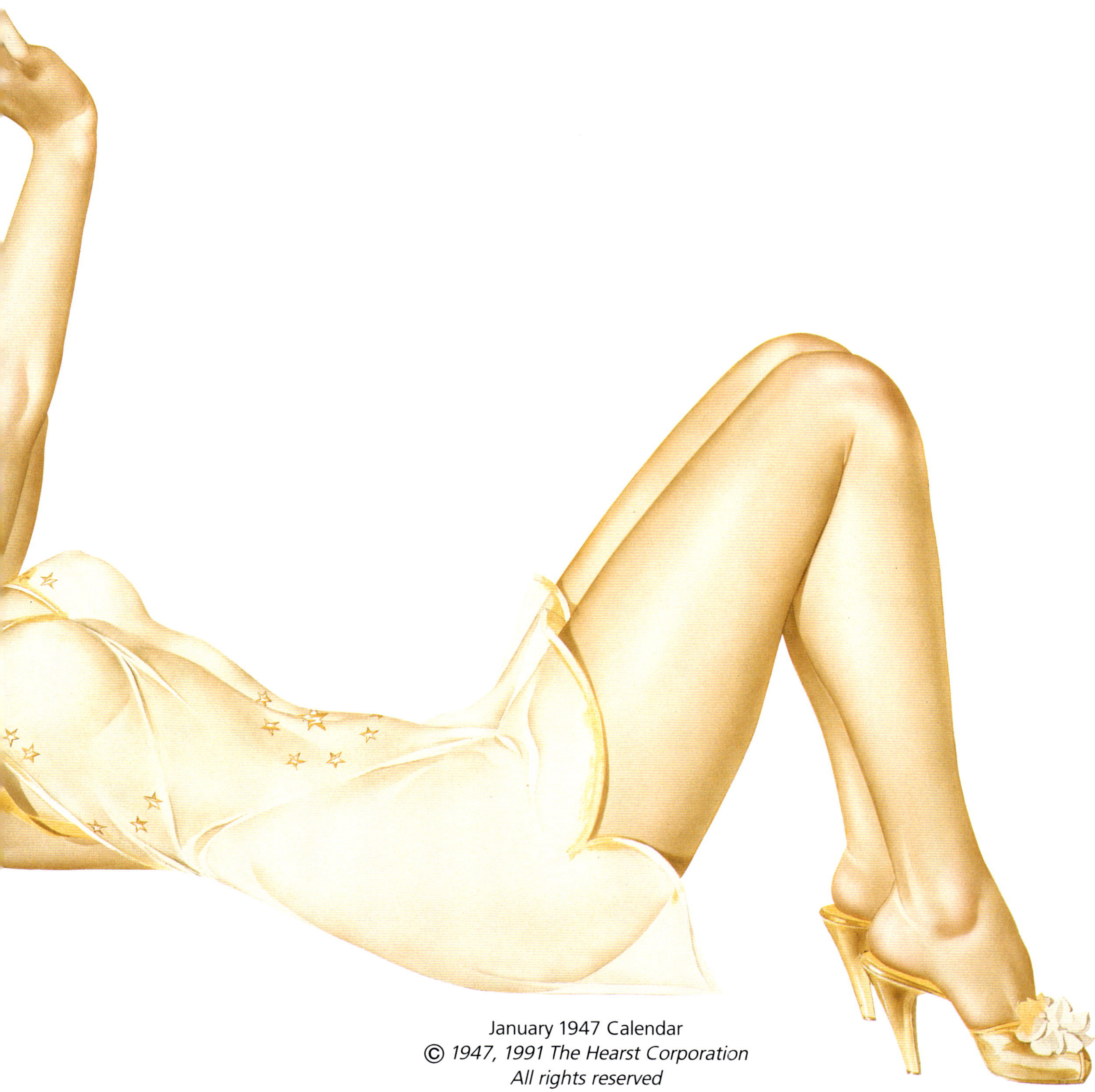

January 1947 Calendar

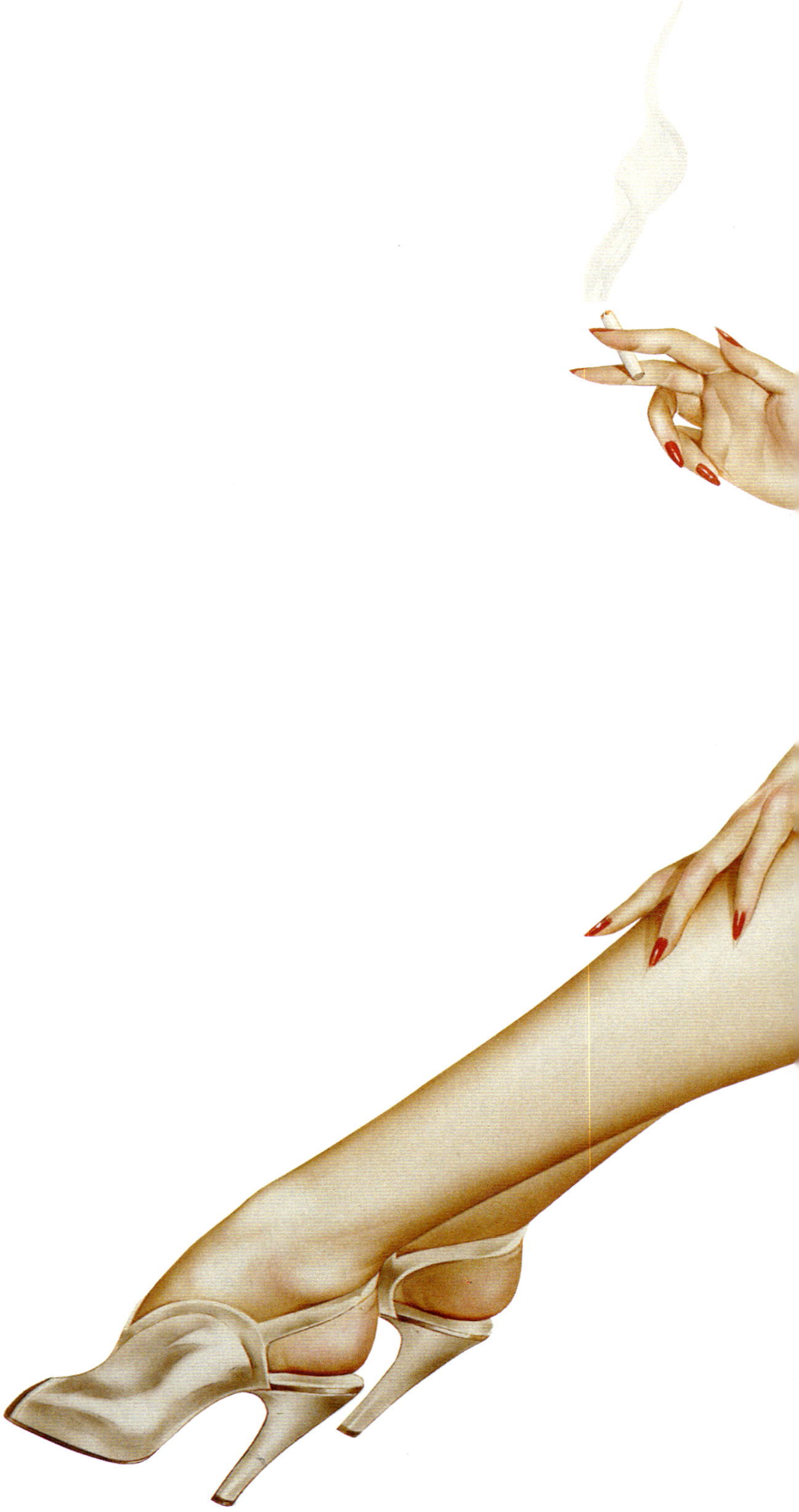

December 1947 Calendar

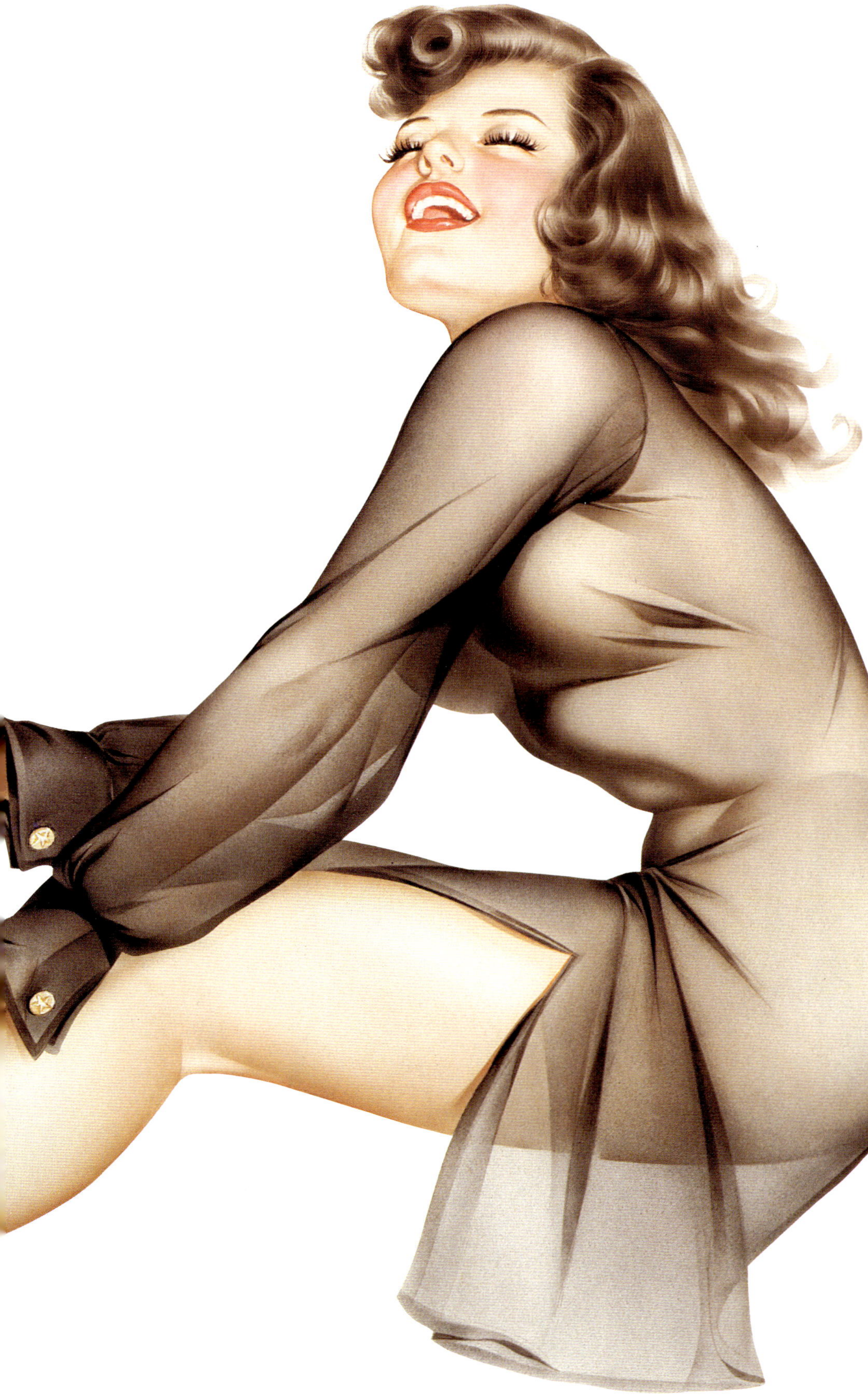

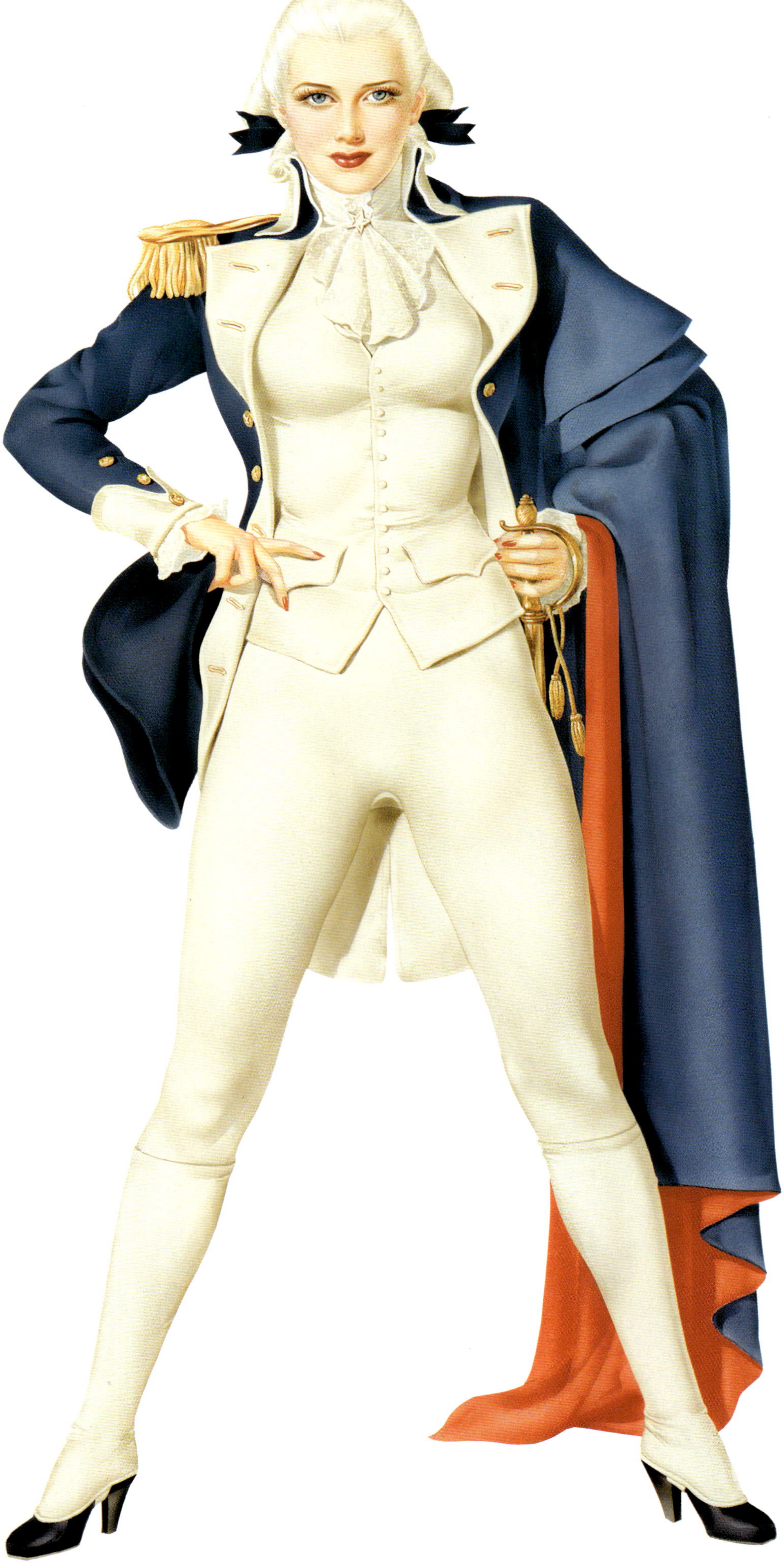

Patriotic Fever

August 1942 Gatefold

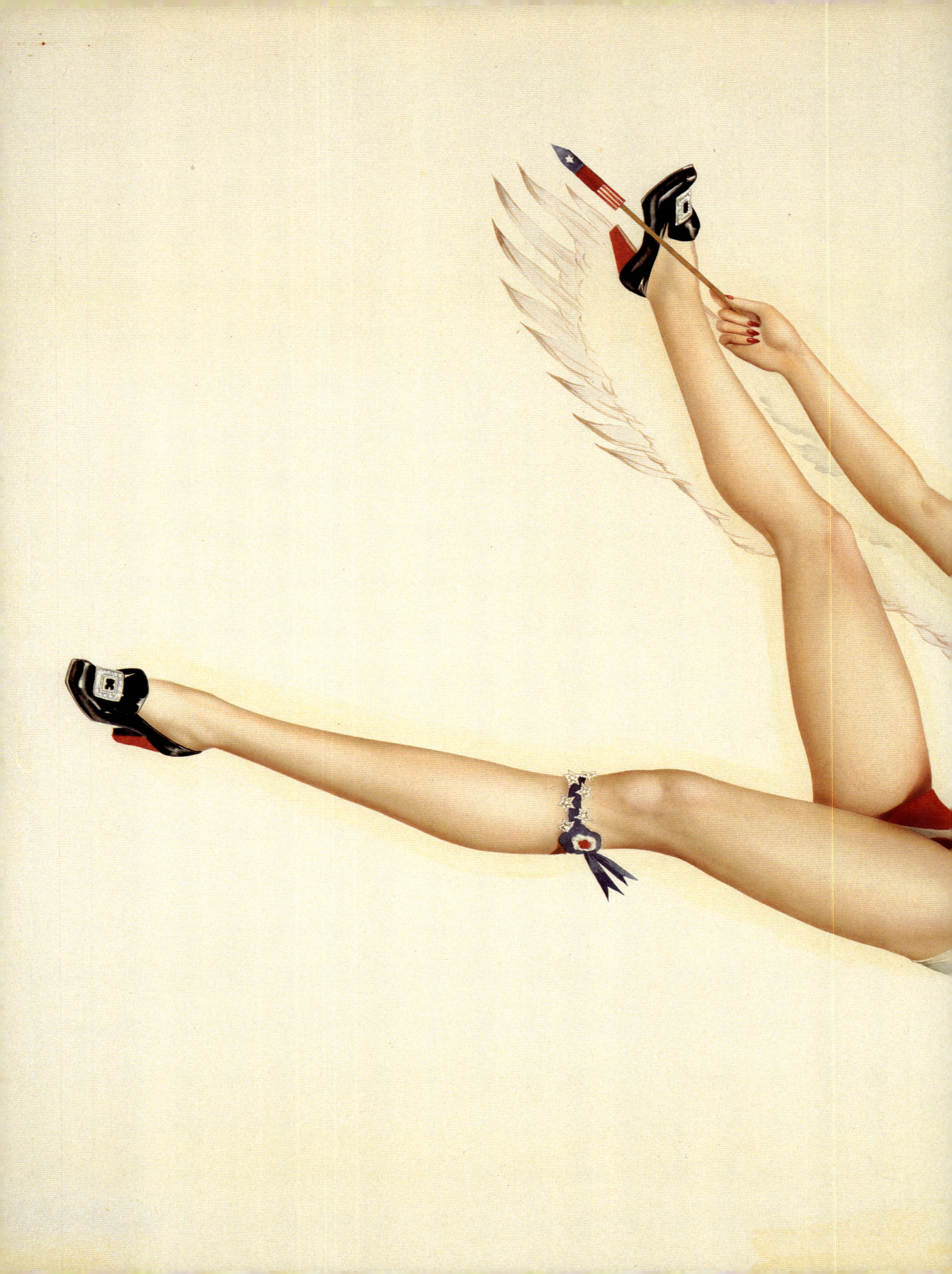

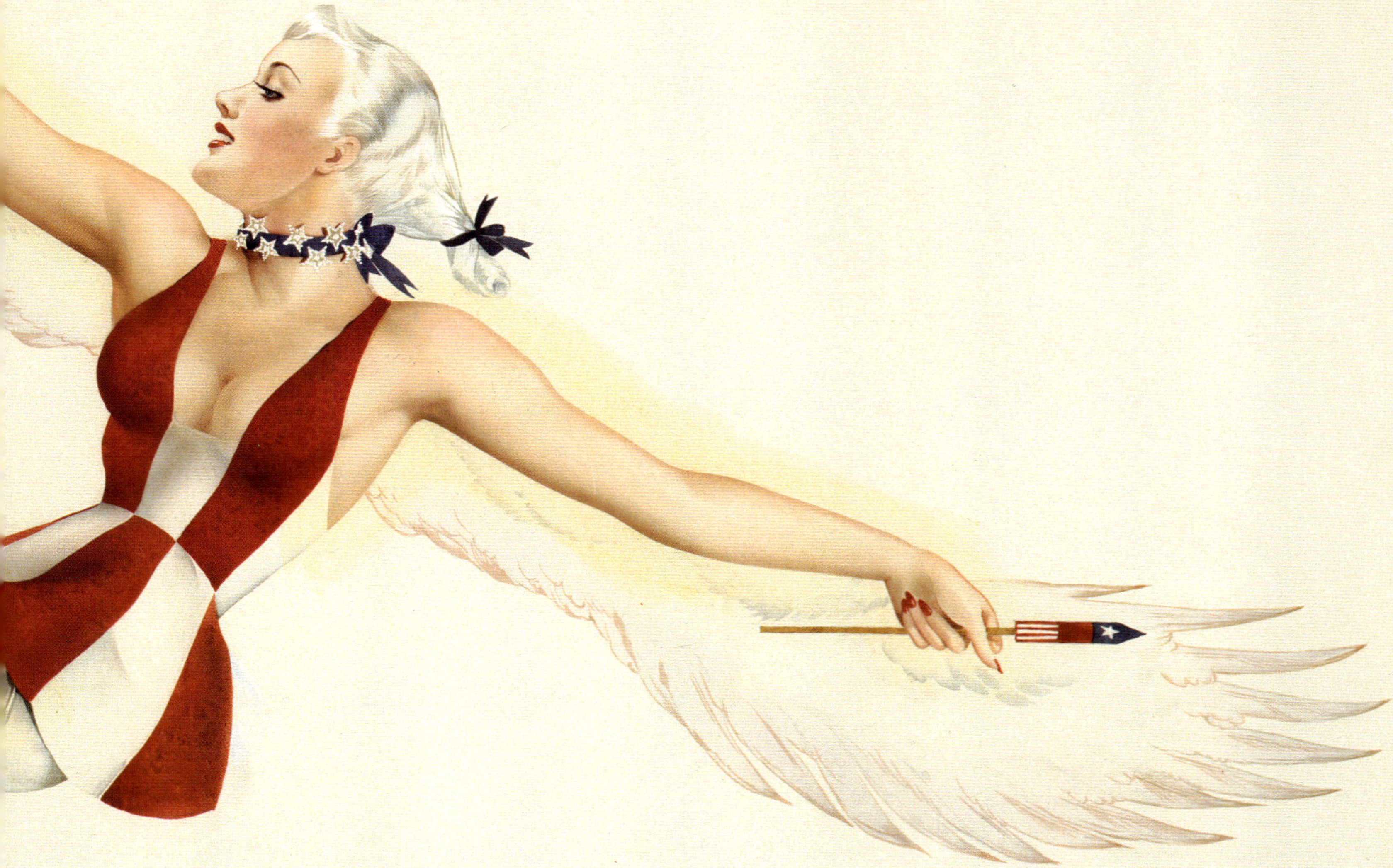

July 1941 Calendar

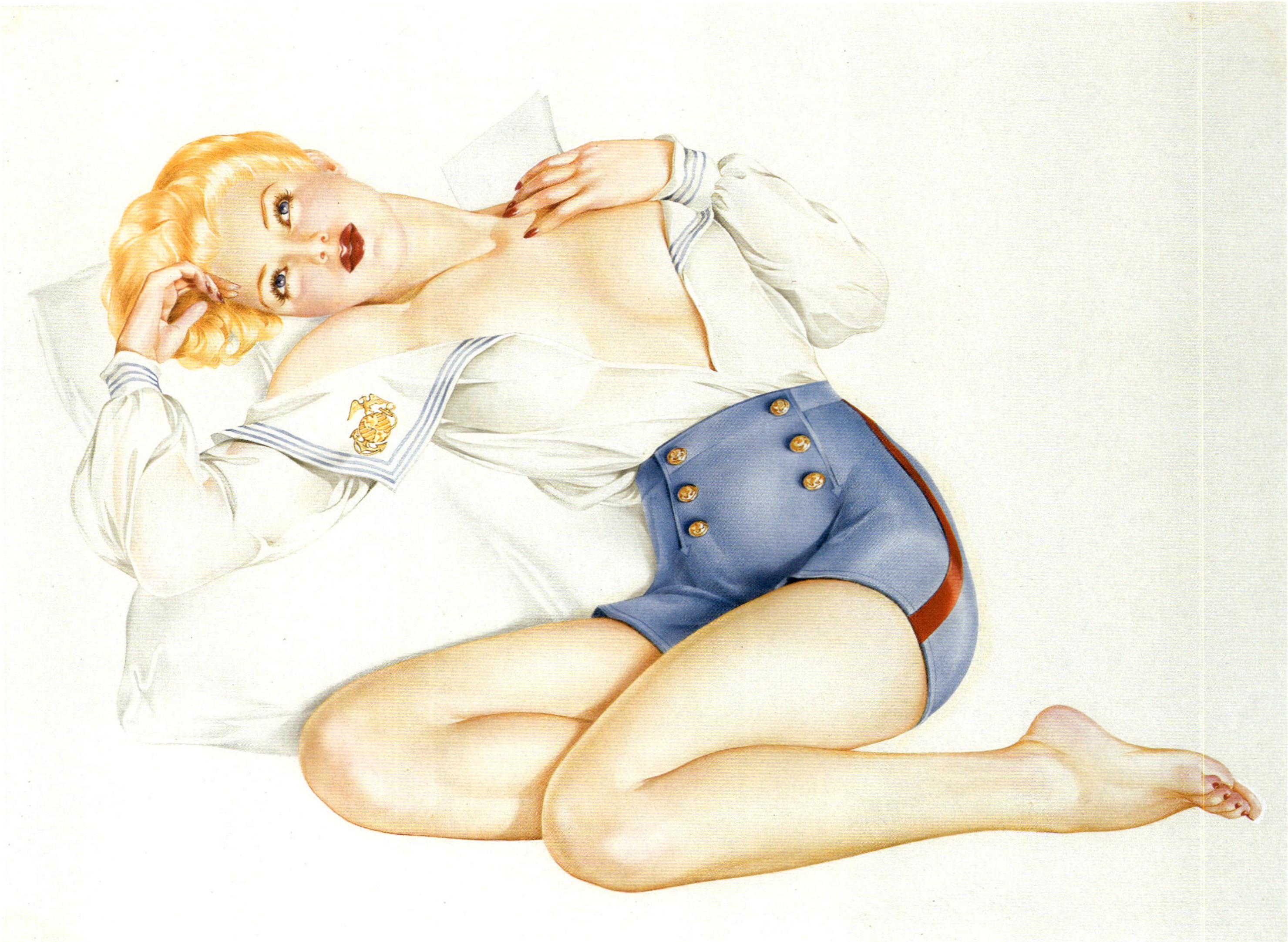

Above: March 1942

Right: July 1942 Gatefold

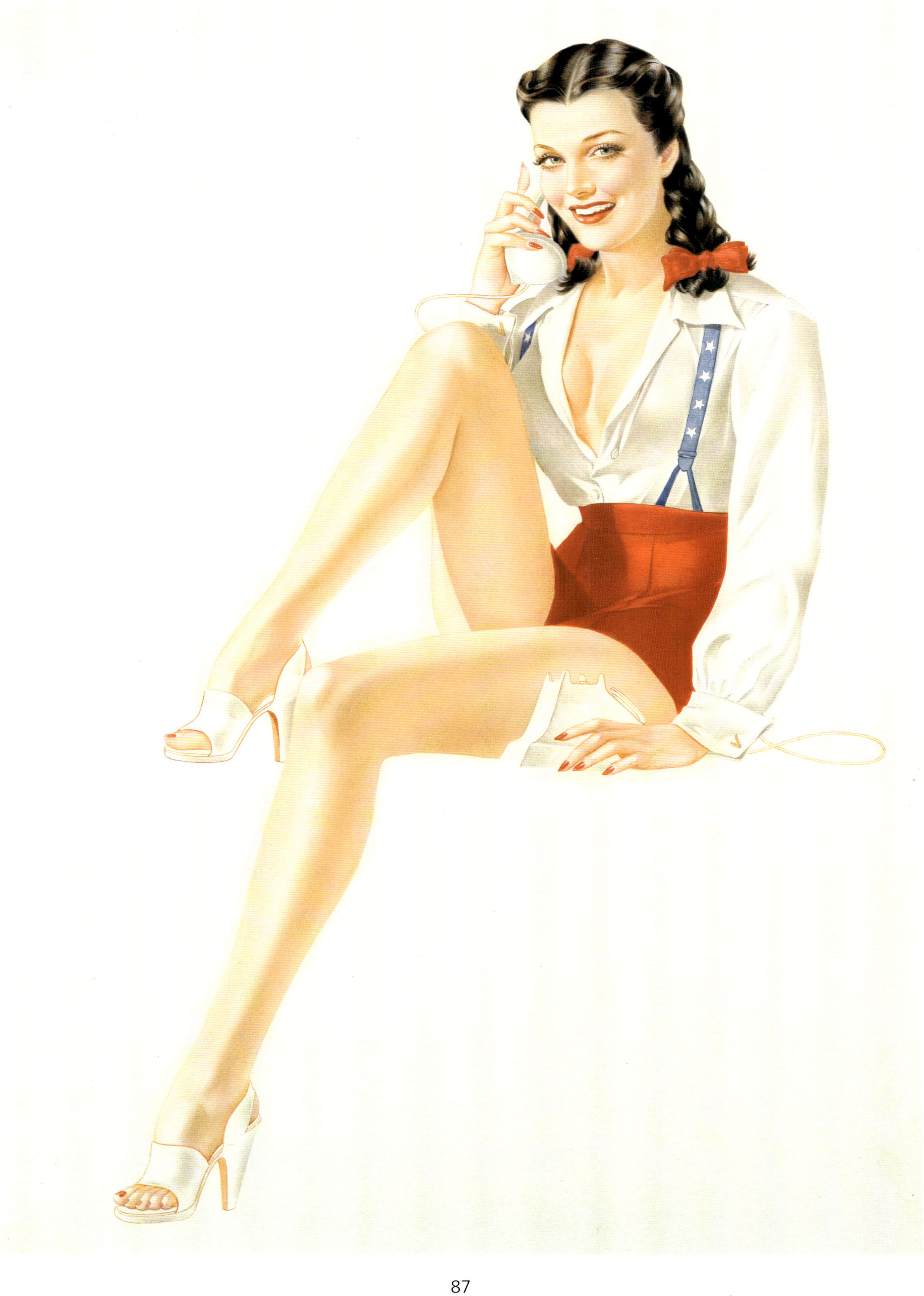

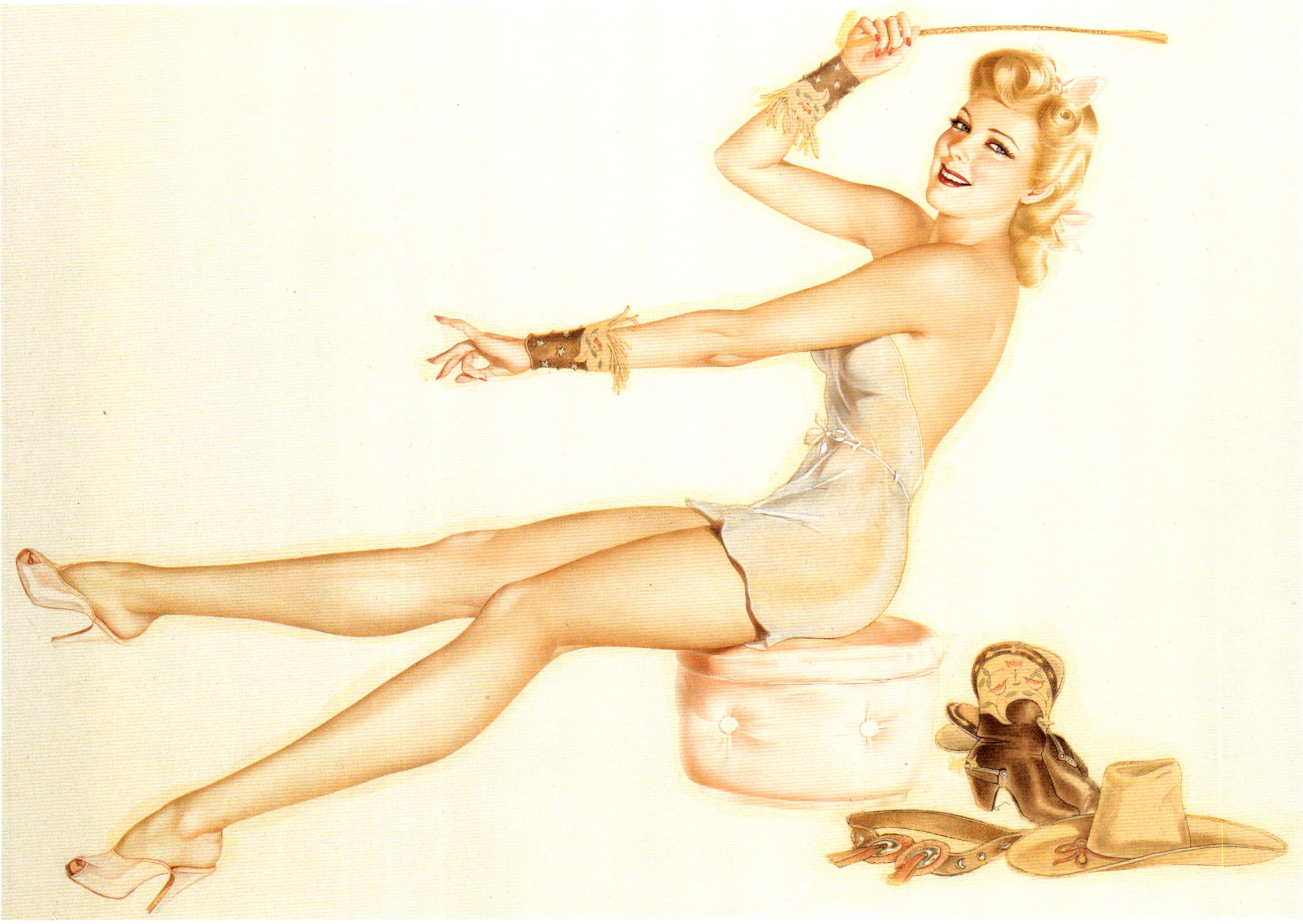

November 1942 Gatefold

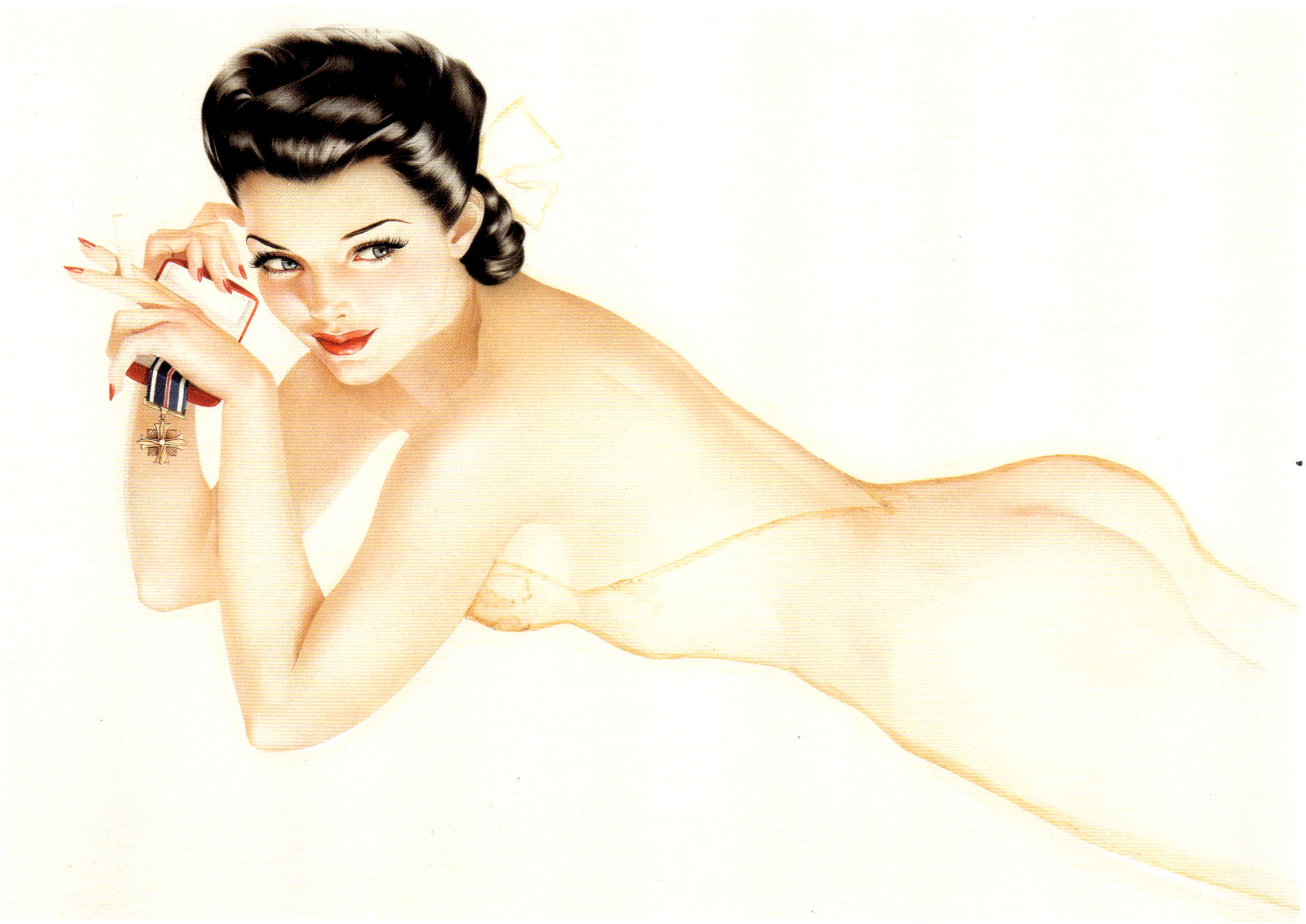

January 1943 Military Edition

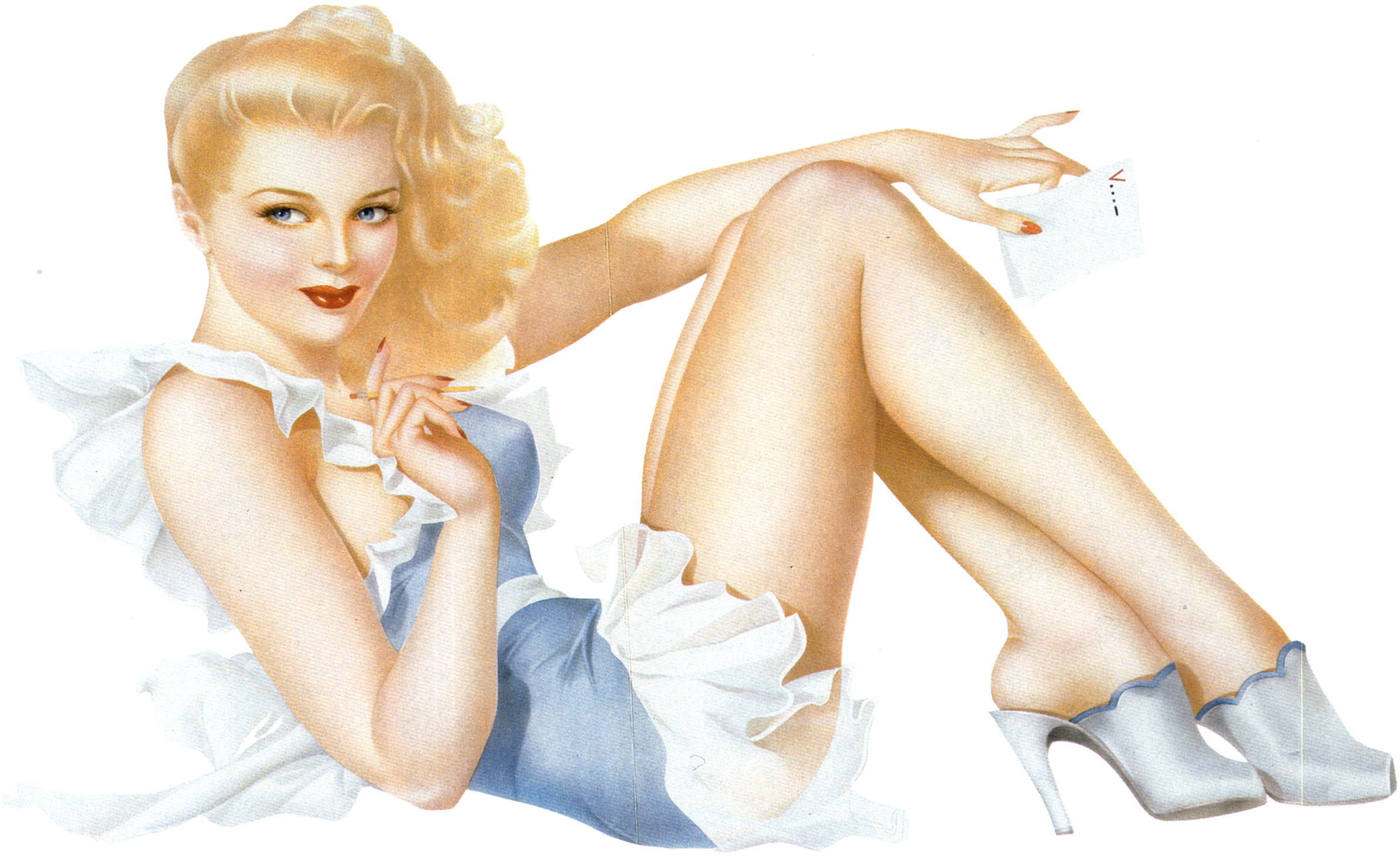

March 1943

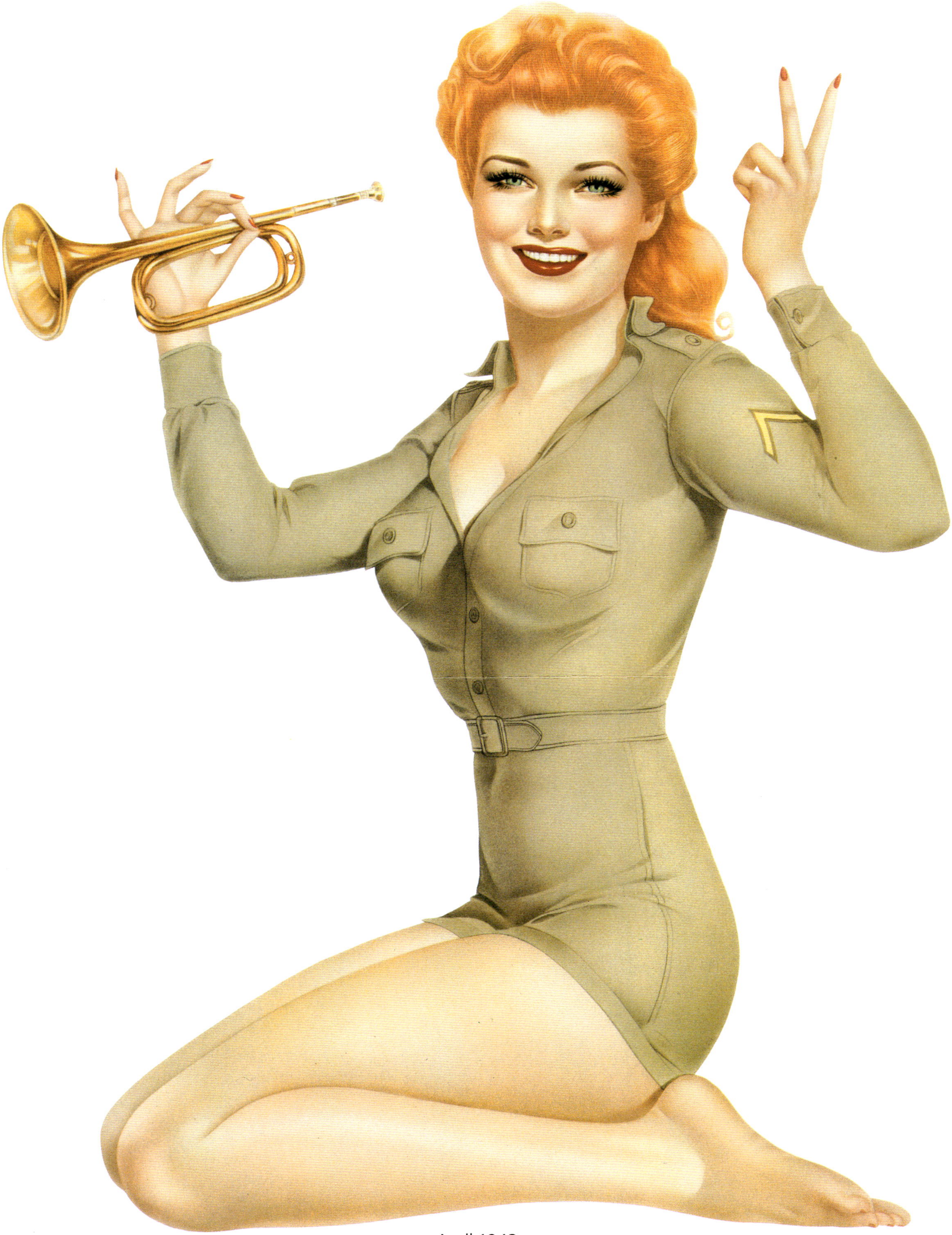

April 1943

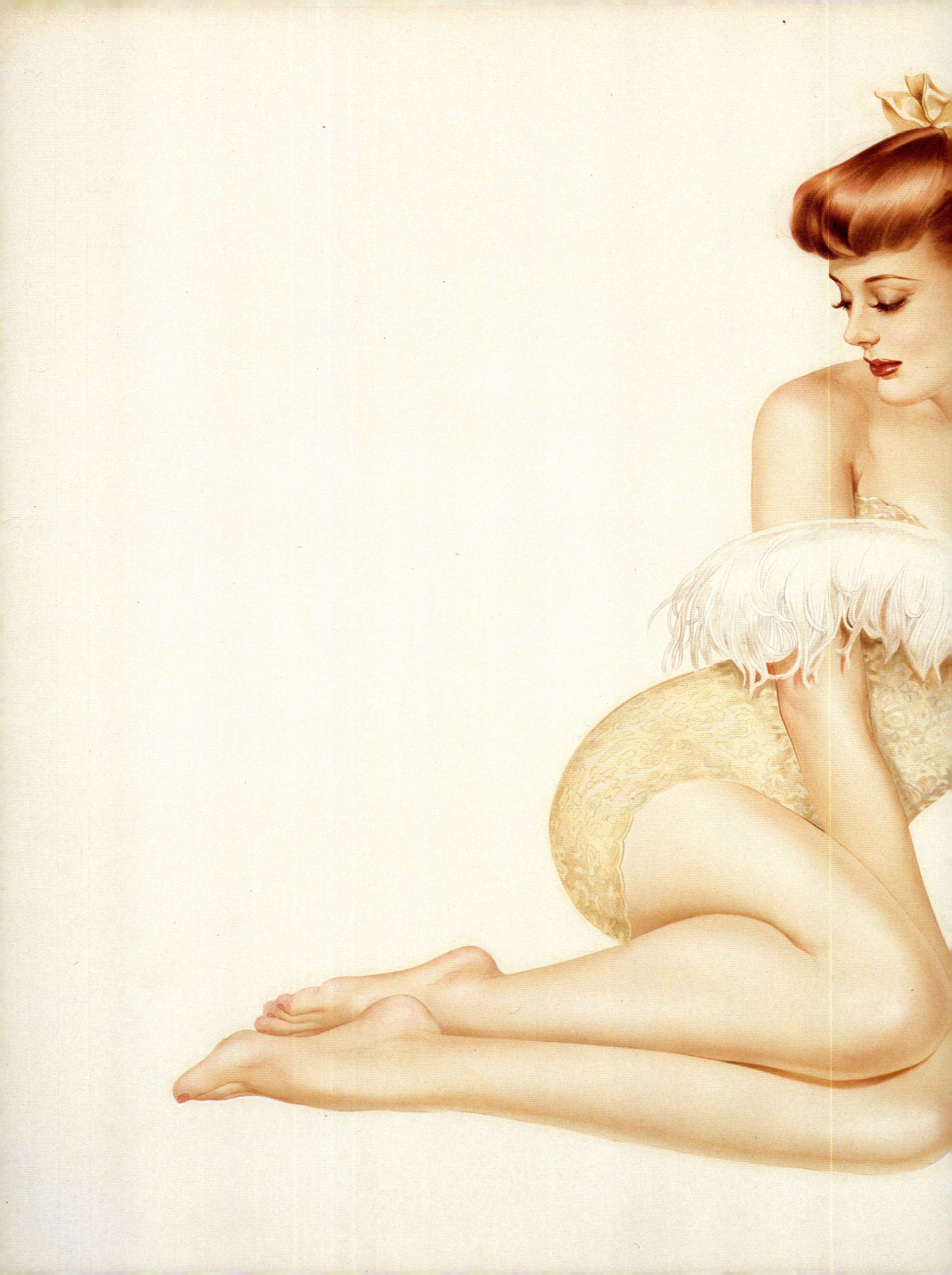

March 1943

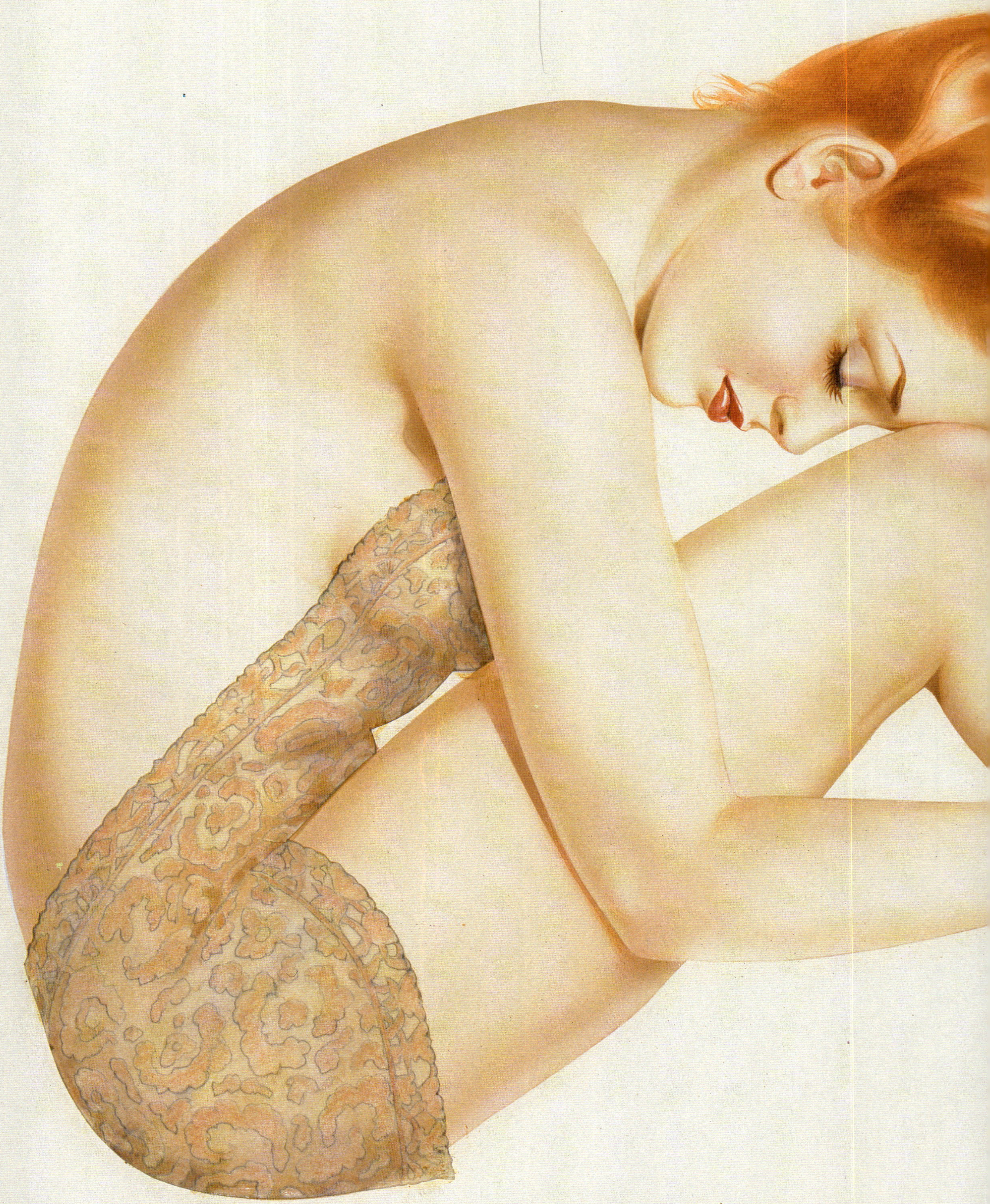

April 1943 Calendar

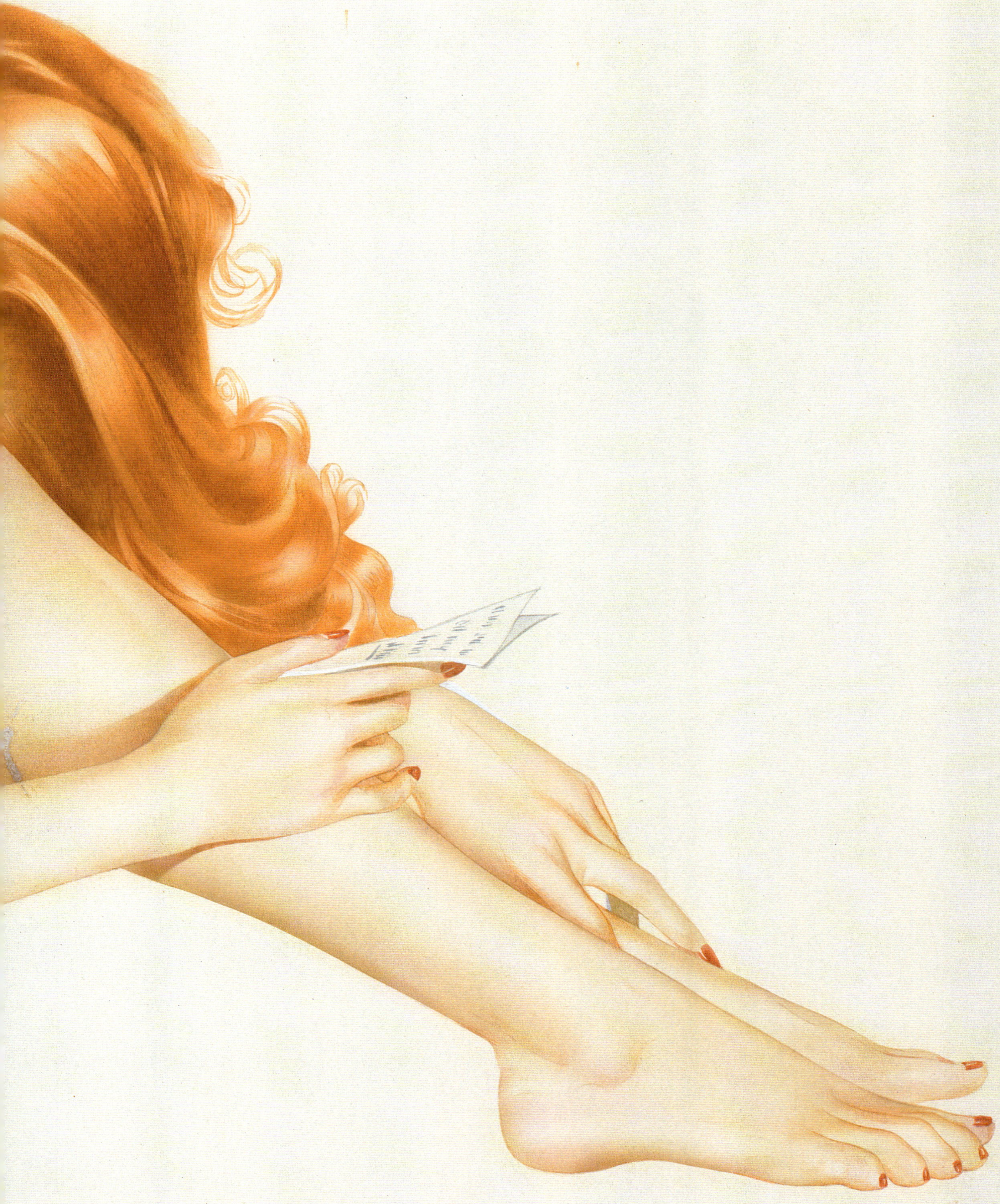

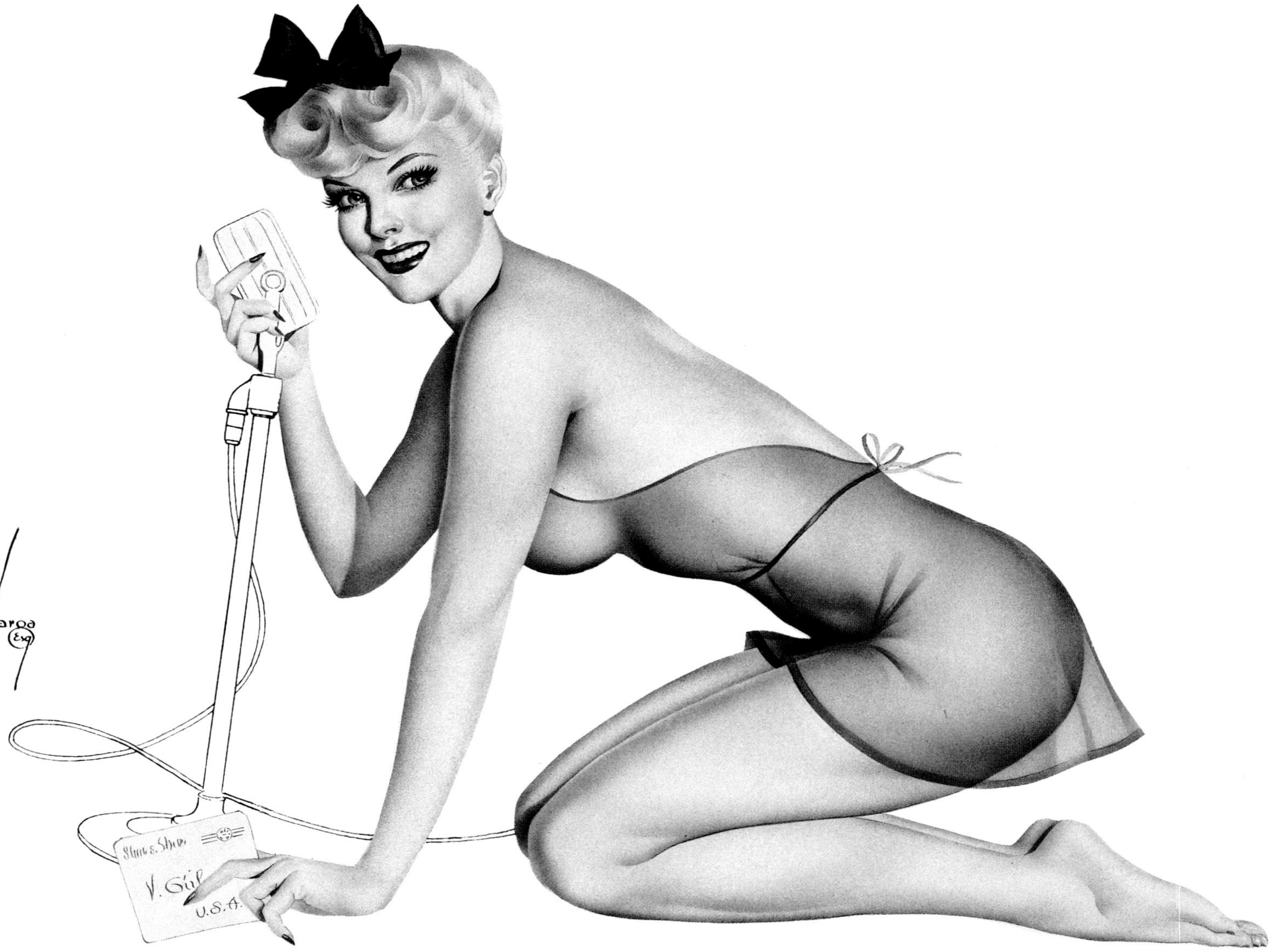

November 1943

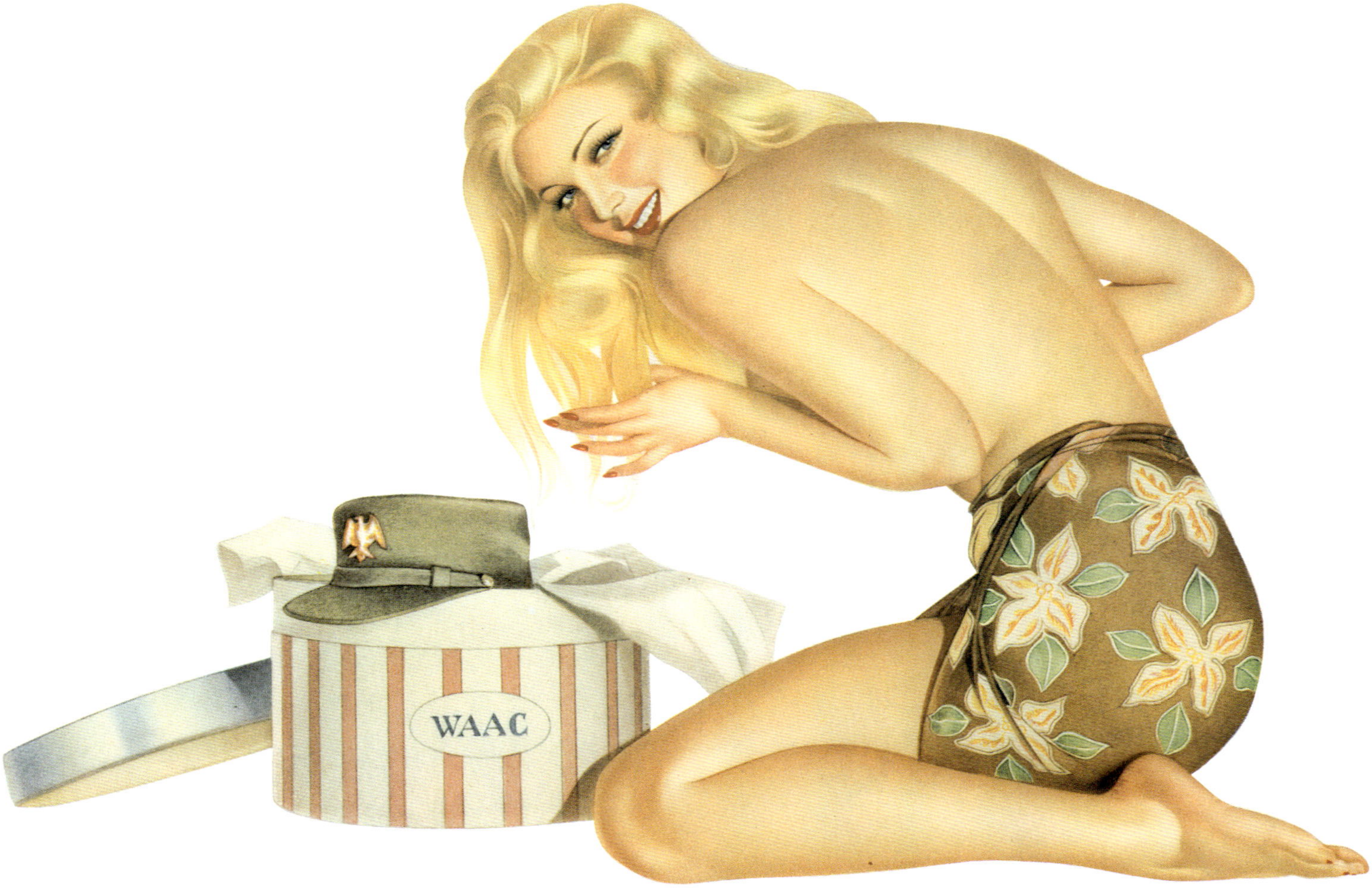

December 1943 Calendar

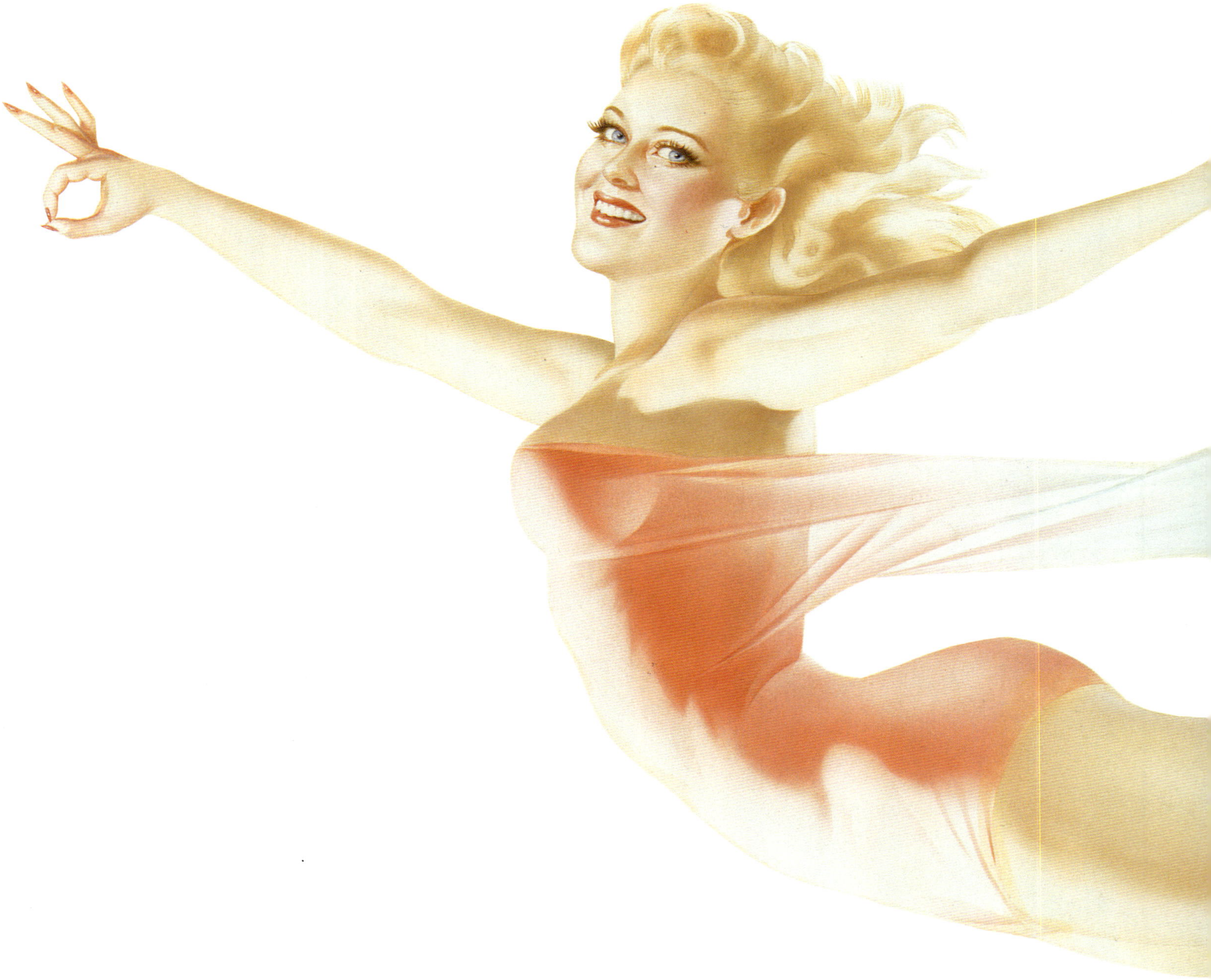

December 1943

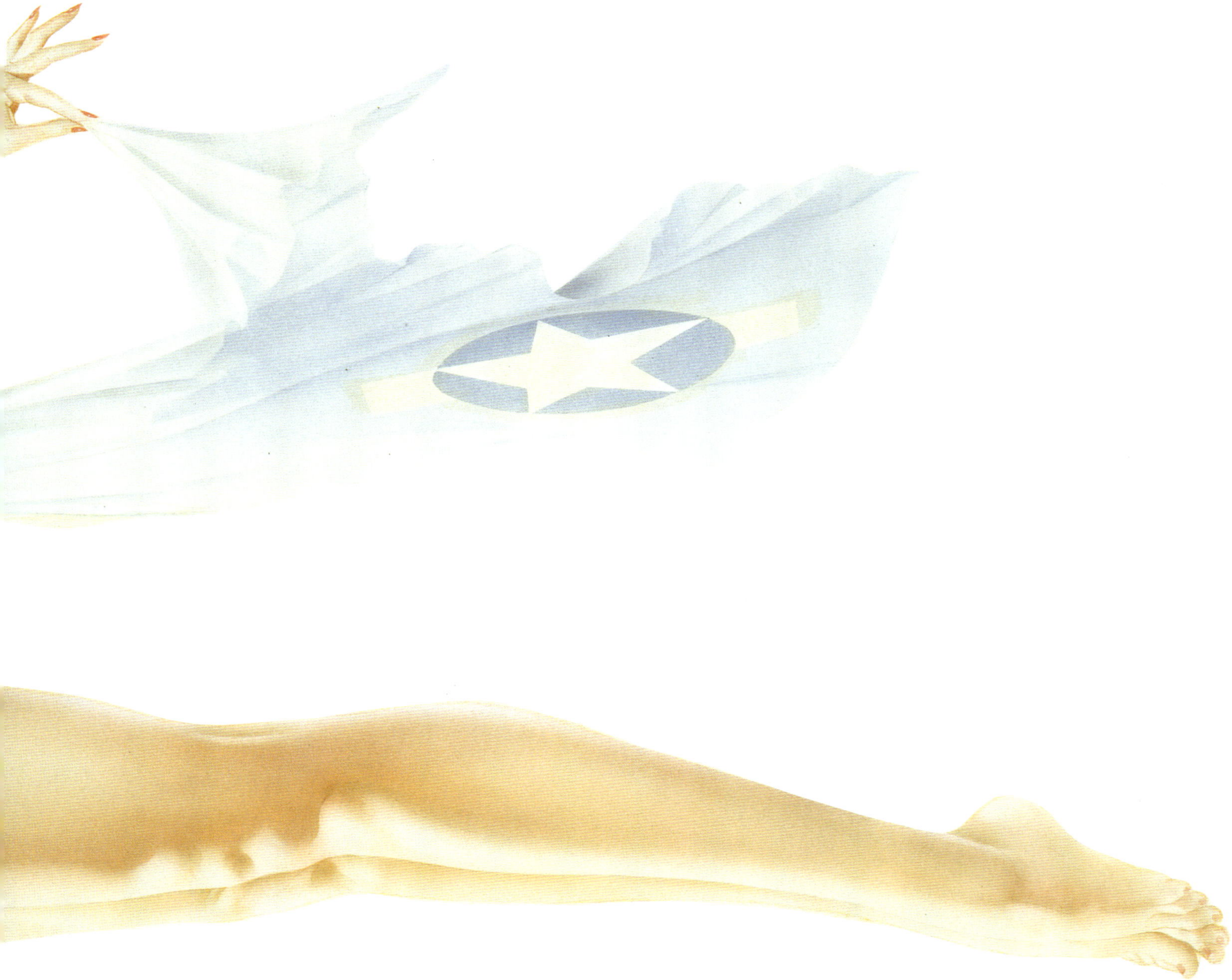

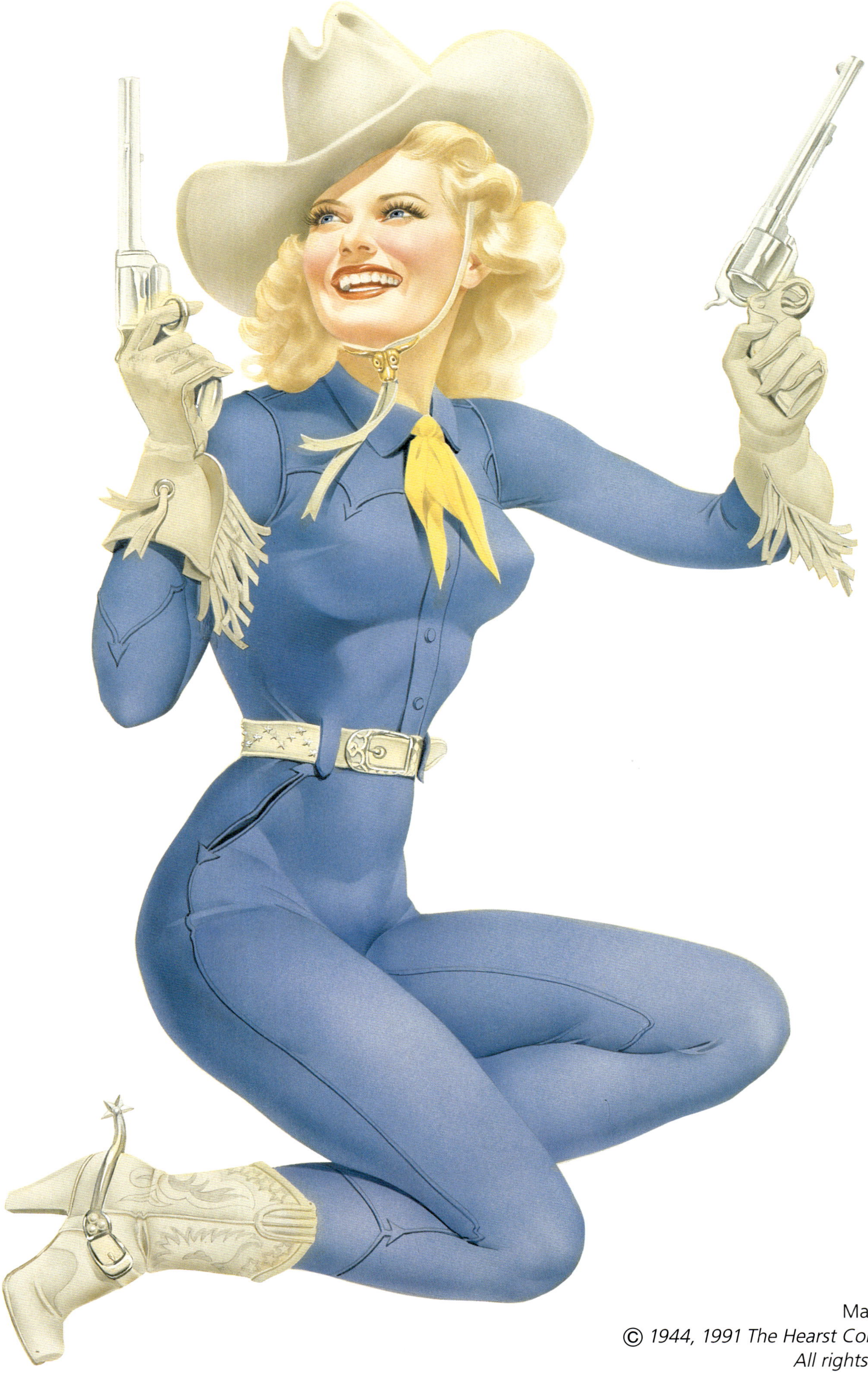

March 1944

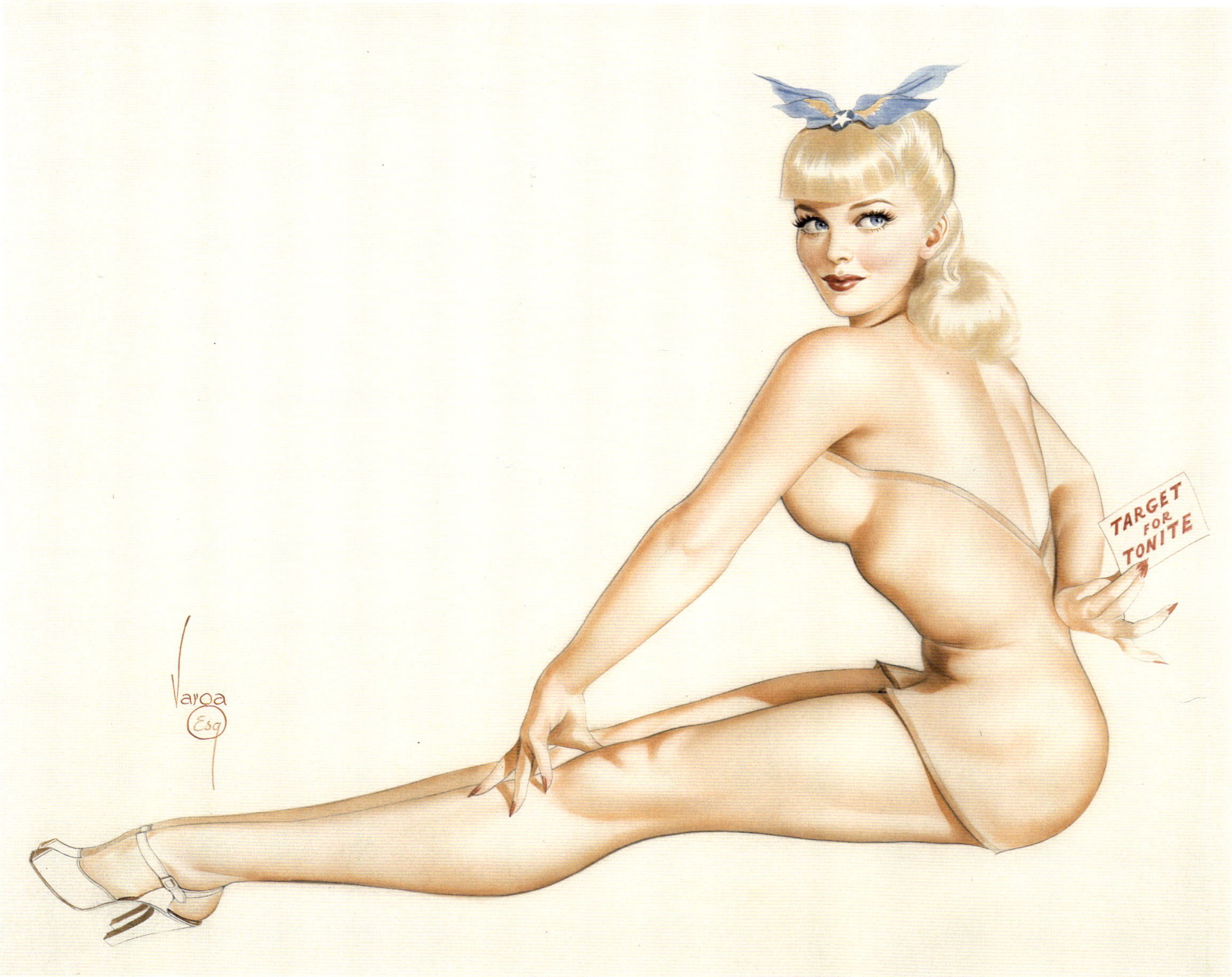

March 1944 Military Edition

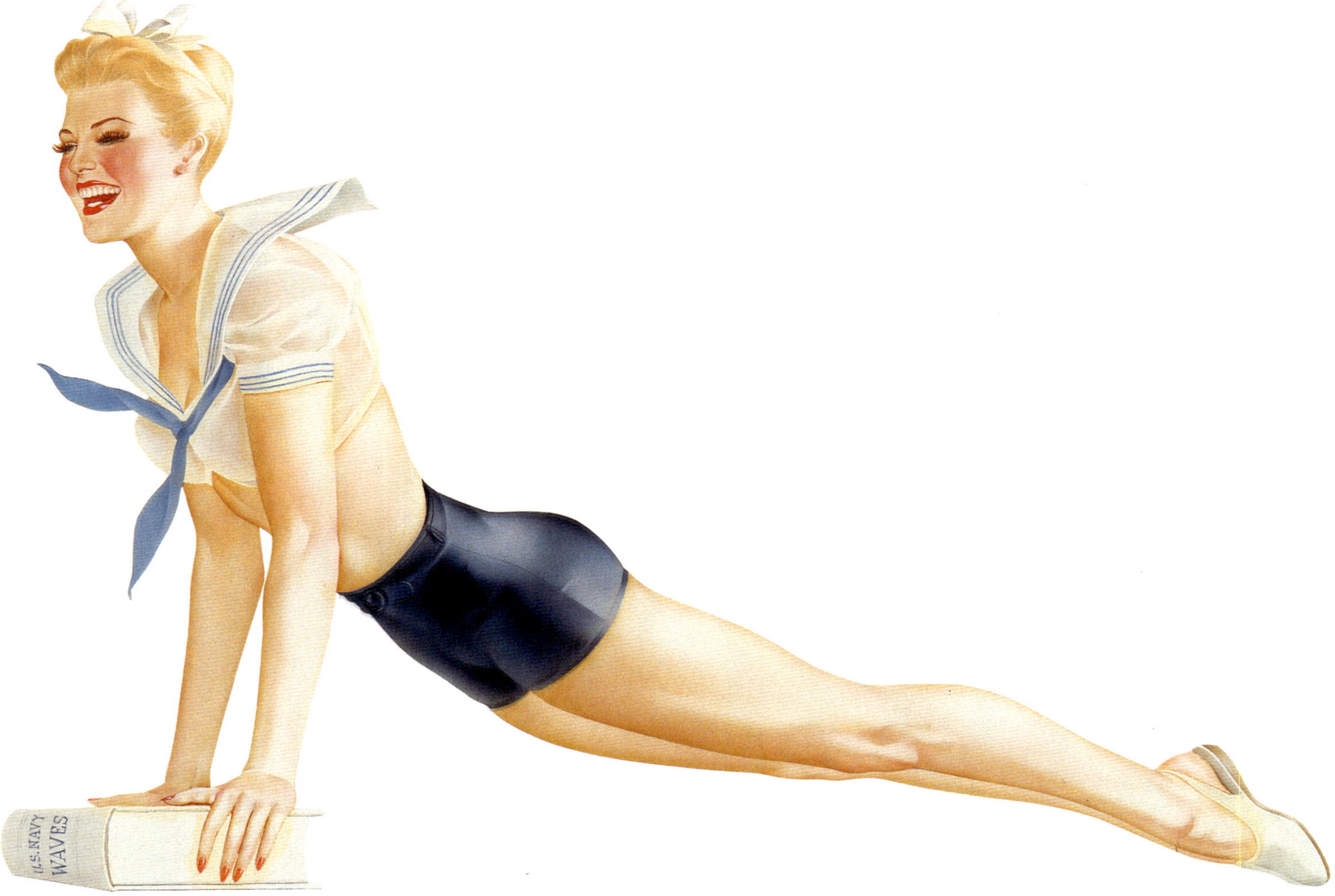

April 1944

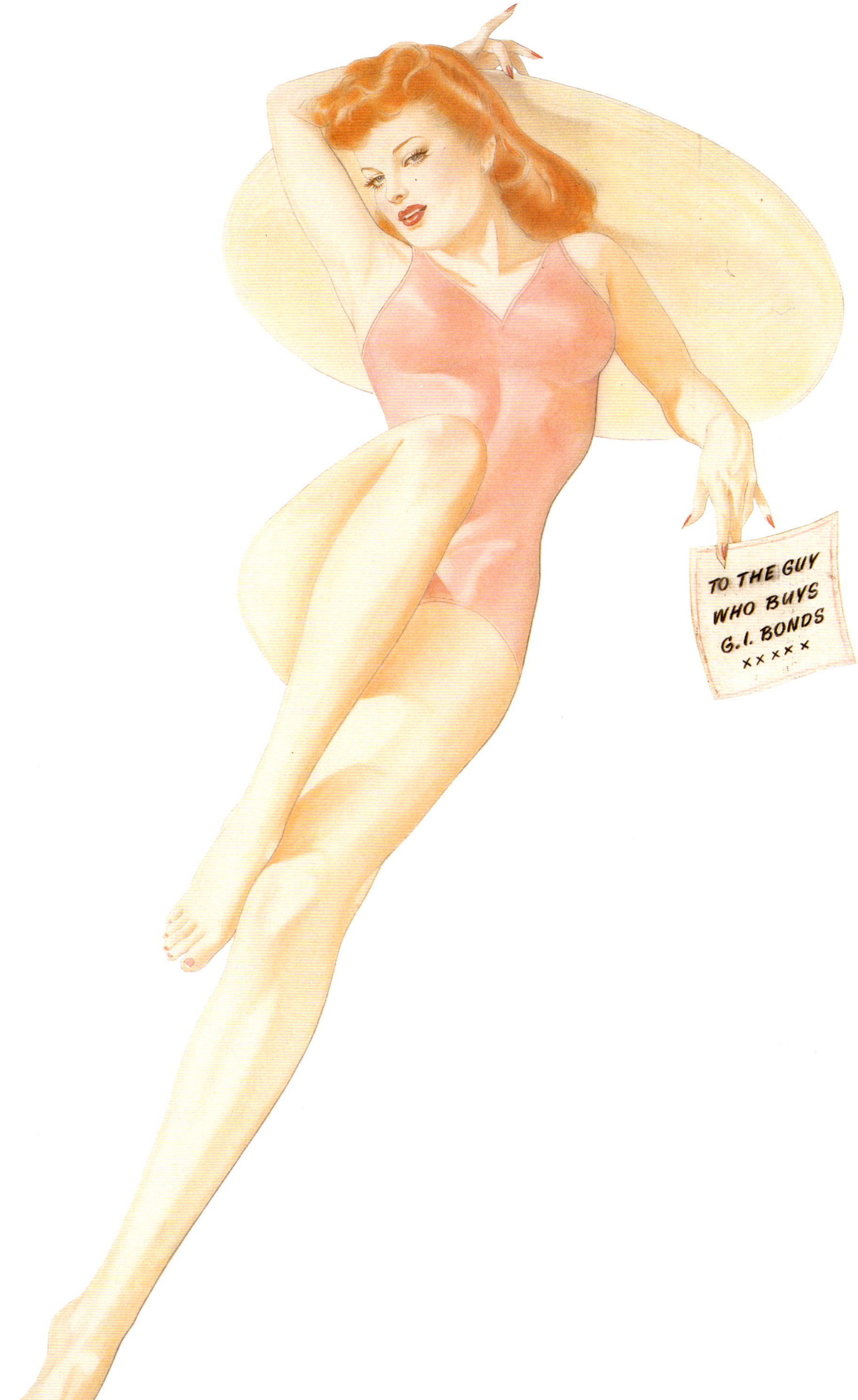

July 1944 Military Edition

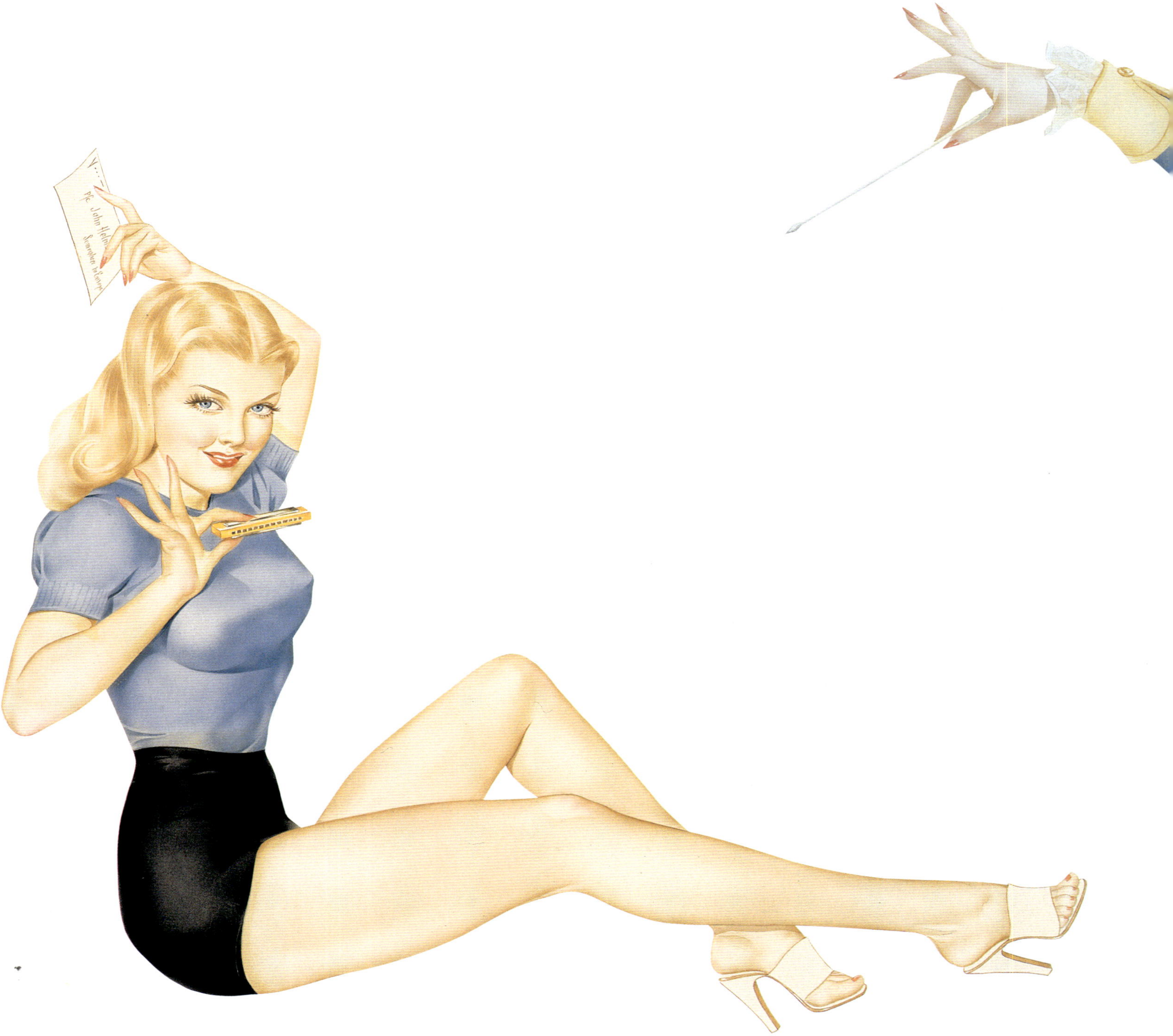

February 1945 Military Edition

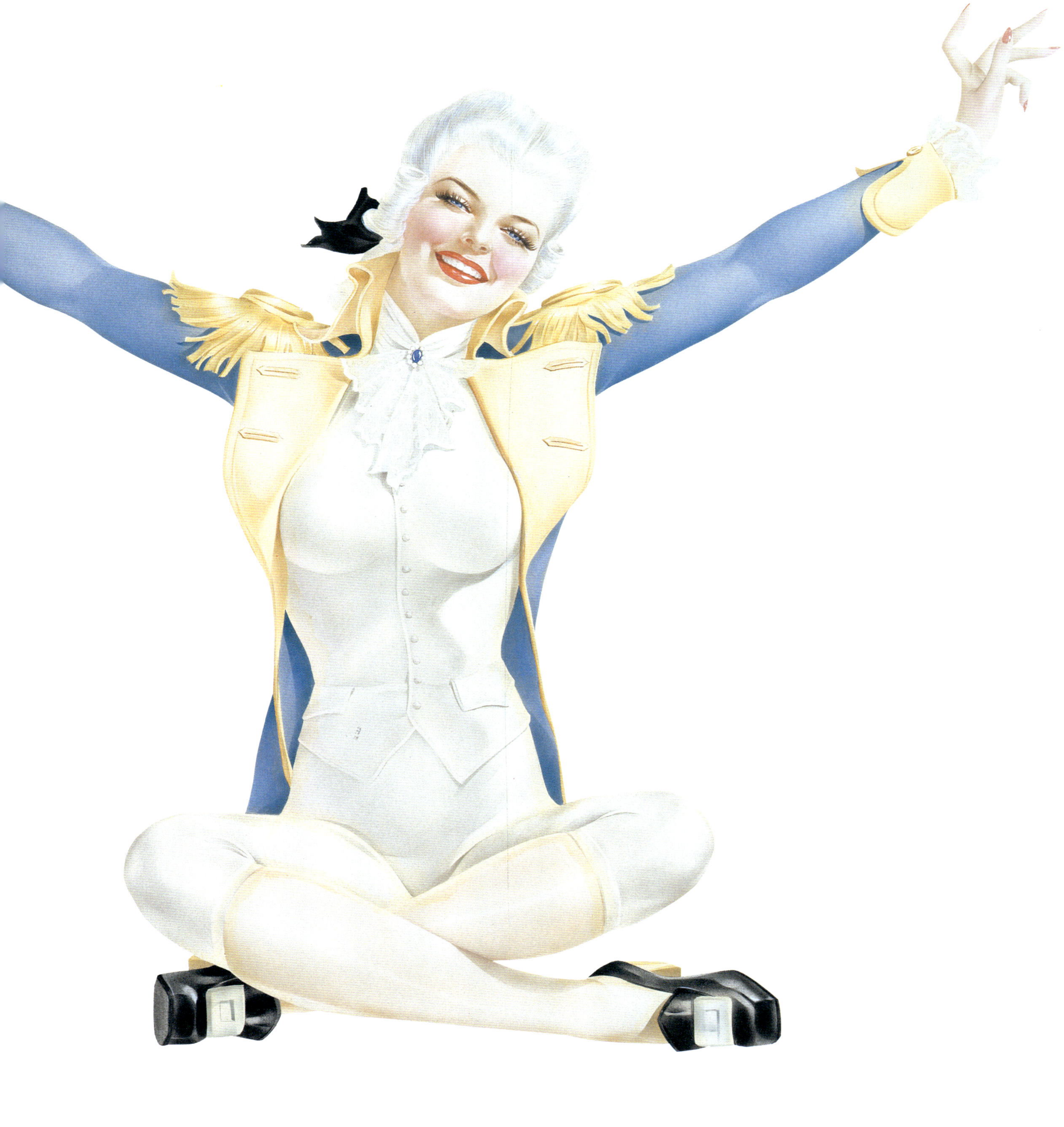

July 1944 Calendar

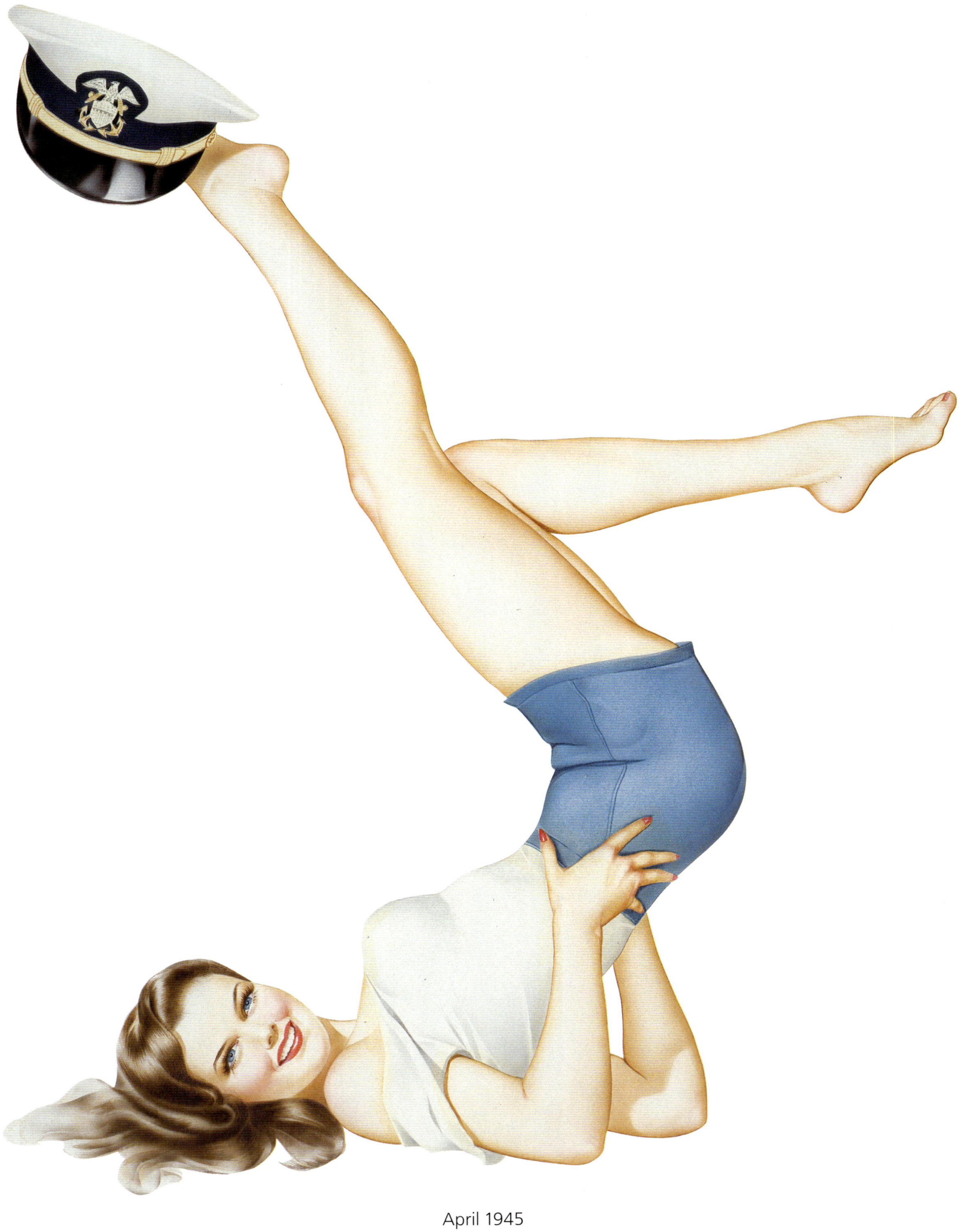

April 1945

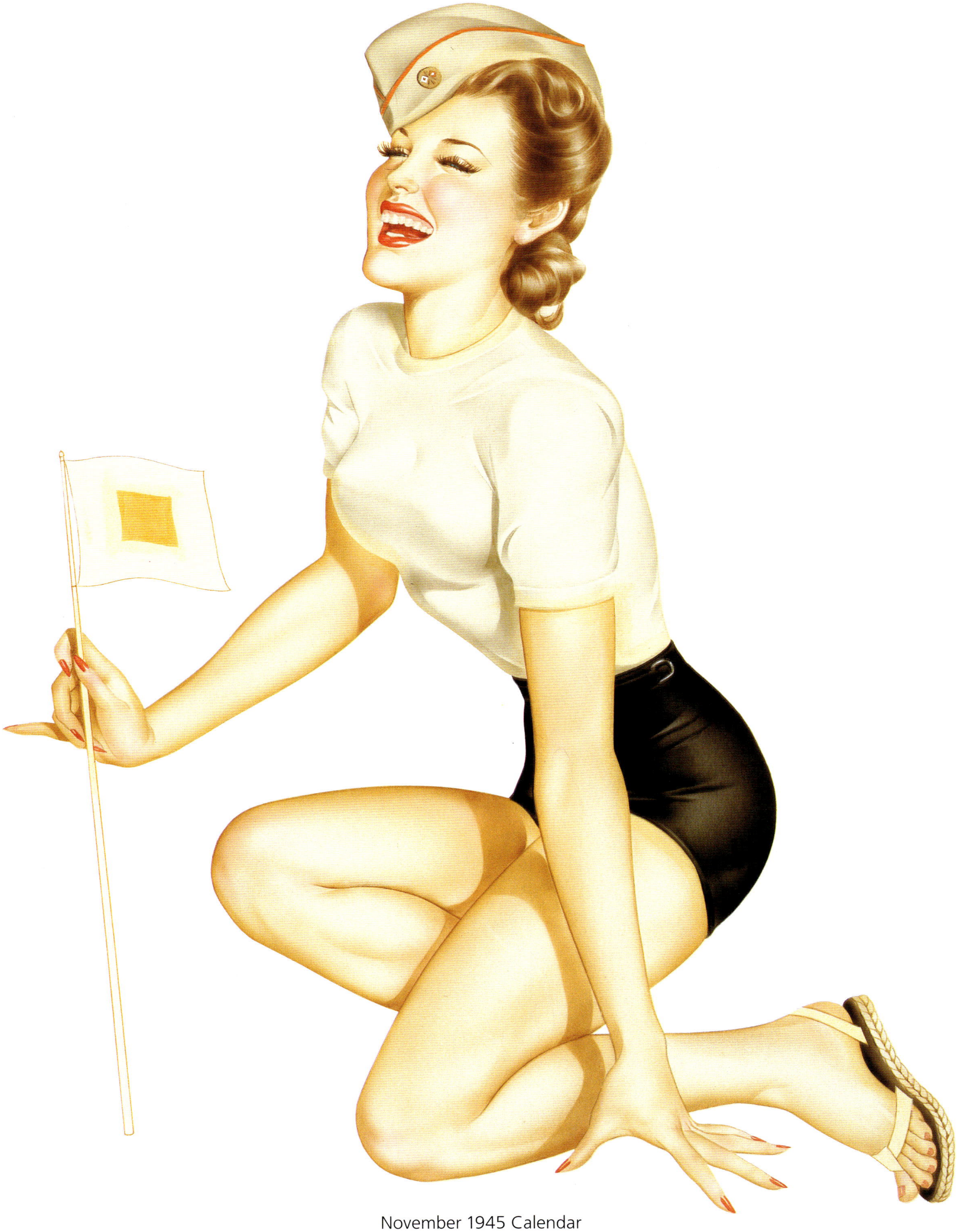

November 1945 Calendar

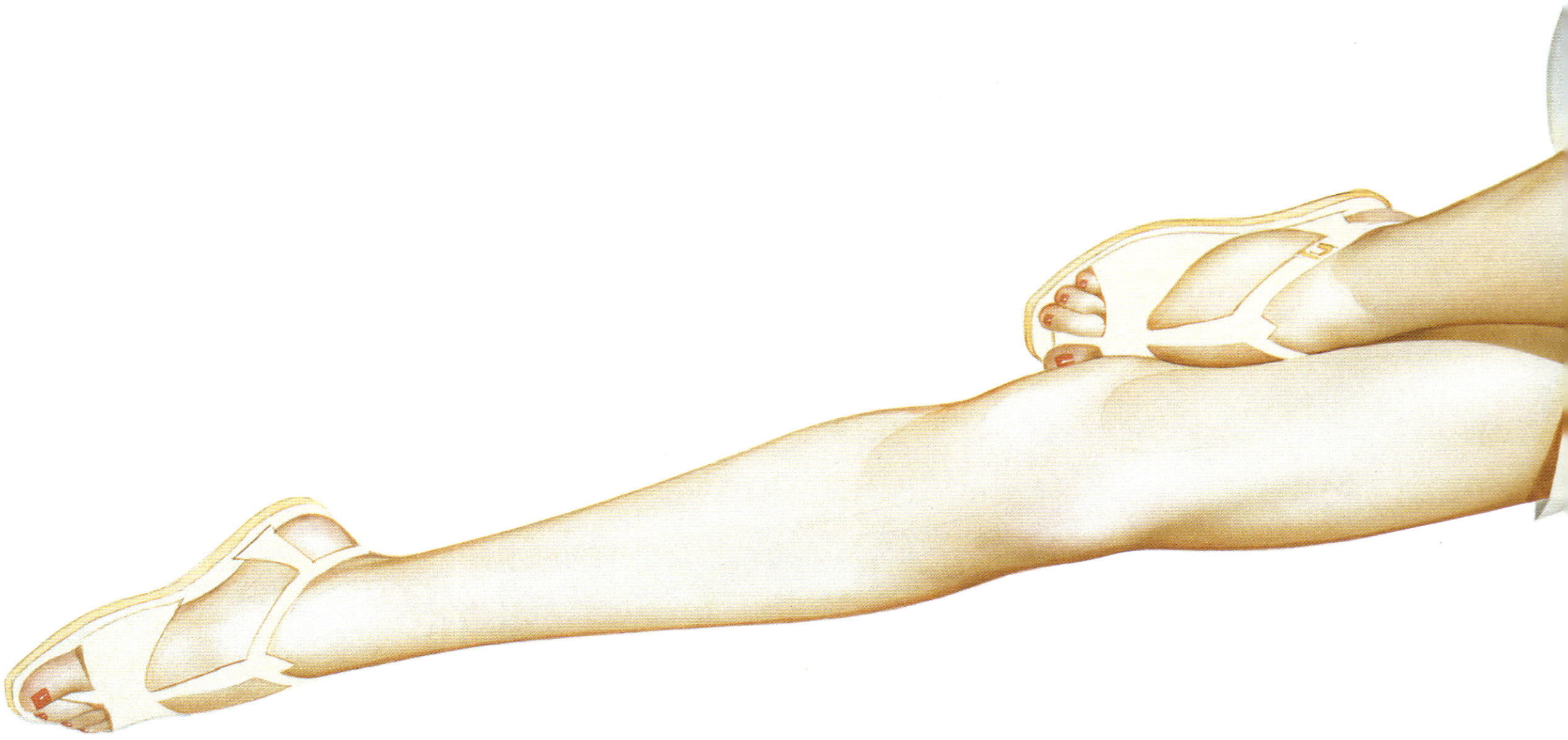

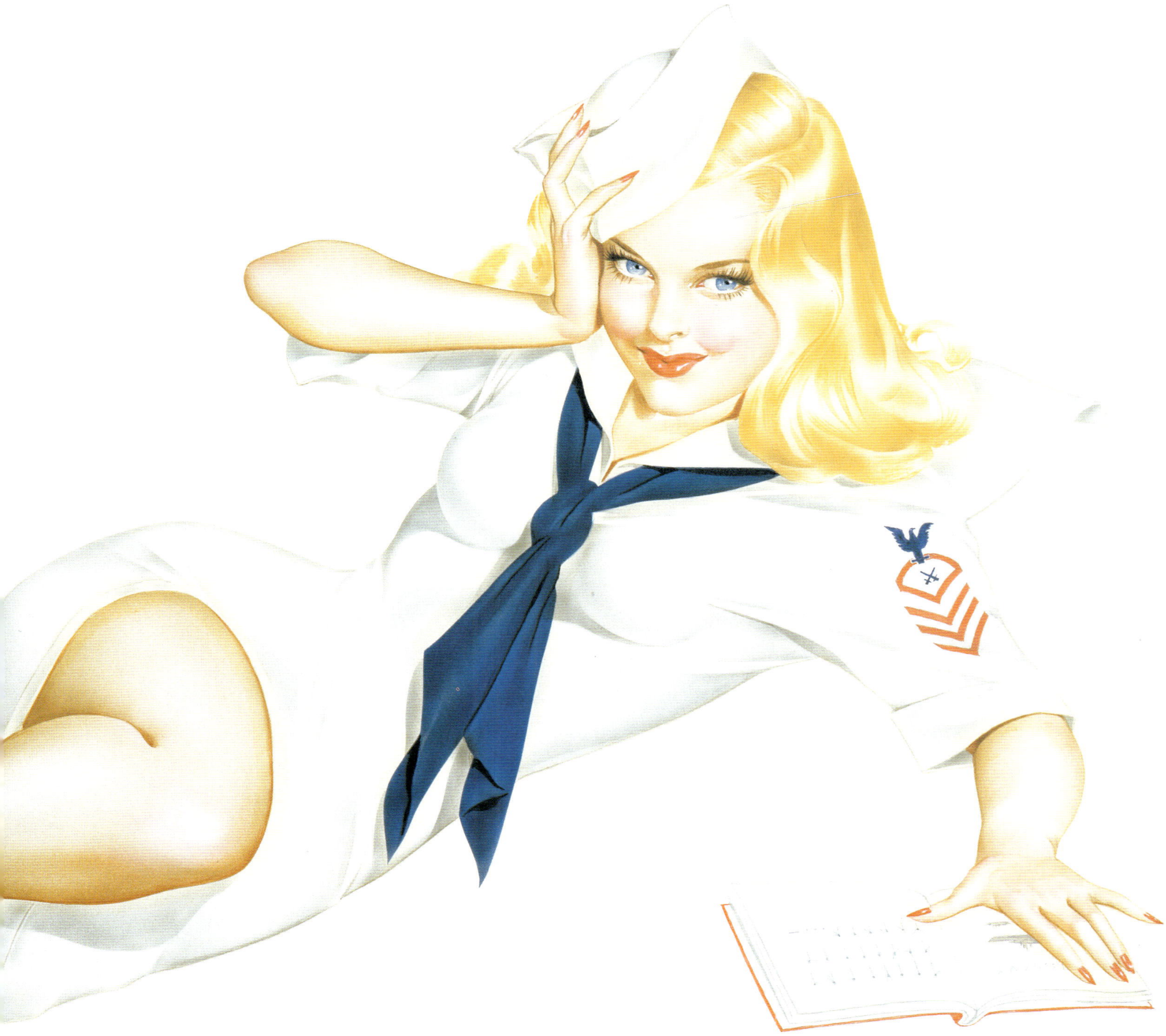

April 1945

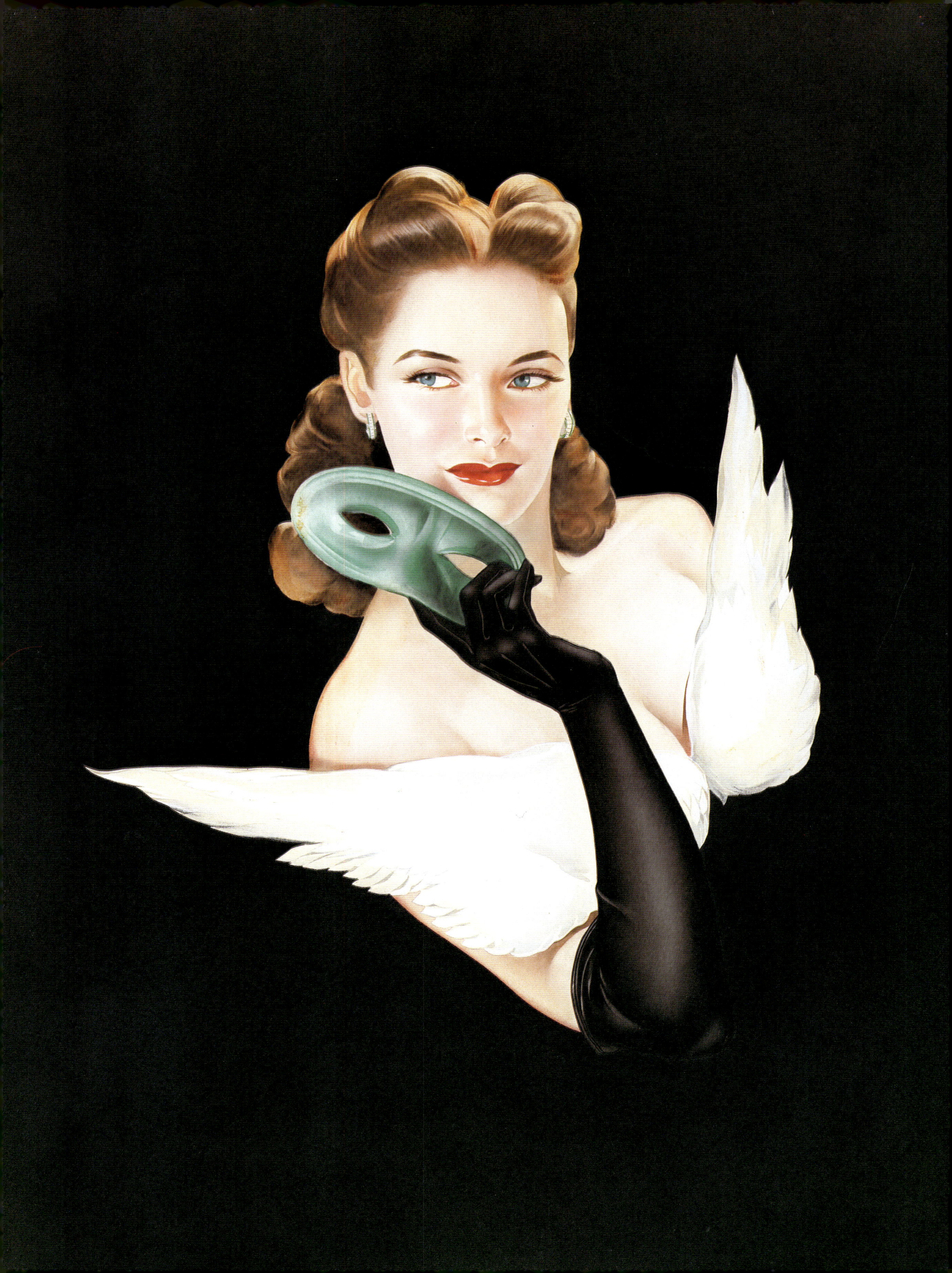

Faces

January 1941

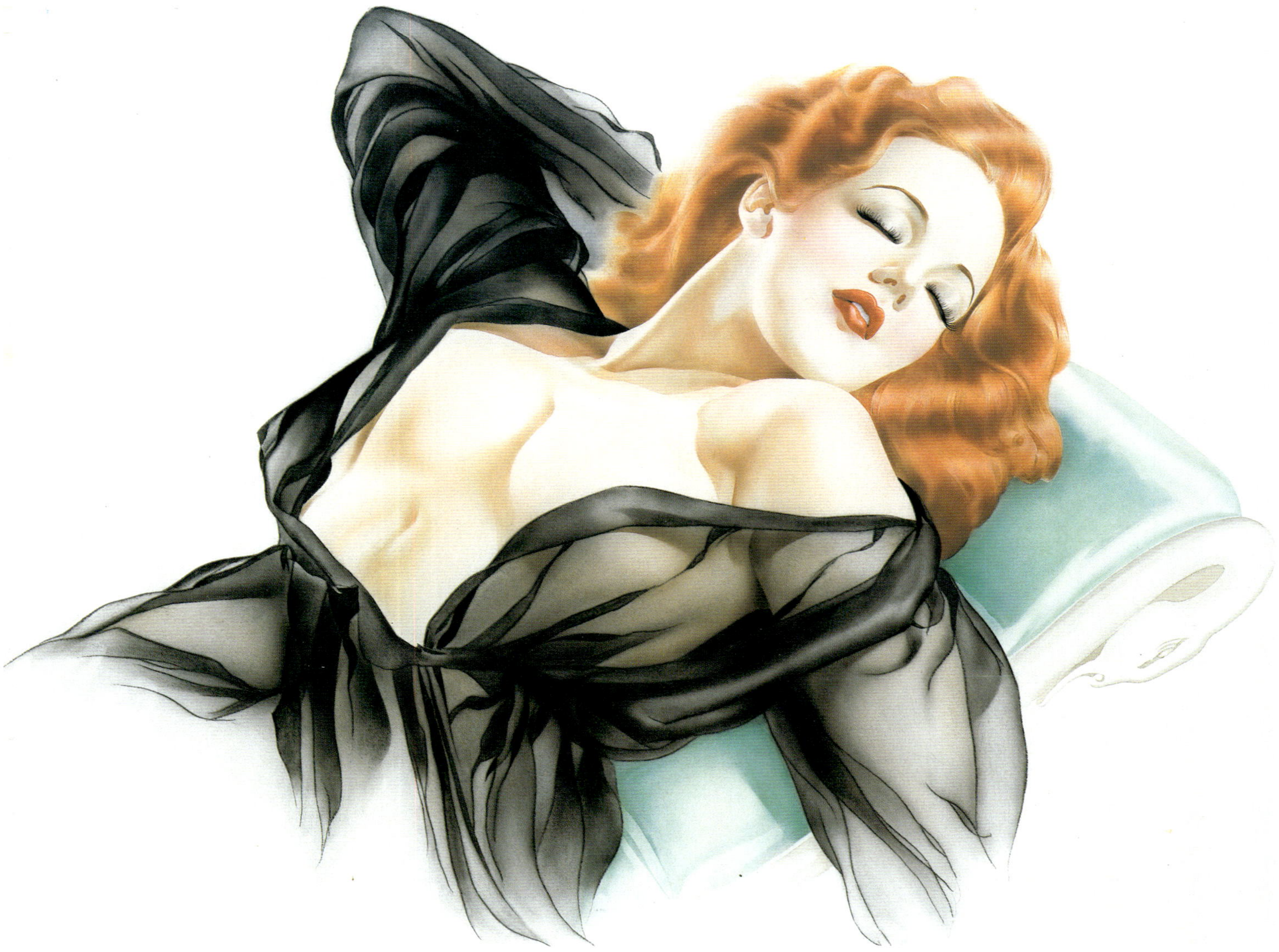

February 1941

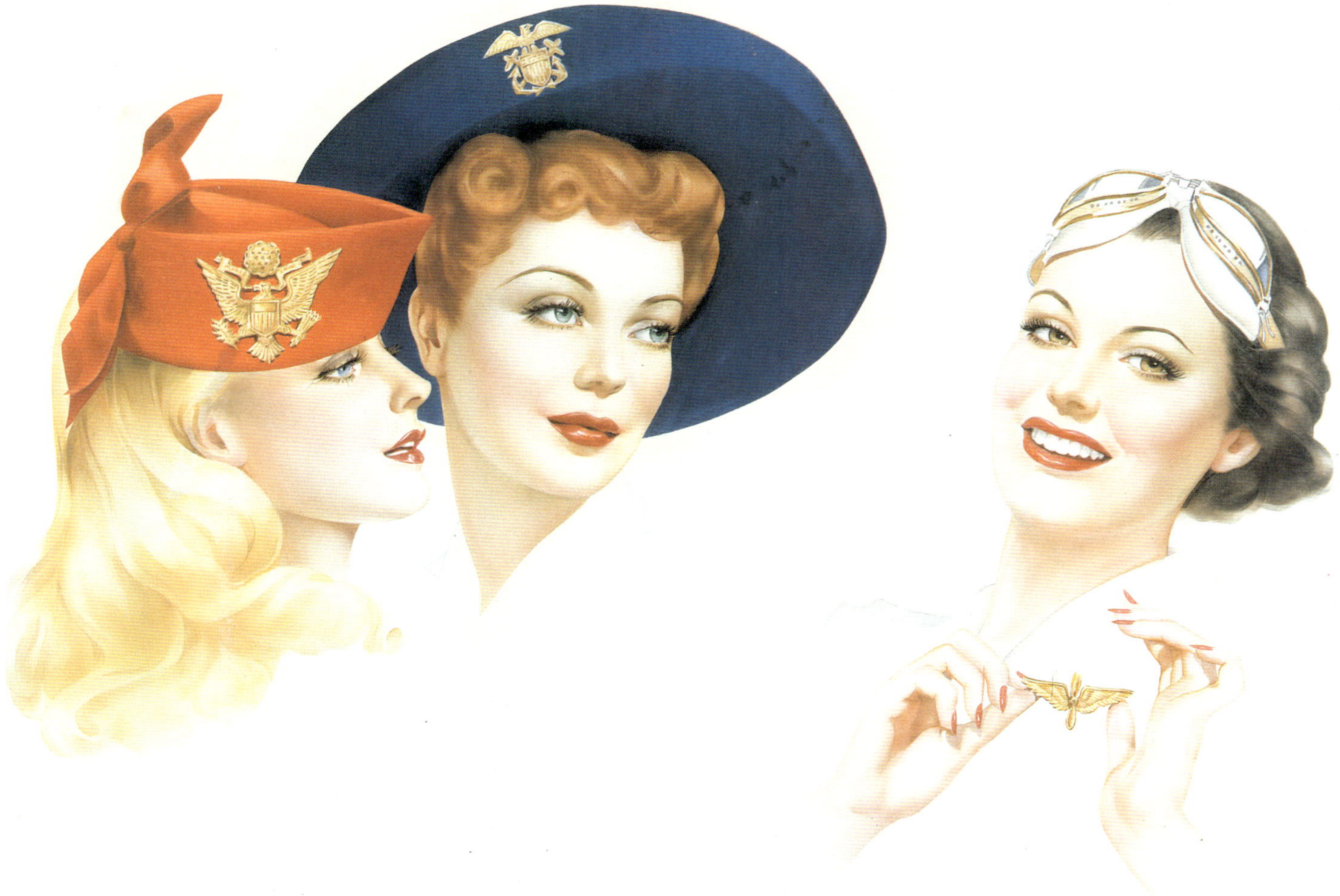

October 1941

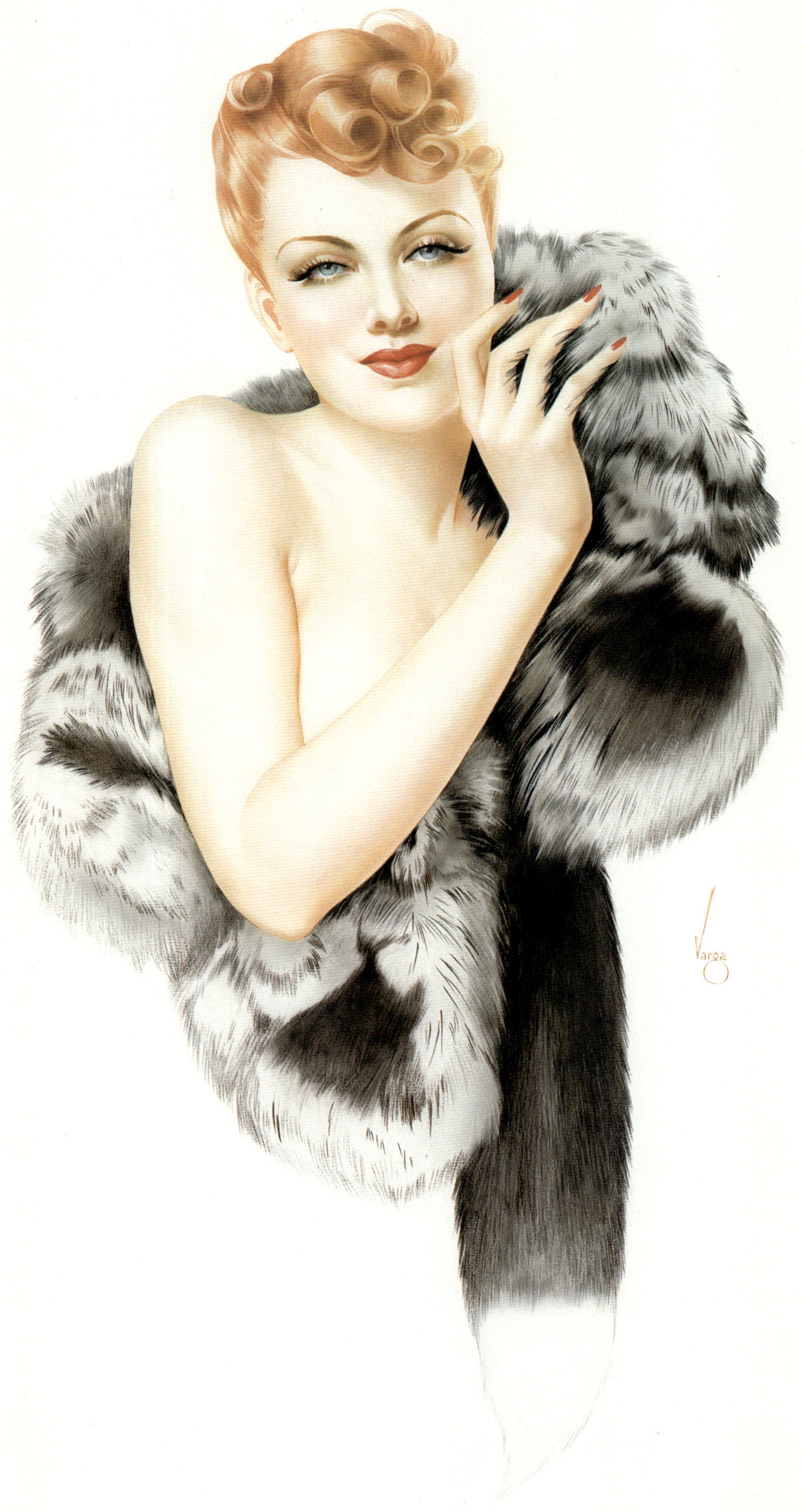
Varga

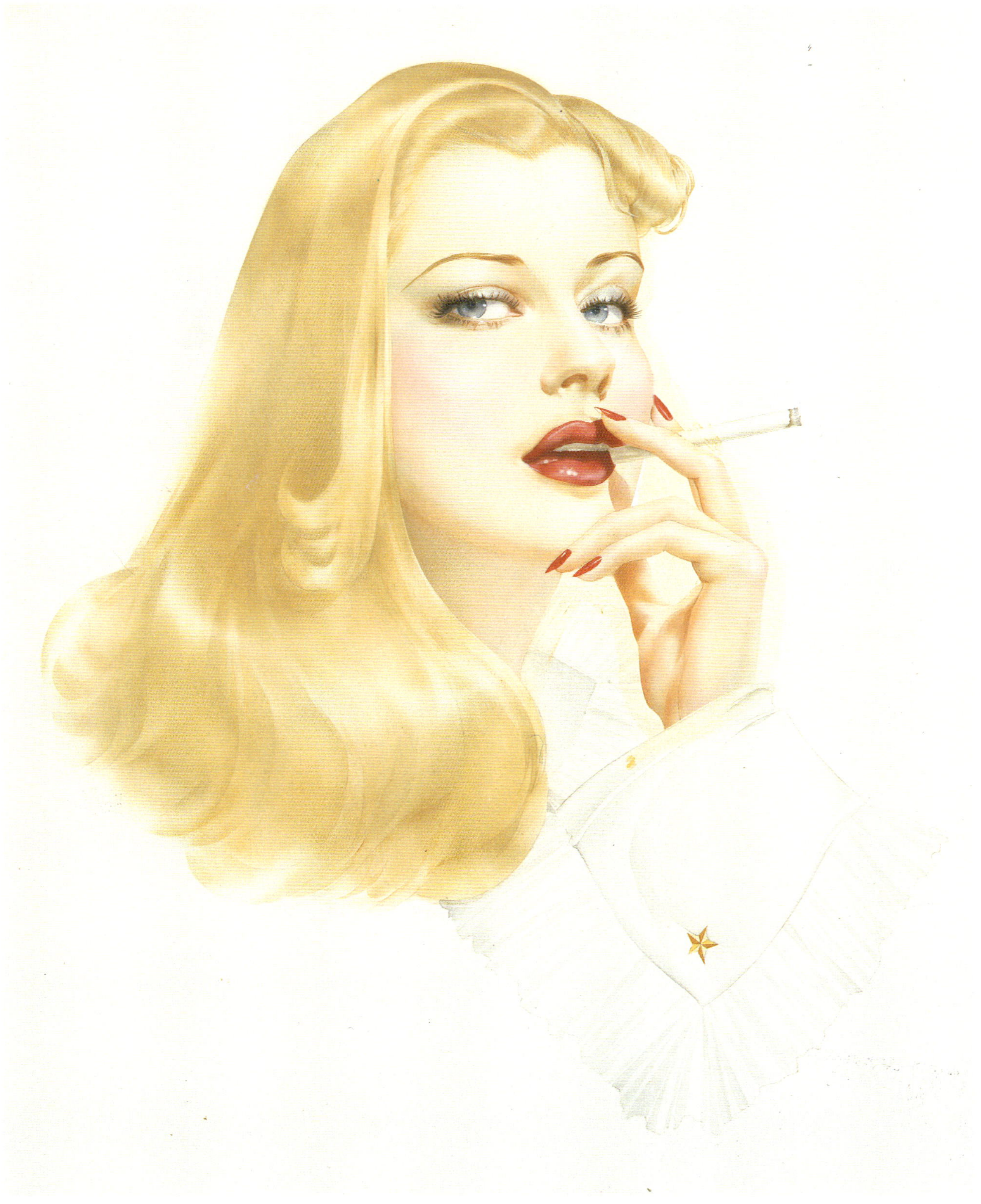

Above: January 1942 Calendar

Left: December 1941 Calendar

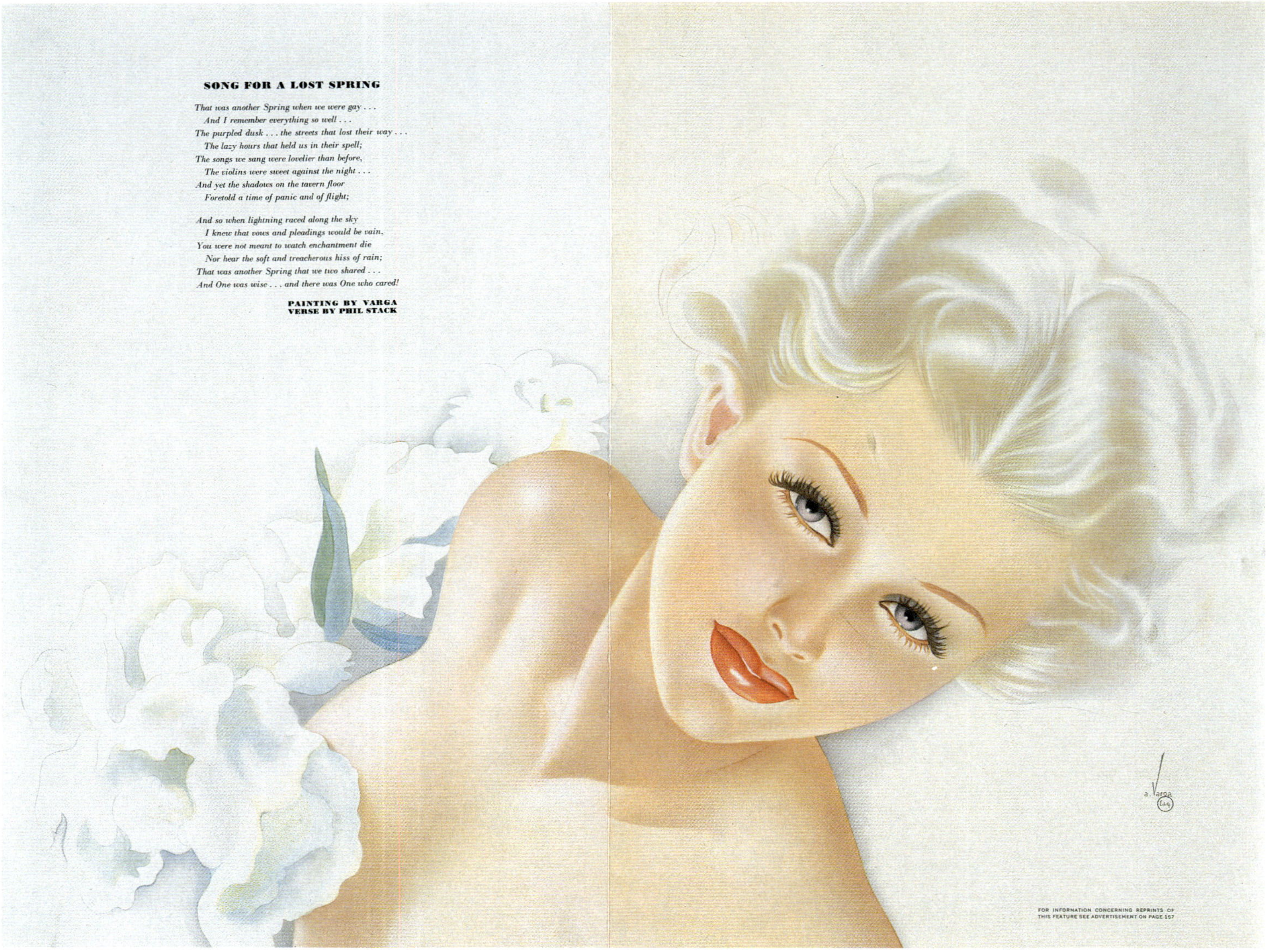

Above: May 1942

Right: Undated (1943?) Playing Card

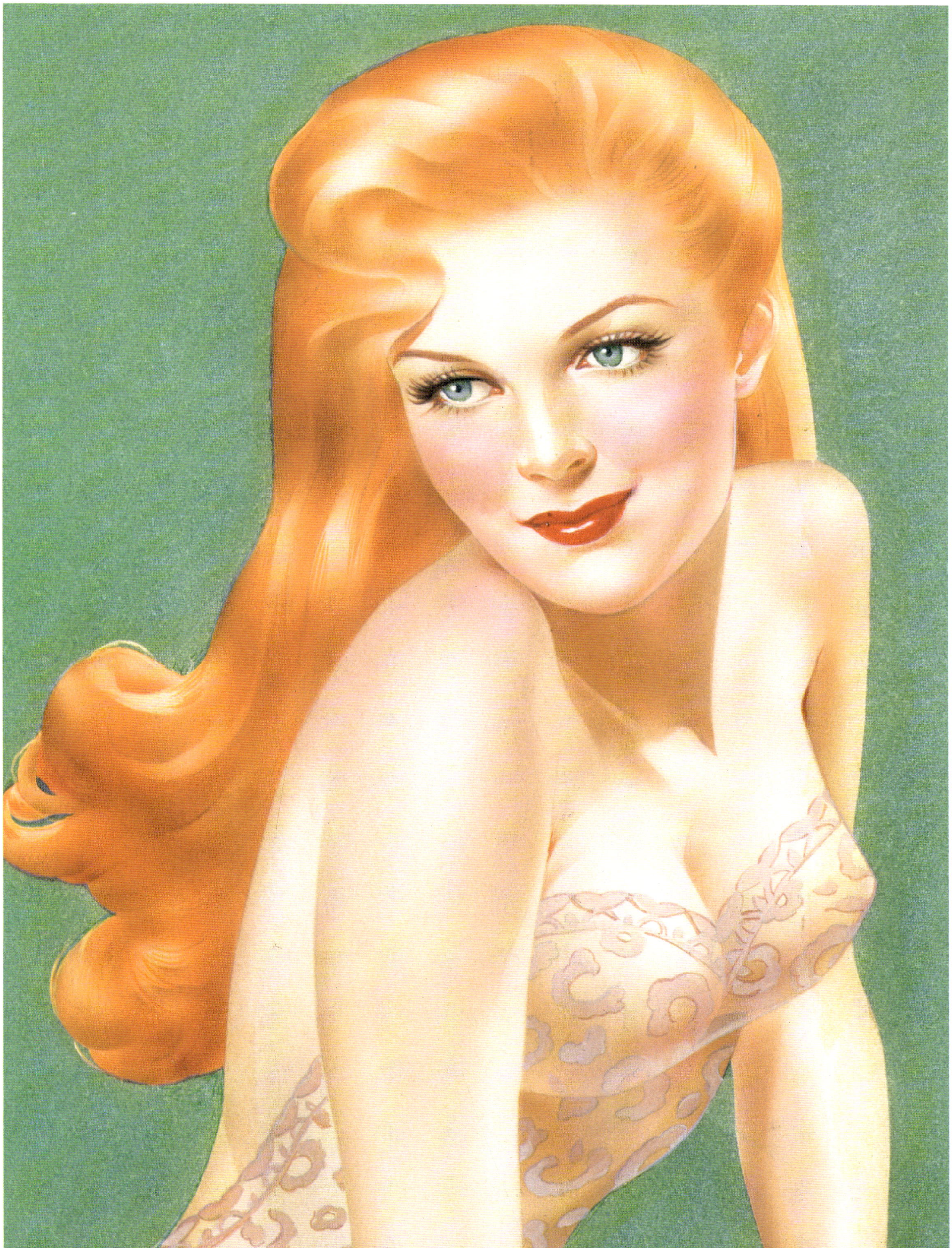

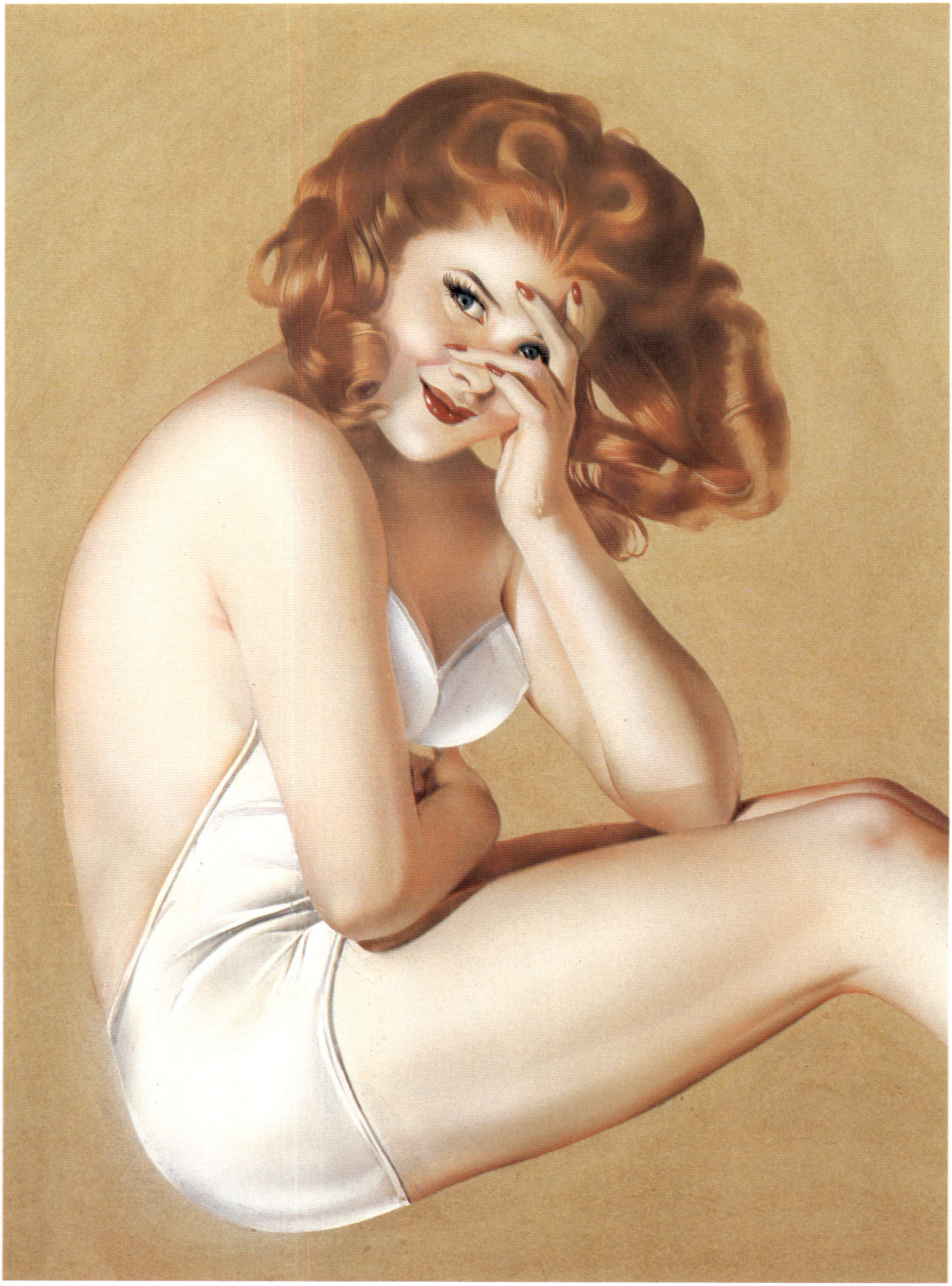

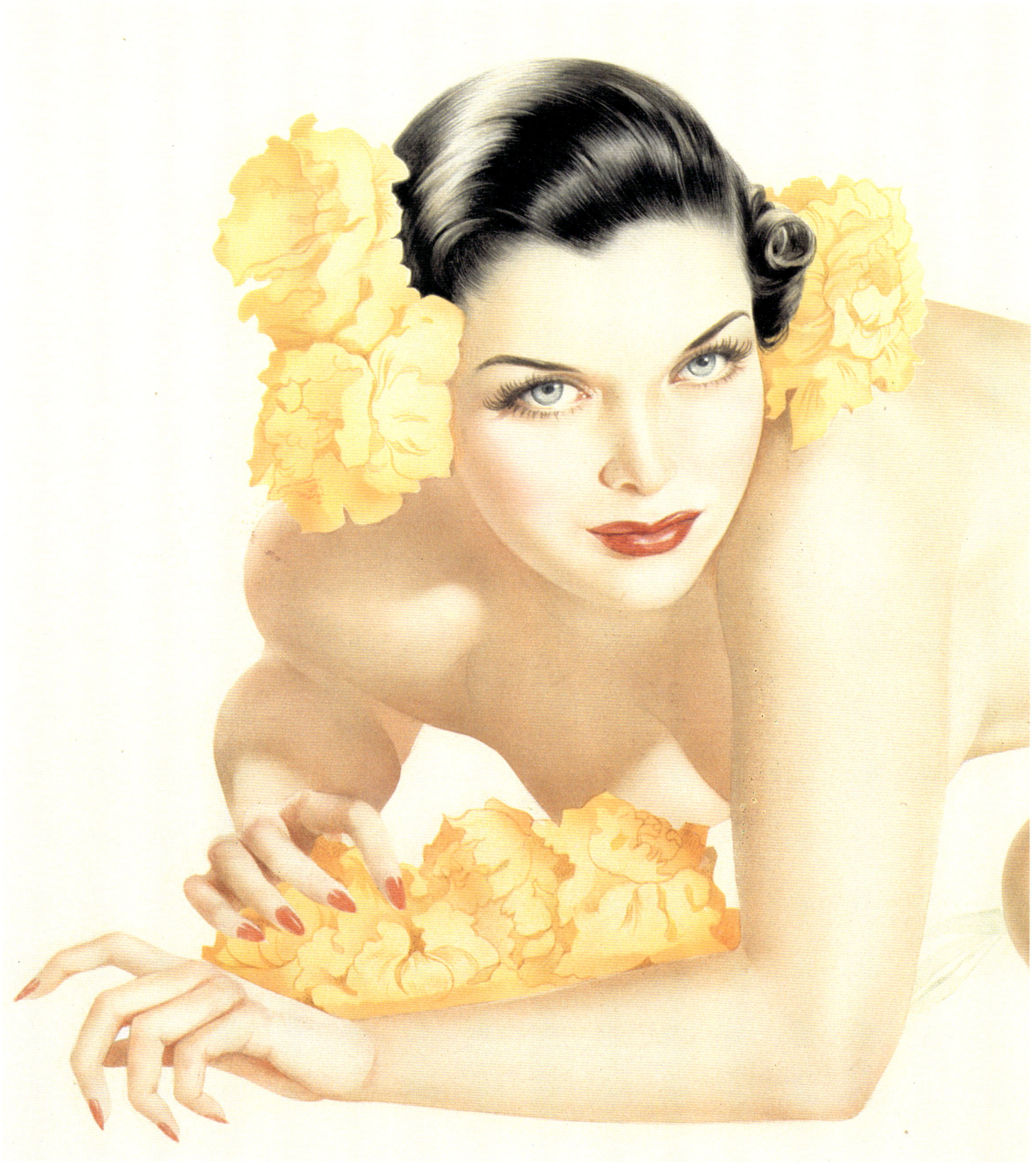

Above: June 1943

Left: May 1943

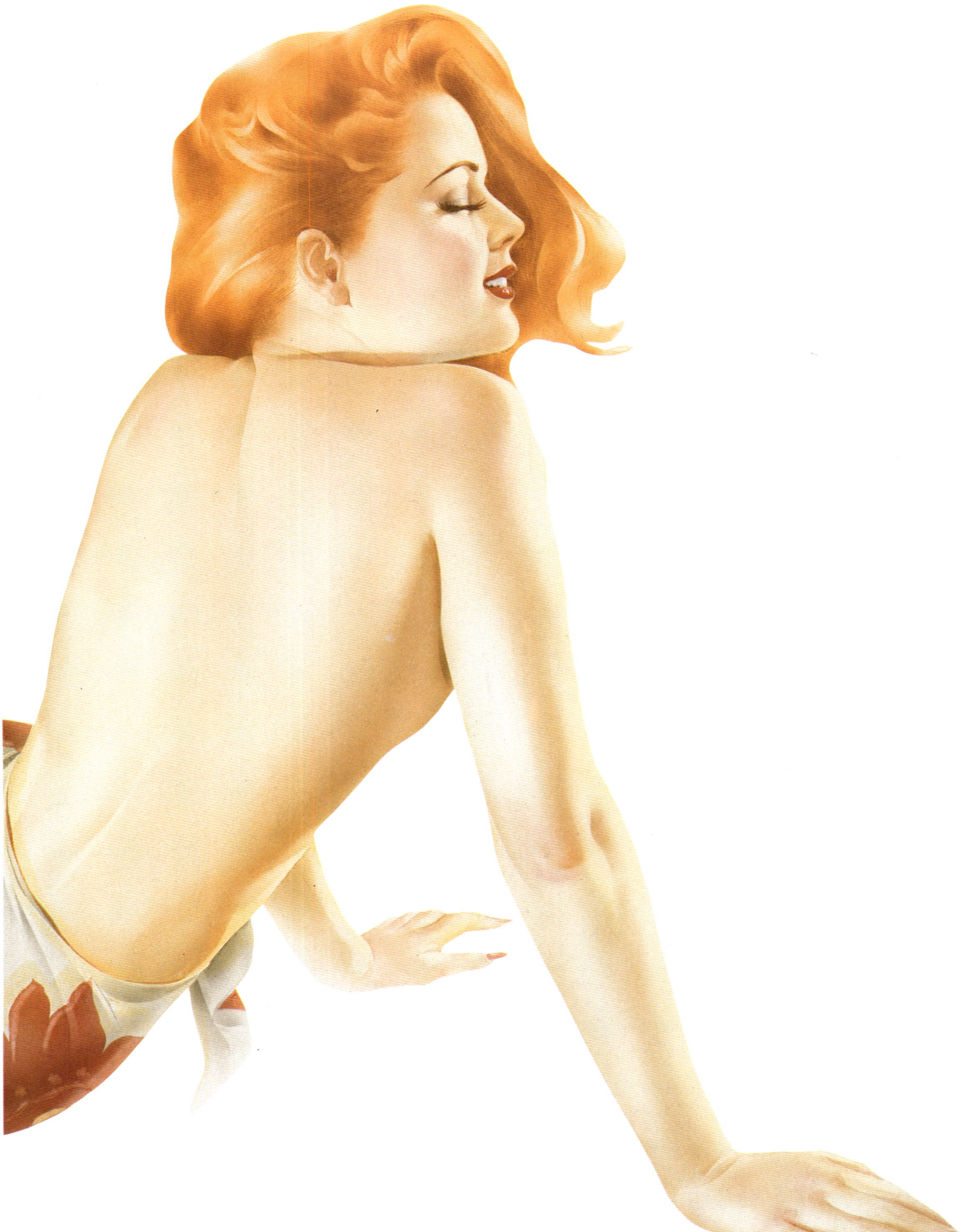

October 1941 Calendar

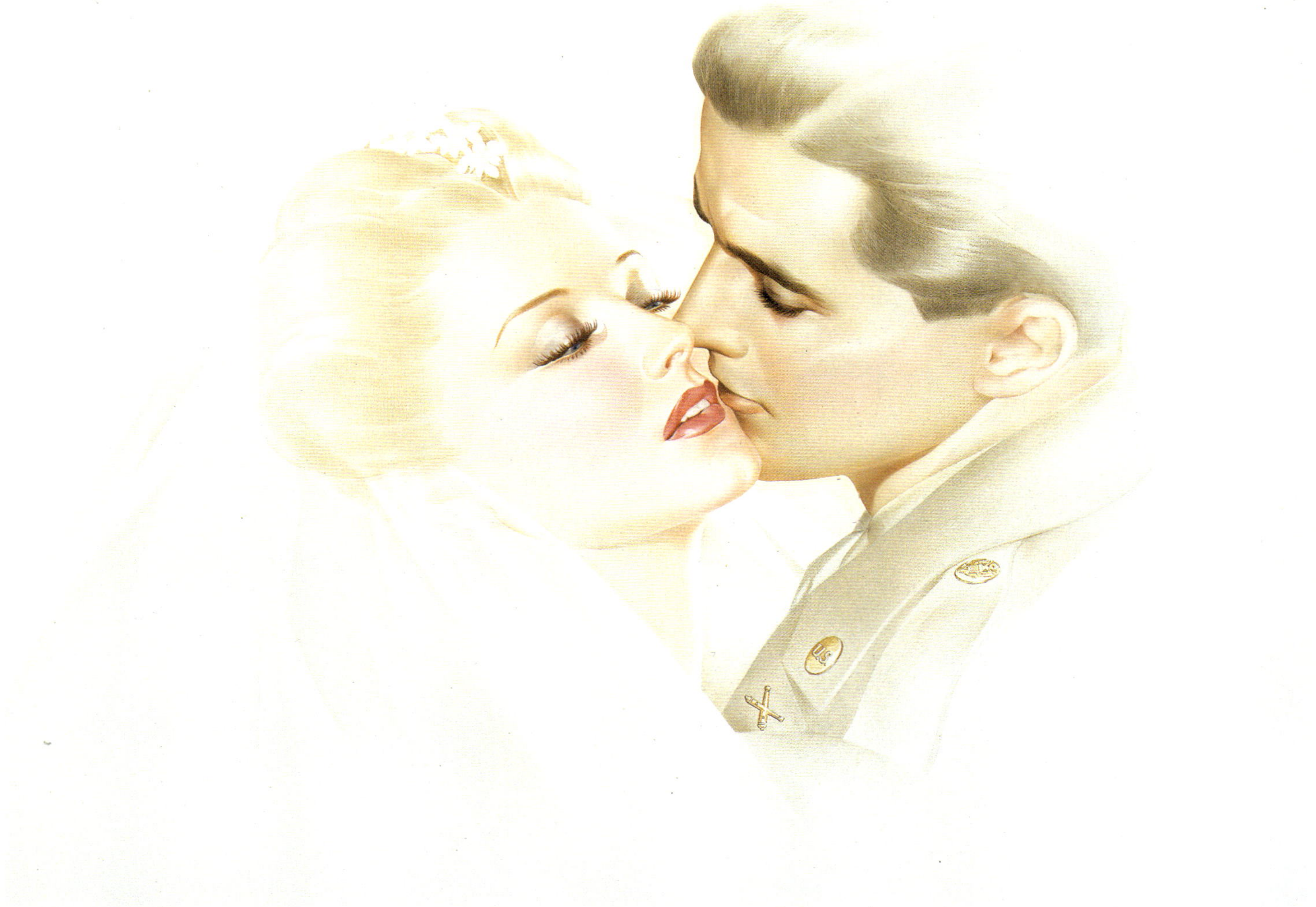

July 1943

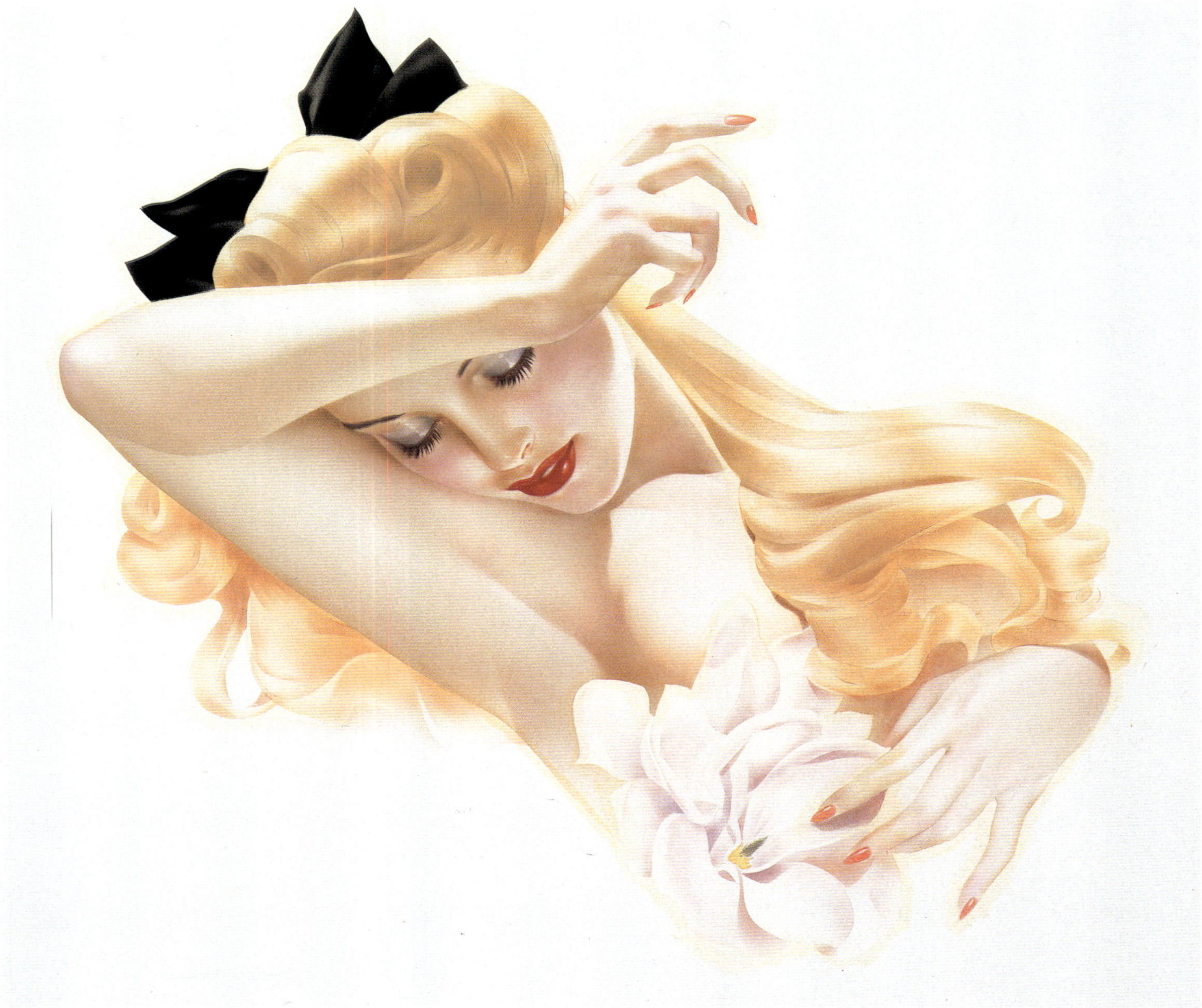

Above: December 1944 Calendar

Right: December 1944

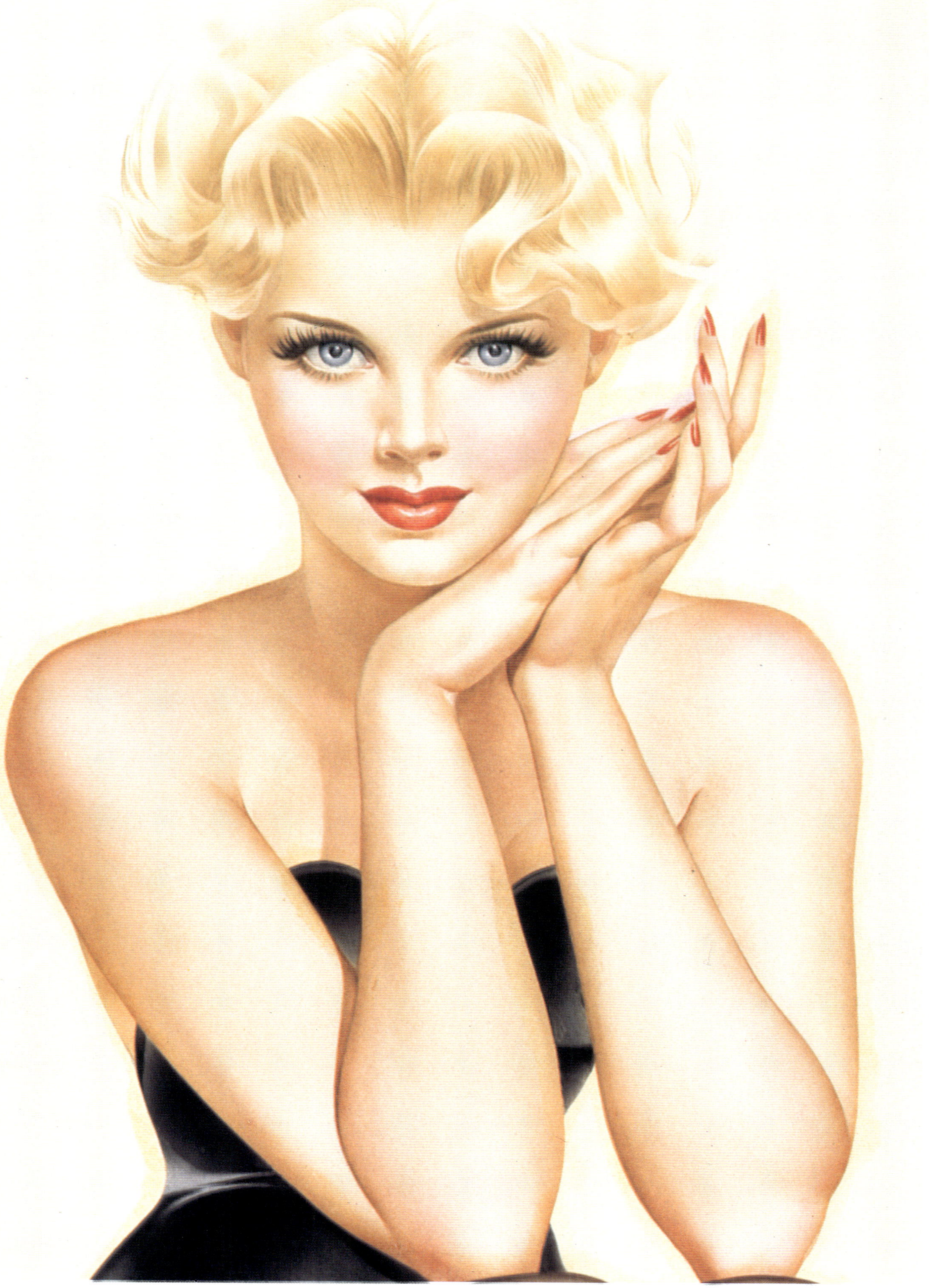

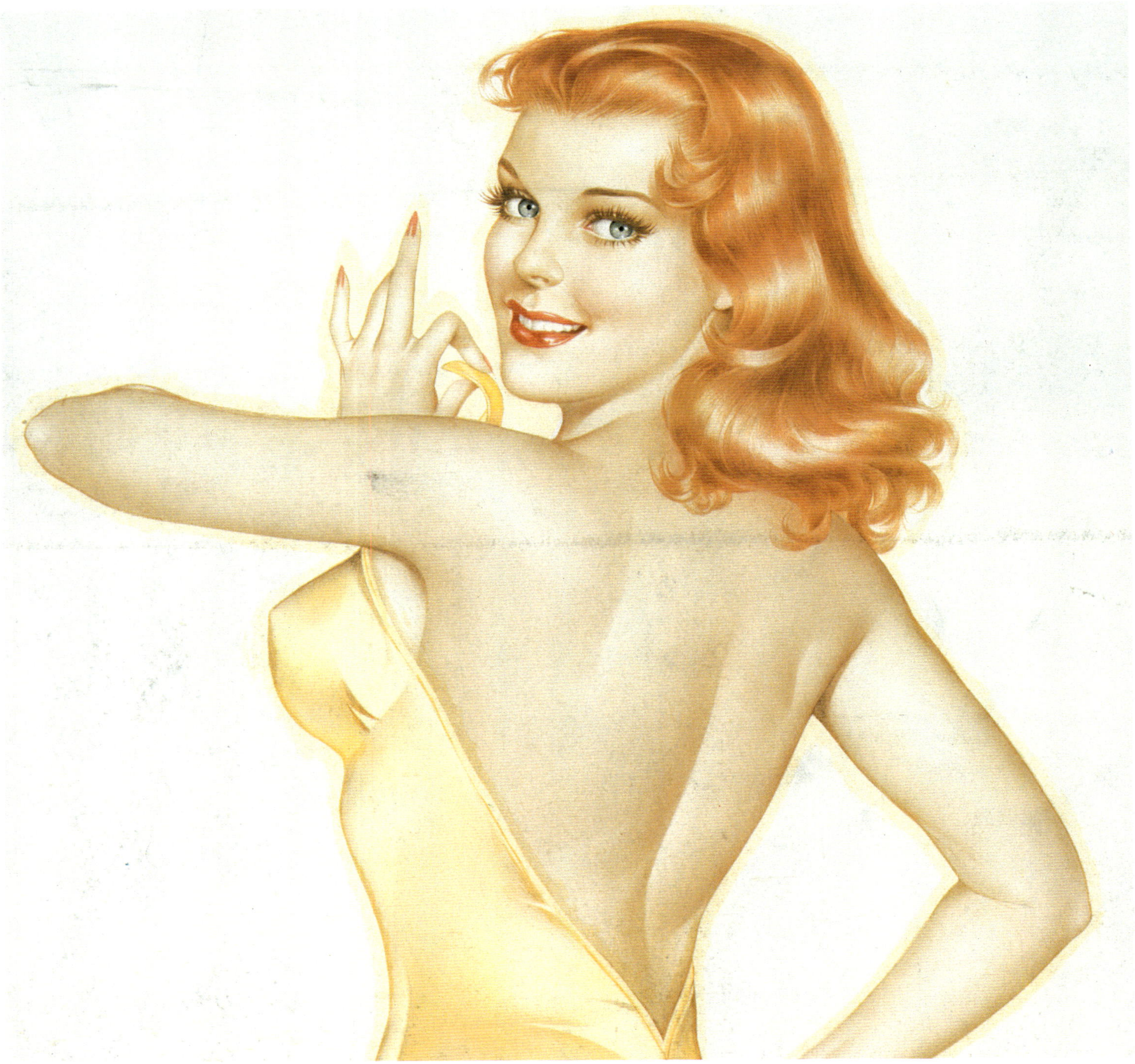

Above: January 1946

Right: Undated Portrait

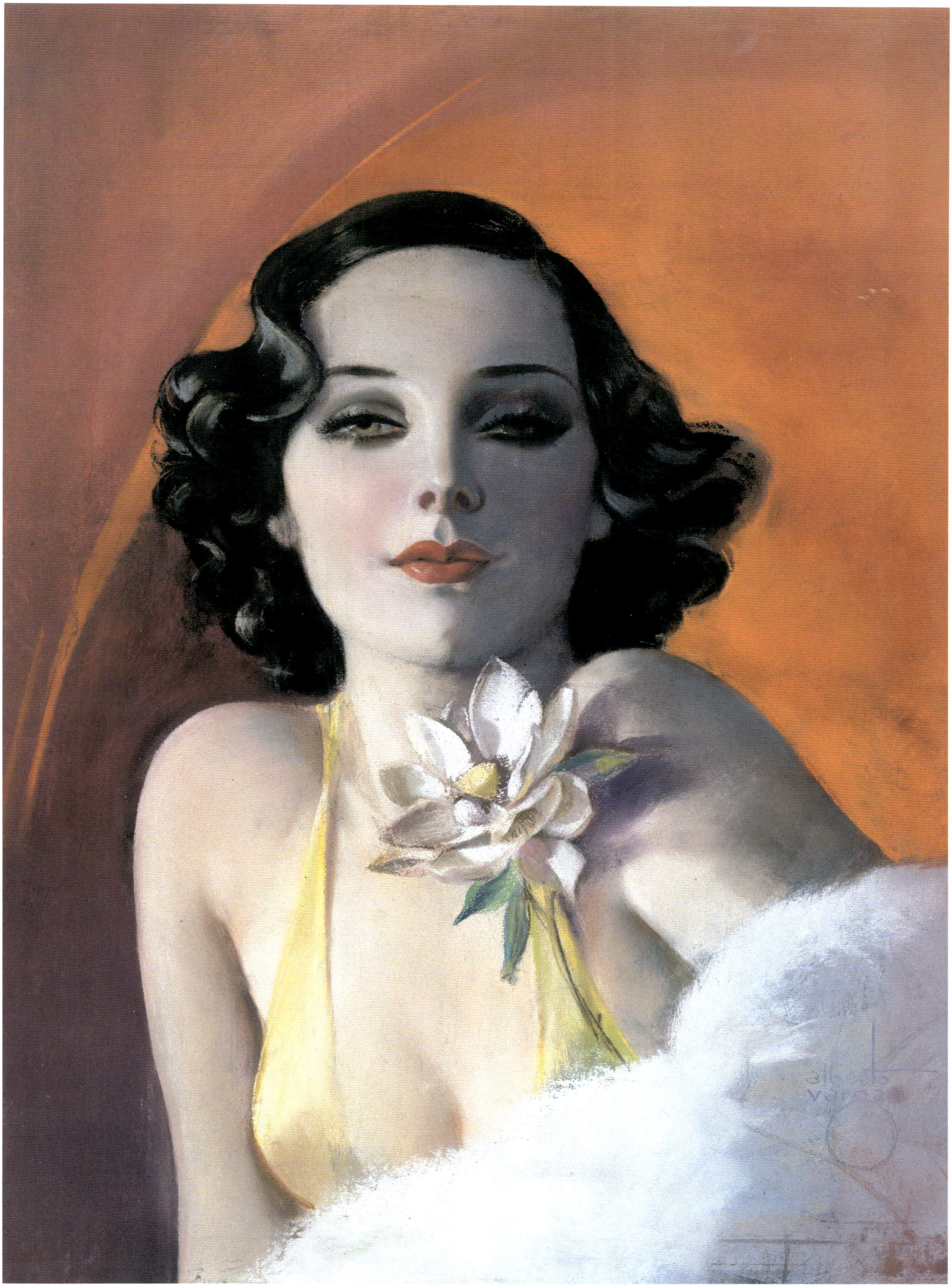

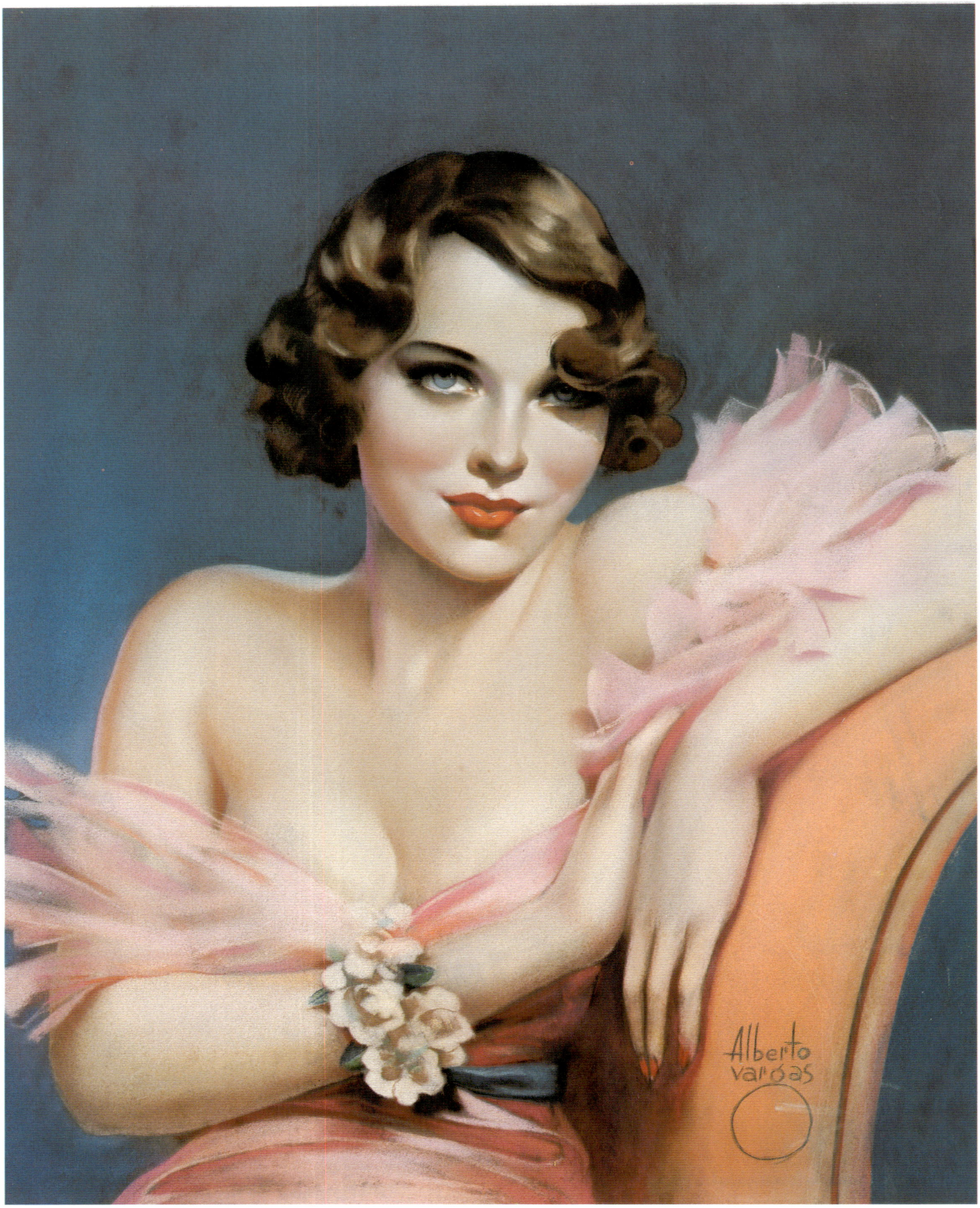

Above: Undated Portrait

Right: 1948

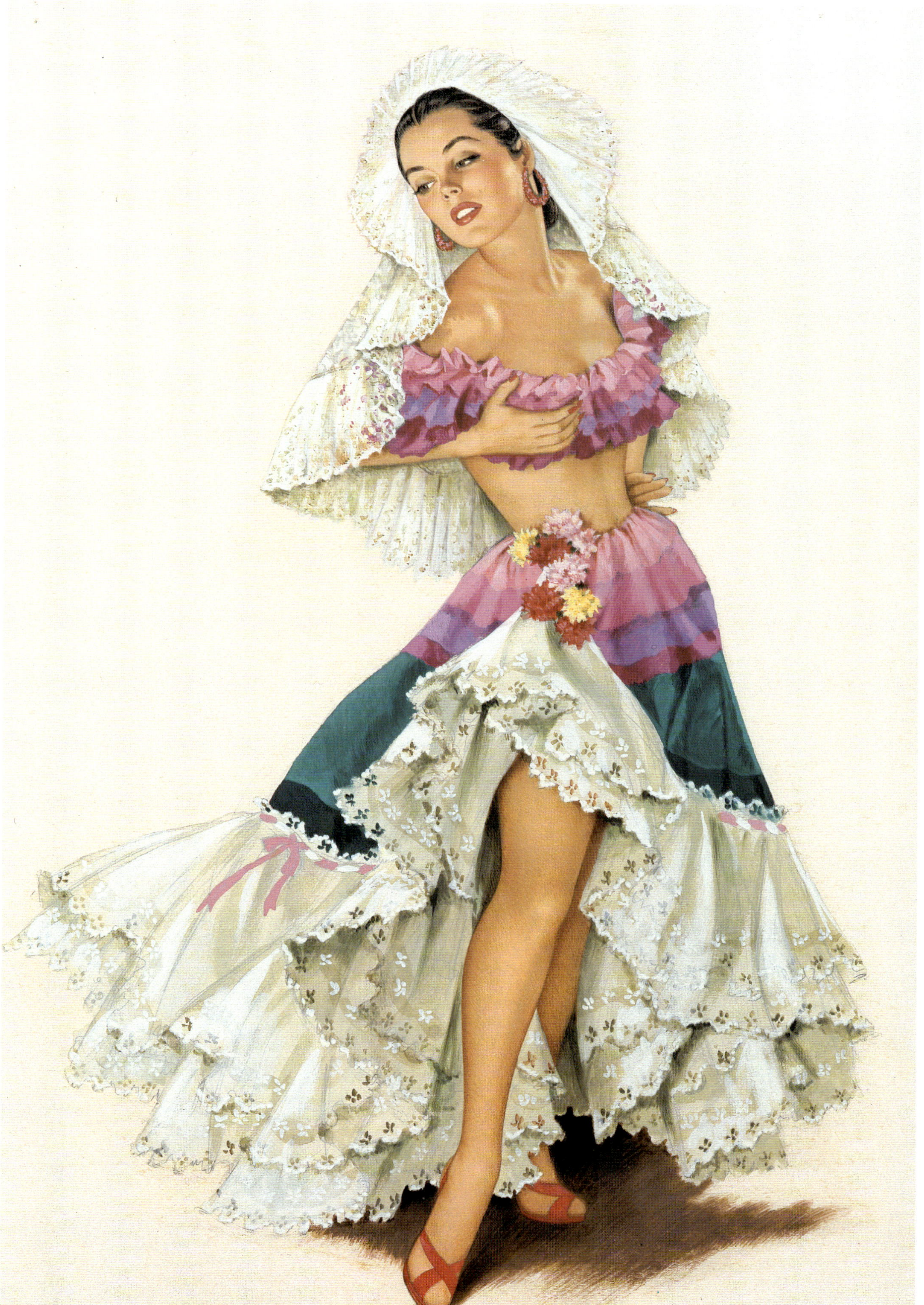

List of Color Plates

November 1940	54-55
January 1941	110
February 1941	112
March 1941	57
June 1941	59
September 1941	26
September 1941	52
October 1941	113
November 1941 Gatefold	61
March 1941 Calendar	56
April 1941 Calendar	58
July 1941 Calendar	84-85
October 1941 Calendar	120
November 1941 Calendar	60
December 1941 Calendar	114
March 1942	86
April 1942	4-5
May 1942	116
July 1942 Gatefold	87
August 1942 Gatefold	82
November 1942 Gatefold	88
December 1942	28-29
January 1942 Calendar	115
April 1942 Calendar	27
June 1942 Calendar	62
September 1942 Calendar	63
March 1943	90
March 1943	92-93
April 1943	91
May 1943	118
June 1943	30-31
June 1943	119
July 1943	121
August 1943	32
September 1943	65
November 1943	96
November 1943 Foldout	24
December 1943	98-99
February 1943 Calendar	64
April 1943 Calendar	94-95
August 1943 Calendar	64-65
December 1943 Calendar	97
January 1943 Military Edition	89
February 1944	67
February 1944	34-35
March 1944	100
April 1944	102
May 1944	70
June 1944	35
July 1944	72
September 1944	33
October 1944	38
November 1944 Gatefold	73
December 1944	123
January 1944 Calendar	66
February 1944 Calendar	68-69
July 1944 Calendar	104-105
August 1944 Calendar	36-37
November 1944 Calendar	74
December 1944 Calendar	122
March 1944 Military Edition	101
April 1944 Military Edition	69
May 1944 Military Edition	70-71
July 1944 Military Edition	103
April 1945	106
April 1945	108-109
July 1945	2-3
September 1945	76
January 1945 Calendar	75
February 1945 Calendar	39
September 1945 Calendar	40
November 1945 Calendar	107
February 1945 Military Edition	104
January 1946	124
April 1946	77
May 1946	78
June 1946 Calendar	41
July 1946 Calendar	42
September 1946 Calendar	43
October 1946 Calendar	44
January 1947 Calendar	78-79
March 1947 Calendar	45
June 1947 Calendar	46-47
October 1947 Calendar	48-49
December 1947 Calendar	80-81
1948	127
July 1949 Calendar	50-51
Undated	51
Undated (1943?) Playing Card	117
Undated Portrait	125
Undated Portrait	126

Acknowledgments

The publisher would like to thank the following:
Martin Bristow, the designer; Clare Haworth-Maden, the editor; Rita Longabucco, the picture researcher; and Simon Shelmerdine for production.

The Reid Stewart Austin Collection: pages 8, 9 (bottom), 10 (both), 11, 12-13, 13 (both), 14 (top), 15 (bottom), 16 (top), 19, 20 (bottom), 22 (bottom), 23 (top left and top right, © Reid Stewart Austin)

The Bettmann Archive: page 9 (top)

© 1989 James W. Hartley and Theron L. Kabrich: page 22 (top)

© 1991 The Hearst Corporation: pages 15 (top), 16 (bottom), 23 (bottom)

U.P.I./Bettmann Newsphotos: pages 1, 6, 7, 14 (bottom), 17, 18 (both), 20 (top), 21